344523

D1579241

Modern typography

Robin Kinross

Modern typography

an essay in critical history

Hyphen Press . London

First published by Hyphen Press, London, in 1992; reprinted
with minor corrections in 1994. This second edition published
by Hyphen Press, London, in 2004

Copyright © Robin Kinross 1992, 2004

The book was designed by Françoise Berserik, The Hague. The text
was typeset and made into pages by Teus de Jong, Nij Beets, in Adobe
InDesign. This text was output in the typeface Arnhem, designed by
Fred Smeijers, Antwerp. Photographs were made by Graham Bush,
London. The book was made and printed in the Netherlands by
Thoben Offset, Nijmegen

ISBN 0–907259–18–9

www.hyphenpress.co.uk

3 4 4 5 2 3

for my mother, who didn't publish

Contents

Preface & acknowledgements

Most of the text of *Modern typography* was written in 1985–6, but it was published first only towards the end of 1992. For this second edition, I have revised and updated the text where necessary, to take account of new research. Putting the work into a smaller format has also prompted a thorough revision of the picture section (chapter 14). The one large change in the text is a completely revised and extended concluding chapter (now chapter 13). In the first edition this final section suffered from the delay in the book's publication. Written in one era and published in another, the closing arguments had to skate over what was just then in process of development. Now, with some better perspective on the tumultuous events of the 1980s and early 1990s, I hope that this new conclusion works better. I have considered extending the scope of the book, to take account of cultures other than the North-European heartland of the discussion – Italy, Spain, Portugal, East Europe, the Scandanavian countries, not to mention the world beyond Europe and North America – but my circumstances have prohibited this. One day *Modern typography* could perhaps be extended in that way; but then it might become another book, with differences in its character and thesis. As to this thesis, I can repeat the words I used in the preface to the first edition, in the three paragraphs that now follow.

This book is an essay, in that its text is brief and its argument condensed. The sequence of pictures included here also has the character of a short, highly selective excursion through a landscape of vast possibilities. But more importantly, the work is an essay in the sense that it 'essays' or 'attempts'. This is perhaps better conveyed by the German word 'ein Versuch': an essay, but, in its primary meaning, an 'attempt' or 'experiment'. What is attempted here is a shift of orientation for the history of typography, and so also for its practice. This proposed shift is, of course, not an entirely new orientation. Elements of this approach have been suggested by existing work in the history of the subject, and in its practice; and one could point to thoroughly worked out precedents in parallel fields, such as architecture. As will be clear, the argument depends on the contributions of a large gathering of previous writers; and the present book is in one aspect a reading of – and a report on – this literature.

It is a report written at a particular time and in a particular cultural context, in which what is 'modern' is frequently held to have come to an end, and to have been superseded – or perhaps just extended and qualified – by some 'postmodern'. This context has provided a setting for the book, helping to define its position. In constructing the work I have taken heart from the proposition (of Jürgen Habermas) that modernity is 'a continuing project', and have tried to see how this might be worked out in the field of typography.[1] If all history is to some extent (though not merely) a response to the conditions in which it is written, it is as well to make this dimension of contemporary reference explicit, so that it can be accounted for and engaged with by readers. The facts and examples that are presented in the book are part of this position: they define, test, qualify, advance the argument. There may be a kind of mythic or fictional quality to this, especially in such a compressed work, so that the examples selected become stages in a story, moved along by a narrative mechanism. I hope, at least, that I have avoided any false imposition of pattern and too much tying of loose ends.

From all this it will be clear that the book does have an argument, and is informed by a critical element. The need for a critical approach in any such undertaking, as giving it purpose, and connecting it to practice and to our ordinary lives, is itself one of the propositions of the book. But rather than expound such theses any further in a preface, I have felt it best to devote the first chapter to a statement of position and approach.

My deep acknowledgements for this second edition are as for the first. I owe much to the Department of Typography & Graphic Com-

---

1. See Habermas's 1980 Adorno Prize lecture, translated into English as 'Modernity: an incomplete project', in Hal Foster (ed.), *Postmodern culture*, London: Pluto Press, 1985, pp.3–15. This thesis about 'modernity' has raised much debate and serious questioning, as I touch on in chapter 13. But I feel that the Habermasian thesis remains useful as a good proposition. It has been starting point for investigations, including the present book, which might otherwise never have happened.

munication at the University of Reading, where I was a student and
subsequently a teacher (until 1982); many of the ideas put forward
here have been everyday currency there. However, neither that
department nor any of its members are responsible for what I have
written, and I imagine – and hope – that the book will provoke them
to argument. I am indebted in particular to a past colleague at Reading: Paul Stiff, who has been a constant friend and discusser. Jane
Howard also gave the text of the first edition thorough criticism,
as well as providing moral support. For further helpful criticism,
I must thank James Mosley, another ex-colleague at Reading, and
(now ex-) Librarian of the St Bride Printing Library, London. This
library is the other institution that has made this book possible.
I hope that it may provide something in return for the friendly and
knowledgeable help of its staff.

The first edition of *Modern typography* was printed and bound
in Zutphen in the Netherlands. It was the first Hyphen Press book
to be produced in that country, and it marked the start for me of a
long engagement with Dutch culture. A number of colleagues there
have been wonderful friends over this period. It would be invidious
to mention names – especially as I look to them and their work as
unwitting exemplifications of the themes of this book.

RK / London, 1992, 2004

Blessed be the inventor of the printing press. It is to him that we owe this wondrous revolution.
    Louis Lavicomterie, 1792

Standardization, instead of individualization.
Cheap books, instead of private-press editions.
Active literature, instead of passive leather bindings.
    Jan Tschichold, 1930

It is through more reason – not less – that the wounds dealt to the irrational totality of humankind by the instrument that is reason can be healed.
    Theodor W. Adorno, 1953

Louis Lavicomterie de Saint-Samson, *La République sans impôts*, Paris: ICS, 1792, quoted by G. Kates, *The 'Cercle Social', the Girondins, and the French Revolution*, Princeton: Princeton University Press, 1985, p.178.

Tschichold, 'Was ist und was will die Neue Typografie?', in his *Eine Stunde Druckgestaltung*, p.7; reprinted in his *Schriften 1925–1974*, vol.1, at p.90.

Theodor W. Adorno, 'Der Artist als Statthalter', in his *Noten zur Literatur 1*, Frankfurt a. M: 1958, p.184; quoted here (with modifications) from its translation in *Notes to literature*, vol.1, New York: Columbia University Press, 1991, p.103.

1   Modern typography

Modern typography?

If the printing process was one of the main facilitators in the development of the modern world, then the phrase 'modern typography' may be an unnecessary duplication of sense. Is not *all* typography modern?[1] Certainly a cultural historian might see 1450, the moment of Gutenberg's movable type, as falling near to the intersection of 'late medieval' and 'early modern'. And, whatever is suggested by large schemes of periodization, the nature of the new process seems to claim the characteristics of modernity. It was a process of mass-production: texts and images could now be made in quantity and in identical copies. Though manuscript texts had been produced as duplicates in sizeable numbers, printing introduced fundamental changes: in quantity, in speed of production, and above all in ensuring the identical nature of the information in copies (allowing for variations of presswork and changes to a text within a printing run). This standardization of the product was as far-reaching in its implications as any of the innovations brought by the new process. It was on the basis of shared, stable and exact knowledge that the modern world came into being.

The process itself implied and necessitated a standardization of materials. A satisfactory product depended on proper alignment and fit of characters, on evenness of printed impression, and these things depended in turn on a normalization of the dimensions of the materials. Early printers may not have had well co-ordinated materials, even within a single workshop, but the implication of such a co-ordination was there in the nature of the process. Similarly, the process suggested a division of labour, although the early printing workshops may often have been small affairs in which work-functions were shared, and although at certain times and in some places the production of manuscript texts was quite ruthlessly

1. The argument that '"modern" typography began around 1440' was suggested by Anthony Froshaug in: 'Typography ancient and modern', *Studio International*, vol. 180, no. 924, 1970, pp. 60–1; reprinted in Kinross, *Anthony Froshaug: Typography & texts*, pp. 202–4.

divided by the allocation of component parts of a text to different scribes (the 'pecia' system).

These qualifications may at least hint at the social grounding of the theme of typography. In this compressed discussion, 'typography' will inevitably tend to become an abstracted idea, shedding the human and material reality of which it is constituted. But, although social realities may qualify generalizations about the fundamental character of typography, the fact remains that writing is a single process, while printing is at least two: composition and presswork. Here lies the source of difference between a unitary activity and one that can be put out to workers who may know nothing of each other.

In these broad respects, then, printing is fundamental to the development of the modern world: as a principal means of spreading knowledge, enabling the shift from medieval attitudes to modern ones; and as itself incorporating modern characteristics, of mass-production and standardization, of specialization and division of labour.

The debate over the history of modernity will always be inconclusive.[2] Different definitions of the concept allow different locations of it, and the proper start of 'the modern' has been placed later than the time of the first printers: with steam power and industrialization, or later still, perhaps with the First World War. This book starts its discussion not at 1450, nor at 1800 nor 1900 nor 1914, but rather at around 1700, and this is a part of its argument. If modernity was implicit in printing, it was not fully or immediately realized by Gutenberg's invention. Printing enabled modernity, but evidence of recognizably modern attitudes in typography only began to emerge some 250 years after its introduction.

The decisive evidence that allows this judgement is of the readiness to articulate knowledge and consciousness. Before the time of this emergence of modern attitudes, printers certainly knew what they were doing. One can see this simply in the fact of successfully produced printed books: for the making of any such extended text requires considerable conscious planning or design. Though little evidence – drawn layouts, marked copy, imposition diagrams – survives to document this, one can surmise that these aids must have been used; one can also assume a process of copying existing formats. But this knowledge was not shared. Early printers, in keeping with the tenor of their times, surrounded their activities in secrecy: for practical reasons (to preserve commercial advantage) as well as in the quasi-magical furtherance of the 'black art'. That this epithet should have survived so long suggests the persistent, perhaps inherent, surprise and mystery that attaches to the process of printing. Paper is passed over a nonsensical, mirror-image surface to produce – in an instant – text and images, smooth and full of meaning; and the process can be repeated again and again. However, the 'black art' has been the practice of a trade organized along masonic lines: a secretive, male preserve, stubbornly resisting change. 'The trade' appears as a principal though usually silent character in this book, as the bedrock of printing. At its best it has been a repository of solid wisdom. But it has also seemed to be an obstacle, especially to bright outsiders who have wanted to take control of the process of production and publication.

The first move in the long process of the break-down of the printing trade was the splitting of the editorial function away from the workshop and into what would become the publisher's office. With this division, printing began to be opened up: its secrets started to be articulated. One might also suggest, as a working definition, that this is the point at which 'printing' separates from 'typography'. This distinction of terms has been latent in discussion of the matter since Joseph Moxon's *Mechanick exercises* was published at the end of the seventeenth century, but has never been fully explained. To over-simplify, the difference is between inarticulate practice with the materials of production ('printing'), and conscious shaping of the product, by instruction ('typography').

One might well argue, with this distinction in mind, that 'modern typography' is indeed a duplication of sense, because when printing becomes typography is also when printing becomes mod-

2. The literature of this debate is huge and various. For some observations from a historian of printing, see Eisenstein, *The printing press as an agent of change*, pp. 683–708. See also a brief survey by H. D. L. Vervliet, 'Gutenberg or Diderot? Printing as a factor in world history', *Quaerendo*, vol. 8, no. 1, 1978, pp. 3– 28, which tends to support the thesis of the present book.

ern. Printing becomes modern with the spreading of knowledge about itself: with the published description of its practices; with the classification of its materials and processes; with co-ordination of dimensions of materials, enabling their exchange and better conjunction; with the establishment of a record of its history. These things, which one begins to see in the late seventeenth century in (especially) England and France, are realizations of the implications of the process of printing: they follow from people using the means of printing to discuss that process itself. With the publication of manuals and histories of printing, with the introduction of common systems of measurement, then the 'black art' is illumined: a process that still continues.

It is as well to make explicit the obvious limitation of this book to the western world, and to typography employing Latin script. This, too, is a part of its argument, for the overlap between 'modern' and 'western' is so great as to make them synonymous. As well as its chronological structuring, the discussion follows a geographical course, moving from country to country (or culture to culture) as each seems to become significant. But the process of modernization is also one of homogenization, and national cultures come to be less distinct. Thus a more extended discussion of current developments would have to consider the situation of typography in the Far East and the effects, throughout the world, of the international manufacturing companies.

Approaches to history

The history of printing and typography has been the subject of different approaches, developed for particular purposes. One may distinguish the following leading strands (representative examples are given in the discussion of sources, chapter 15).

First, there are histories of printing. These have taken technical development as their main subject, tending to be histories of printing machinery. Printing history of this kind has been a phenomenon of the last few decades, and it has been prompted by the need to preserve and record the materials and practices of past techniques.

Bibliographical history has a longer tradition, beginning in the late nineteenth century. This is the study of printed texts and their transmission. It has been conducted as a branch of literary scholarship, taking an interest in processes of printing as the necessary material underpinning for knowledge of a literary text.

A third kind of history has recently emerged from within the ranks of professional historians, as an aspect of cultural history. This has come with the realization that printing and especially 'the book', as it is hypostatized, have been key factors in historical change. Besides this intellectual emphasis, there is the social one: the printing and publishing trades are relatively well provided with surviving documents, and examination of this material has been able to provide rich insights into past life.

The last category is the vaguest and has often been the least substantial: history of typography. Where printing history has focussed on machinery and on the trade, and has been largely produced from within the trade, typographic history has concentrated on the printed products and their design. A special field of examination here has been the history of typefaces, which has also received some attention from bibliographic historians interested in authenticating texts, but the major motivation for this specialization has come from the need to fuel the production of adapted or recreated versions of past letterforms. Typographic history has largely been produced by practising typographers, whose emergence it has closely followed. The connection with practice has been of mixed benefit. While one may point to shining examples of the fruitful interplay of practice and historical scholarship, it would be possible to fill shelves with works crippled by an absence of historical skills and by superficial notions of design. This kind of history is the only one to recognize the aesthetic factor in printing, but it has had the tendency to do little else but view. One may deride printing history for its blindness to the visual and its fixation on details of machinery, but it has at least done its time in the archives; typographic history has tended not to get beyond the reproduction of products, with accompanying rituals of admiration and distaste.

This book belongs to the category of typographic history, though it is an attempt to criticize the existing model for the genre. This critical effort has been conducted partly through incorporating insights from these other kinds of history and from enquiry outside typography: in architecture and design, and in historical and theoretical discussion more generally. But the opening out of typograph-

ic history can here be only a matter of hints and suggestions: its full
elaboration would require years of investigation into the everyday
interactions of typographers, printers, their customers, and the
public at large. (And this last above all: for the major absence, in this
book as in all works of typographic history, is the reader or user of
printing.) A more immediate and more achievable task is the suggestion of new directions for typographic history, within its existing
terms, by way of rapid outline and substantiated by necessary detail.
It is this that the present essay attempts.[3]

An approach

To take the theme of the modern as central at once questions the
prevailing pattern of typographic history. This pattern has been
most evident in Britain, but Britain has been the main home of this
history and an exporter of it. The norm for existing history is traditional typography, so conceived; modern typography, where it is
recognized, is isolated as 'modernist' and then treated, briefly, as an
eccentricity. Modernist typography is held to be an incursion of artists blundering into the quiet preserves of book-printing and there
violating the wisdom of tradition and convention. (The assumption,
usually unspoken, that all typography is book typography is another
characteristic of existing typographic history.) This view, expressed
most clearly and influentially by Stanley Morison, has come to colour all discussions of the subject, even the few extended treatments
of modern or modernist typography. Thus books about 'the pioneers of modern typography' or 'Bauhaus typography' situate their
subjects in a vacuum, without historical precedent and without
relation to the unmentioned but implied contemporary traditional
norm. The hope of this book is to break down such separations, and
to show that there are modern elements in what has been regarded
as traditional, and that there is a tradition behind what has been
taken to be just 'modernist'.

A difference of emphasis of this essay arises from a shift of
attention, away from products (and the untroubled reproduction
of images of them) and towards the ideas that inform production:
though a strategy for dealing with the evidence of artefacts is attempted in chapter 14. The products that are discussed here are
sometimes made from printed paper, sometimes they are printing

presses, sometimes 'typefaces' (a troubled notion), sometimes computer languages, or whatever material the essay-discussion finds it necessary to take account of. This emphasis on ideas relates to the thesis of what constitutes modernity: the discussion, description and ordering of practice, rather than mere practice and mere products. It is clear that, on this view, the subject of such a history is as much what people have said as what has issued from their practice.

There are other aspects to the stress on ideas. It enables the historian to move closer to the processes of design than does the simple reproduction of products. This may appear odd to those who assume that the design is the product. That is a view superficial in the literal as well as metaphorical sense of the word, and which ends in equating design with ornament: the border of printers' flowers that pleasantly divert from dull text. In this essay, 'design' is understood not as a noun but as a verb: an activity and a process. And, in this light, ideas become as real as inked sheets of paper.

Such an emphasis on thought and intention also has the advantage of generating a clearer view than one that gives priority to products: a summary becomes more possible. This is something that is hard to achieve when contemplating the vast numbers of products that might conceivably be discussed, or the arbitrary and perhaps very small selection that is actually available for inspection. Limits on the material available to the typographic historian have encouraged the formation of a canon of products considered to be exemplary: images that are passed, without recourse to an original specimen, from book to book.

There are, of course, important objections to a history that would rest on ideas. People do not do what they say, and to take their words as unquestioned truth and to deduce action from words leads to idealization and falsity. And such an emphasis gives improper prominence to those who are articulate and who have access to the channels of publication.

The first of these objections will be met by a realistic attitude,

3. The necessary speed and relatively high level of the discussion make it inappropriate to provide any extended explanation of technical processes or of the terminology of typography. Readers new to the field will find help in the plentiful introductory literature to printing and typography.

which can understand the context of discussion and which knows the arbitrariness, muddle, ambitions, deceptions and naive hopes that surround any human endeavour. The goal must be a total history that relates ideas to products, and not just to final products. These are the visible tip of designing. But beyond and beneath them is the mass of material (marked copy, layouts, dummies, and so on), which could – if it can be found – reveal the process of design and production as no finished item can. That histories of typography – not excluding the present text – should pay so little attention to intermediate products is another sign of their superficiality.

The second objection to an emphasis on ideas – that it gives undue prominence to the articulate – amounts to an objection to the positive argument of this book: that typographers need to incorporate critical reflection into their own practice. This informs the judgement implied in the selection of figures for discussion here: special attention is paid to those typographers who have been articulate about practice. The risk may then be that one replaces a cult of great creators by one of great articulators. No cults of the individual are intended here, though individual people are allowed an honourable place in this history. A way between a history of hero-worship and its opposite of a history devoid of all human presence lies in the critical examination of individual cases. Merely to utter is not enough: what is said has to be evaluated. This argument does not suggest that writing about the activity is a necessary qualification for its proper practice. But it does assert that enquiry, reflection, discussion, are activities that enhance designing and making. The thought that accompanies making need not issue as printed or written words, nor even as speech, but it may still be traced in the product. In this way products can themselves be 'articulate', though their makers may not have spoken. One thinks of certain pre-industrial punchcutters, or of countless unknown compositors.

This essay, then, does have a certain polemical purpose in its preference for the articulate. And, in the same spirit, it assumes that value lies in editorial quality, in the content of text and images, in their accurate transmission, and that notions of 'beauty' are best left undiscussed, or, at least, construed in the light of these primary tasks of printing. This may explain the selection of subjects discussed here, and the short shrift given to some of the staple subjects of typographic history – Baskerville, Bodoni, the post-Kelmscott private presses – whose reputation rests on superfluous books of doubtful textual accuracy, meant for viewing rather than for reading, or as investments. The cult of 'fine printing', with its fetish of the title-page, has been questioned often enough, and by celebrated typographers (Jan Tschichold, Eric Gill), but it seems to persist. Faced with its complacent monuments, one turns rather to work that shows some life.

One means of circumscribing and rooting the ideas discussed in this history is through reproduction of artefacts. This is a purpose of the illustrations that comprise the visual component of the essay. The intentions and methods in making these images are outlined in the note that follows the sequence (pp. 234–5).

The text of this essay depends very heavily on printed sources, including much material that is secondary to its subject, or is even further removed. This is not a very happy state of affairs: there is a strong risk of retailing stories that have been told (and distorted) many times before. The least an author can do is be frank about this, disclosing and discussing sources. Chapters 15 and 16 are devoted to this matter: they are meant to provide readers with some help in extending their knowledge, and to suggest that this book is the product of one voice in dialogue with many others. It has been written in the desire to prompt critical discussion and critical practice.

2   Enlightenment origins

The first manual

The beginnings of a separation between 'printing' and 'typography' can be located in the famous first definition of 'the typographer'. In the preface to his *Mechanick exercises: or the doctrine of handy-works applied to the art of printing* (1683–4), Joseph Moxon wrote: 'By a typographer, I do not mean a printer, as he is vulgarly accounted, any more than Dr Dee means a carpenter or mason to be an architect: but by a typographer, I mean such a one, who by his own judgement, from solid reasoning within himself, can either perform, or direct others to perform from the beginning to the end, all the handy-works and physical operations relating to typographie'.[1] One could apply this sense of 'typographer' to some of the earliest printers, who, although commonly called 'printers', played a directing role, rather than working as part of a production team: Aldus Manutius and other scholar-printers would provide the clearest examples. Moxon is thus articulating a function that has its origins at the start of printing: the process was by its nature one that required a co-ordinating or overseeing figure. We are thus returned to the idea, raised in chapter 1, that printing has within it the seeds of modernity.

The importance of Moxon's definition is that it came at the opening to the first extended published discussion of printing. With the *Mechanick exercises*, printing received its first extended theoretical treatment, and thus moved out of a state of unconsciousness. The book was primarily an intensely practical manual, with minutely detailed descriptions of the operations of making, composing, and printing from, type; but the dimension of theory could not be avoided. Thus the preface included a sketch of the invention and progress of printing. For the first time, printers could acquire some sense of the history of their practice, which was thereby raised above the level of blind 'practice'. And the whole effort of describing methods of work and of formally naming mechanical parts inevitably introduced a new sense of order into the practice. As a process of multiplication and of proto-mass-production, printing might imply system and standardization, but between individual operations (typefoundries and presses) there was little or no compatibility of materials. The essential modularity of printing could not be fully realized, and capitalized on, until common standards of description and manufacture had been worked out and adopted. Progress towards this state depended on published information and discussion. This brings us near to an essential constituent of the sense of 'modern' as it is here being used. Modern typography exhibits a rational impulse, both internally in ordering its own workings, and externally in the face it presents to the world.

In Moxon's book there was no concerted advocacy of ways of rationalizing typography: he was concerned simply to describe and to pass on knowledge of methods. He stands at the start of a line of purveyors of 'useful knowledge': a British empirical tradition that operated without the larger (notably French) ambition of constructing systems. The nearest that Moxon comes to advancing an explicit theory is in his description of designing and cutting letters as type. He wrote in a context in which there was no agreement among typefounders on standard sizes for printing type: neither the 'height to paper' nor size of body (and thus of image). Despite the predominance of a few large typefoundries and an international market in type, there was no common nomenclature. Even less was there a system of typographic measurement. But, in any case, general (non-typographic) systems of measurement were still casual and unco-ordinated even within state boundaries. The method that Moxon proposed as an aid to designing letters was to 'imagine (for in practice it cannot well be perform'd, unless in very large bodies) that the length of the whole body is divided into forty and two equal parts': seven parts, each of which had six subdivisions (Moxon, *Mechanick exercises*, p. 91). This then became the system by which proportions of letters were calculated, so that regularity was introduced into their appearance, over a set of characters and in different sizes. But there was no attempt to relate this scale to any existing system of measurement, nor to devise a system of measurement internal

1. Moxon, *Mechanick exercises*, pp. 11–12 (spelling and punctuation of the edition retained). Moxon's reference is to John Dee and the preface to Dee's edition of Euclid (1570).

to typography. A principle for relating typographic elements (type
and spacing material) to one another existed then only residually
and casually, in the names given to sizes of type, which were by this
time agreed in the main printing languages. Some order is evident
in these names, and it can be seen as lying at the foundation of the
system of point-size designations that finally emerged in the twentieth century. Thus the traditional English name of Pica was translated into '12 point', Double Pica into '24 point'. Moxon did suggest
numerical values for these designations, in relation to the English
foot, but he was doing no more than roughly summarizing existing
practice. (Moxon, *Mechanick exercises*, p. 21, and the editors' note.)

Rationalization of letters

After Moxon, and without any reference to his book, steps towards
further ordering the practice of typography came during the following century in France. The first of these, the design of the 'romain du
roi', is still often seen just as an episode in the history of letterforms,
though the project was conceived with wider ambitions. It arose
as part of a proposed study of craft techniques (for their eventual
improvement) to be undertaken by the newly founded Académie
des Sciences. A committee was set up in 1693, and a report of 1699
described its progress: 'We have begun with the art which preserves
all others – namely printing. Monsieur Jaugeon, who took it upon
himself to describe one aspect, has first of all gathered together
alphabets of every language, both dead and living, with a supplement to each one, showing characters peculiar to certain sciences
such as astronomy, chemistry, algebra, and music. Next, no longer
restricted to simple description, he showed the Academy a new
French alphabet that had been chosen to please the eye as far as was
possible.'[2] By this time, therefore, what had set out as an investigation of all trades, and printing first of all, was now concerned with
the design of a particular set of letterforms: the 'romain du roi'.
This existed first as a set of engraved plates, which were added to
and modified over the years (up to 1718). And it existed also as a set
of punches and types, which seem to have followed the forms of the
early plates, and which were used to print a book: the *Médailles du
règne de Louis XIV*, published in 1702 from the Imprimerie Royale.
The committee of the Académie was thus, in effect, working for the

King: the Imprimerie Royale had been established by Richelieu in 1640, thereby formalizing the long tradition of nominating 'printers for the King'. The collaboration shows clearly the centralization of political and academic authority that was peculiar to France. In England, Moxon, though he became a Fellow of the Royal Society, wrote and worked simply as an individual, living by his trade.

Two features of the work of this committee introduced new elements of system to printing. In the first phase of their work, Sébastien Truchet, for the committee, drew up a table (dated 13 June 1694) of the proportions of the types at the Imprimerie Royale. This goes further than Moxon's correlation of names and feet-equivalents, in giving unit values for the bodies of each named size: from 7.5 units to 192 units (poster types) in 20 steps. The unit was not then explicitly related to any system of general measurement. But a later document (6 August 1695) gives the relation of these sizes to a current general unit, the 'ligne' (a twelfth part of a 'pouce' – the French 'inch'). This system was developed further and presented in an undated summarizing plate, headed 'Calibres de toutes les sortes et grandeurs de lettres' (see example 1, pp.184–5). This diagram was not formally published, but proofs of this and other plates in the set to which it belongs survive in some libraries.

The 'Calibres de toutes les sortes et grandeurs de lettres' lives up to its title. It presents a vision of an ordered sequence of sizes of type, and also of parts of characters and their position on the faces of types: their x-height, capital or ascender height (the same value in this case), descender height, and the space above and below the character on the face. All this was now calibrated to a unit of 1/204 of a 'ligne'. Although the committee has often been seen as an unworldly and impractical group of theoreticians, the system being developed here was a sophisticated view of typography, with profound and highly practical implications. In one remark in his manuscript

2. A. Jammes, 'Académisme et typographie: the making of the romain du roi', *Journal of the Printing Historical Society*, no.1, 1965, p.73. My sources in this section are primarily this account by Jammes, with Mosley's recent splendidly detailed articles, especially his 'French academicians and modern typography: designing new types in the 1690s', *Typography Papers*, no.2, 1997, pp.5–29.

account of the work, quoted by his principal historian, Jacques Jaugeon showed himself to be 'an open-minded and appreciative experimenter': 'Experience has shown us that it is in the harmony of parts that an agreeable letter consists, and that often enough it depends on an indefinable quality – "un je ne sais quoi" – that can be felt rather than defined.' (Mosley, 'French academicians and modern typography', p.13.)

The second and more celebrated feature of the 'romain du roi' was the grid against which the letters of the engraved plates were represented, and by means of which they were constructed. In its first form, this grid comprised 64 squares (8 x 8) for capital letters; later, each unit was subdivided into 6, to give 2,304 squares. Even in its simpler form and in the largest sizes, this system could not be of much practical use in cutting punches. And, in any case, the type of the *Médailles* was produced before the majority of the plates had been engraved. The plates were important rather as theoretical demonstrations: suggestions of what might happen if letterforms were designed according to rational principles, and with less regard for what were by then established conventions. Thus, in some of the plates, the italic forms become 'sloped romans', by a consistent deformation of the rectangular grid. The 'romain du roi' can be seen as an innocent anticipation of the conditions of type design and text composition in the later twentieth century.

The first French printing manual appeared in 1723: *La Science pratique de l'imprimerie* by Martin Dominique Fertel (see example 2, pp.186–7). The author, who was also the book's publisher, was primarily a jobbing-printer, printing books only occasionally. Fertel worked in Saint-Omer in the north of France and, in this provincial situation, he was quite without the advantages of the centrally placed and powerful Académie. He also provides a striking contrast with the metropolitan Moxon. Though both wrote manuals of practice, addressed to fellow printers and to apprentices, where Moxon emphasized materials and 'handy-works', Fertel's book is notable for its stress on the organization of the text (it is largely concerned with book printing). With Fertel there appeared for the first time a conscious concern with the structuring of verbal information through the devices of typography: size and style of type, headings, subordinated text, space, ornaments, symbols. Some specimen pages showing typical configurations were included, and were annotated with explanatory comments. The author also takes his own text as material for instruction, pointing out how he is using the typographic repertoire: thus the list of errata in the book is given as an example of such a list. In all of these aspects, Fertel's manual exemplifies this new attitude of rationality: concerned to understand how typography works and to explain it to others.

Point systems

Some of the proposals of the committee of the Académie reappeared as elements in the work of Pierre Simon Fournier ('le jeune'), together with his mocking comments on the impractical nature of its endeavours. Fournier started his working life in the typefoundry of his elder brother, who at this time (around 1730) had acquired the materials of the Le Bé foundry. This had been the major foundry in France, and possessed the authentic types of Garamond and Granjon, cast from sixteenth-century matrices. Fournier set up his own typefounding business in Paris in the 1730s, issuing a first small specimen in 1736. In 1737 he published a table of proportions for printing type. This followed the table of the Académie, but there is no evidence to suggest that Fournier had seen that earlier scheme, which existed only in manuscript. The situation of starting afresh would have provided the right encouragement for this proposal; and Fournier was working in a climate of growing consciousness of printing, as the publication of Fertel's book suggests. And in 1723 there had been issued a decree to the French book trades which sought to fix a standard for the 'height to paper' of type: without success, for established foundries and printers would naturally resist the necessary reinvestment costs, though Fournier adopted it.

In Fournier's proposal of 1737, a system of graded body sizes was now expressed in terms of units. Fournier's typographic unit was simply related to the 'pouce' and 'ligne': the 'ligne' into was divided into 6 'points'. There were thus 72 'points' in the inch; and this proposal provided the foundation of the system eventually adopted as a standard in the English-speaking world. In 1742 Fournier published his *Modèles des caractères de l'imprimerie*, in which was reprinted the table of proportions. (That the system depended on a scale rather roughly printed on paper suggests the lack of critical accuracy that was then acceptable.) The *Modèles* was principally a specimen of the types that he had cut for his foundry, and it also included a little history of printing, and remarks on the types shown and on the advantages of systematizing body sizes. Though Fournier has been celebrated for the ornaments he designed and, sometimes rather grudgingly, for the forms of his typefaces, one should also notice that the first suggestion of the 'family' of types comes in his work: three variants ('ordinaire', 'moyen', 'gros œil') of a 'cicéro' type were shown in the *Modèles*. The veins of systematization and of decoration were thus interwoven in his work: ornaments were cast on standard bodies, for easy combination. It was natural that Fournier should be involved with the *Encyclopédie* (providing material for the article on 'caractère') and that he should publish, towards the end of his life, as a 'summa', a *Manuel typographique*. He envisaged this as comprising four volumes: on type, on printing, lives of the great typographers, and specimens of type. Only the first and fourth were done (in 1764 and 1766) before his death in 1768. The *Manuel* contained a simplification of Fournier's point system: the 'ligne' was discarded and a scale of 2 'pouces' divided into 144 parts was shown. The specimens also showed considerable elaboration of the idea of variant forms of a given size and style of type: the co-ordinates of variation cannot be exactly defined (or couched in twentieth-century terminology), but, roughly expressed, they were those of the vertical proportions of the letterforms, relative to the body of the type, and of the width of the appearing letterforms.

    Modern letters

Pierre Simon Fournier may be seen as standing at a mid-point in the development of a more rational, enlightened typography. One can perhaps adopt the term 'transitional', sometimes used to categorize his types: transitional, that is, between the 'old faces' of – above all in his context – the school of Garamond, and the 'modern' typefaces that were to become the fashionable norm in France towards the end of the century. With this latter term one is brought back to consider the question of 'modern typography'.

    In typography, in the English language only, 'modern' has come to be used to describe that category of type design whose beginnings may be seen in the 'romain du roi', and whose first proper appearance has been located in a type of François Ambroise Didot of 1784. One finds the word acquiring this sense in such phrases as 'modern-cut printing types' (Caleb Stower, 1808) and 'modern or new fashioned faced printing type' (Richard Austin, 1819).[3] And even in Fournier's *Manuel typographique* there is a display comparing his 'italique moderne' against an 'italique ancienne'.[4] As a term of stylistic categorization, 'modern' now describes the treatment of serifs (flat and unbracketed), modelling of stroke width (abrupt and exaggerated), and the shading or stress of letters (vertical). This development followed the greater presence and fashionable success, during the eighteenth century, of letters printed from engraved plates: the departure from the old-face norms of these letters was partly entailed by the nature of the engraving process. And the fashion for very thin strokes in type may also be attributed to the development of smoother papers and of presses that could be operated with greater precision. 'Modern' in the typography of the Didot family and of Giambattista Bodoni describes this kind of letterform deployed in arrangements that were unornamented or decorated only with the patterns and devices of the neo-classical style (see example 4, pp.190–1 below). But, beyond polite fashion, the style carried with it a vision: that of a shedding of rococo baggage, a return to fundamentals and to the order of the classical age. It was, indeed, entirely appropriate as the style of the new republic in France.

If the term 'modern' as a hard and defined category of type design dates from well after its first appearance, the shift from an old to a new was certainly a conscious matter for those who were making it. In 1771, towards the end of his life, Louis Luce published his *Essai d'une nouvelle typographie*: a specimen of types he had cut while employed as a punchcutter at the Imprimerie Royale. The newness of this 'new typography' lay in the forms of letters and of ornaments, and in their systematization (of the ornaments especially). Luce had published his first specimen in 1740 and seems to have slightly preceded Fournier in taking up the idea of condens-

---

3. Caleb Stower, *The printer's grammar*, London, 1808, facing p. 530; Richard Austin, quoted and reproduced by Johnson, *Type designs*, pp. 74–5.
4. See the reproduction in Updike, *Printing types*, vol. 1, facing p. 264.

ing letterforms. This development appeared first in types from the
Netherlands, an association that Fournier perpetuated in his phrase
'le goût Hollandais'. The motivation for this turn towards narrower
letterforms may have been – as the term suggests – a matter of taste.
But the style entailed economic advantages. Luce gave no hint of
this in the 'Avertissement' to his *Essai*, being there principally concerned to differentiate his letters from those of the 'romain du roi'
(which he would have worked on in its later stages); he suggested
that his types related more closely to contemporary handwriting
than those of his immediate predecessors at the Imprimerie Royale.
The economic advantages became more explicit with Fournier, who
used the name 'poétique' for some of his condensed types, thus
suggesting their advantage in setting the long (twelve-syllable) lines
of the Alexandrine verse form without the need to break. But elsewhere he indulged in some disparagement of 'le goût Hollandais'
– condensed forms and with large faces on the body of the type – and
of the Dutch, whose concern to make money 'has led them deliberately to acquire types of a cramped, starved look, so that they may
get in more words to the line and more lines to the page. They are
not troubled by their ugliness, provided they are profitable.' (From
an article of 1756, quoted by Hutt, *Fournier*, p. 46; see also example 3,
pp. 188–9.)

Apart from developments in letterforms, Fournier's work in
systematization was taken up and developed by members of the
Didot family, who dominated all aspects of typography – typefounding, paper-making, printing and publishing – in France in
the later eighteenth and early nineteenth century (see example
5, pp. 192–3). François Ambroise Didot, primarily a typefounder,
adopted Fournier's point system but related it to the general system
of measurement then standard in France: the 'pied du roi'. In this
modification, 72 points were made to equal the standard French
inch. And further in the spirit of rationality, he proposed that the
traditional names of body sizes be discarded in favour of point-size
designations. Didot also suggested that the 'cicéro', the standard
for determining sizes of type (6 point, 8 point, 12 point, and so on),
be changed from 12 to 11 points, to compensate for the larger value
that the departure from Fournier's point had brought. But 11 is not
exactly divisible and does not allow the modular approach that is

necessary to typography. This proposal was not taken up; but the 12 point 'cicéro' and the relation to the 'pied du roi' were generally adopted, and it is this 'Didot' system that became current in typography, outside the English-speaking world. With an irony that has dogged attempts at standardization in printing, soon after F. A. Didot's proposal had been formulated and accepted, the metric system was established in France: its terminology had been devised by 1795 and the system was given legal status in 1801. In 1811 an attempt was made by Firmin Didot (son of François Ambroise) to introduce a metric point (with a value of 0.4 mm), but by then the inch-based point was too well established, and the proposal did not command the support of the Emperor. The next steps in the history of typographic measurement were taken in the USA, and belong to another phase of systematization, in the context of further mechanization of printing.

Another element in the rationalization of typography appeared fleetingly at this time in republican France. This took the form of a law of 1798 for the regulation of the sizes of stamped papers.[5] Sizes were to be derived from a sheet 0.25 square metre in area, with lengths of sides having a constant ratio of $1:\sqrt{2}$ (1:1.41). Two years before this, the scientist and writer Georg Christoph Lichtenberg had put forward this principle of constant ratio for book formats, though without suggesting measurement values.[6] There is no evidence to suggest that Lichtenberg's proposal was known in France; and once the principle of constant proportion had been formulated, the solution of $1:\sqrt{2}$ could be found, as Lichtenberg remarked, by 'any beginner in algebra'. This system was nowhere generally adopted, and paper sizes remained subject only to the rough and differing systematizations of separate makers: until the unified standard along these lines was instituted in Germany, to become a central element of twentieth-century new typography (see chapter 9).

5. The 'loire sur le timbre' of '13 Brumaire an 7' (3 November 1798), reprinted in: J. B. Duvergier (ed.), *Collection complète des lois*, 2nd edn, vol. 11, Paris: Guyot, 1835, pp. 33–41.
6. G. C. Lichtenberg, 'Über Bücherformate', Göttinger Taschenkalender, 1796, pp. 171–8; reprinted in the *Vermischte Schriften* of Lichtenberg (Göttingen: Dieterich, 1803, and later editions).

Style and serviceability

The question of a modern typography was given some illumination in a document from Paris in 1800.[7] The printer and typefounder Joseph Gillé ('fils') had submitted for comment a specimen of his ornaments and types to the 'Societé Libre des Sciences, Lettres et Arts' in Paris. In a climate in which awareness of printing seems to have been quite notable – the climate of the *Encyclopédie*, above all – one might imagine that such an event was a normal occurence. However, in his address to the Societé, Citizen Sobry, a printer, noted that Gillé was 'the first artist in typography to consult scholars', and, he suggested, 'it was high time for such a move to be made' (Updike, 'A translation', pp. 175, 176). He then went on to appraise the specimen and especially the roman and italic letters: 'To say that Citizen Gillé's types are engraved [cut] in the style and according to the system of the present day, that is, of Didot, and that they are executed with all Didot's refinement, would be equivalent to saying that Citizen Gillé had reached the zenith of his art, if renown were a sufficient title to pre-eminence. But what happens to be the fashion is not always perfect, and to come to a decision in a case like this, the proper thing is to follow principles rather than the vagaries of taste.' (Updike, 'A translation', p. 178.)

Sobry's objection was that Didot (presumably François Ambroise) had pushed the art of printing and of cutting letters 'to a destructive ultra-perfection. In lending it certain secondary qualities he has taken from it the one essential quality; and Citizen Gillé, who works in his style, may, like him, be praised for his efforts but hardly for his achievement.' (Updike, 'A translation', p. 178.) In text set in the most refined Didot moderns, the reader's progress was impeded by the sheer formal beauty of the letters, which were too light in colour and in which similarities of form were emphasized. By contrast, old face types were darker and their letters more differentiated: one read without being conscious of reading. This had seemed to be proved in an experiment cited by Sobry:

> When Didot was beginning to bring his system into vogue, the last of the Anissons, who always refused to adopt it for the Imprimerie Nationale, established a comparison, which, if the report had not been hushed up, would have enlightened the

general public as to the defect, in principle, of the innovation. Anisson took a page printed from the types in the Didot manner, and had it copied with the same spacing, in types of the same body, but in Garamond's manner. He put the two pages beside one another on a reading desk and placed the experts in front of them. At first they read the two pages without noticing any great difference. Anisson made them read the pages again and again, each time at a greater distance, until they could not distinguish the print at all. It turned out that the page which it was possible to make out longest was the one printed on Garamond's system, and this was readable several stages after Didot's characters had become indistinguishable. This experiment, which every-one can make for himself, is a fact which peremptorily decides between the old and the new types.
(Updike, 'A translation', p. 181.)

This is the first reported experiment into legibility, and though, like many experiments since, it was crude, it did embody the critical spirit in typography. Modern typography in the eighteenth century, while incorporating an impulse towards rationality and system, also issued in a style that exceeded the limits of reason. The address of Citizen Sobry was a call to order, for a typography that served the reader, and against a self-regarding stylism. If he spoke against the 'modern', he was in favour of a truer rationality, and perhaps a truer modernity: 'The printer's art will soon be restored to its pristine splendour if an artist, anxious to do as well as is Citizen Gillé, takes upon himself the task of bringing it back to its first principles by putting aside the sort of superficial prettiness that some have intro-duced into it, to its obvious degeneration.' (Updike, 'A translation', p. 183.)

7. See: D. B. Updike (ed.), 'A translation of the reports of Berlier and Sobry on types of Gillé fils', *The Fleuron*, no. 6, 1928, pp. 167–83. One might observe that Sobry's argument exactly confirms Updike's own preferences.

3   The nineteenth-century complex

Nineteenth-century typography has commonly been characterized in terms of loss of standards under the pressures of industrialization, and then regeneration. In this version of typographic history, 'modern' typefaces became ever thinner and spikier, until the return of 'old face' types: first in the revival of Caslon typefaces, and then in the more full-blooded reaction of the Kelmscott Press, which sent shock waves across the world. And, in Pevsner's famous thesis, it was William Morris's decision to take up design that, by some dialectical shifts, led on to the twentieth-century 'modern movement'.[1] Any examination of the question of what was modern in nineteenth-century typography must include both technical and stylistic changes, but there are other factors too. A consideration of these other aspects, especially of attempts to describe and rationalize typography, suggests that the story of decline and regeneration is too simple.

Mechanization

The major phenomenon of the period is certainly the introduction of powered machinery into the printing trade, and its consequent industrialization. As has often been remarked, in 1800 most printers were working with processes and equipment that had not changed for 300 years. By the end of the century, in a printing shop of any size, in Europe and the USA, the press would be power-driven, paper would be machine-made, finishing processes (collating and binding printed sheets) would usually be done with the aid of powered machines, and typesetting would quite possibly be carried out with Linotype or other composing machines (and certainly so within another twenty years). This modernization of printing entailed a greater division of labour, as individual operations grew in size, and as work-processes became more specialized with the introduction of complex machinery. But this tendency should not be over-exaggerated: even in the most industrially advanced countries (Britain and the USA), a large rump of small printers, setting by hand and printing perhaps by foot-driven treadle press, remained active well into the twentieth century. So too, the finishing processes continued to require a large contribution of hand-work from unskilled and sweated (usually female) labour.

The mechanization of the printing processes might plausibly be imagined as a leapfrog race, with each component process being speeded-up in turn: development in one part forcing a quickening of pace in others, and the whole being stimulated to supply a demand for more printed matter, and the greater output in turn seeming to encourage greater demand. The pace was forced by the newspapers (and, in Britain, especially by *The Times*), where success was critically dependent on large runs and rapid production. Dates of invention and patenting bear no simple relation to dates of widespread application, which are the most interesting and significant indicators, but also the hardest to discover. However, something of the progress of mechanization in printing can be suggested by listing the order of major inventions. The first successful paper-making machine (a water-powered mill) was patented in 1799 in France, in 1801 in England. Iron platen hand-presses were developed from 1800; the first powered cylinder press was in use at *The Times* in 1814. The first effective typecasting machine was patented in 1838. A machine for cutting punches was developed by 1884. Machines that both cast and composed type began to be produced in the 1880s. The mechanization of finishing processes – cutting, gathering, sewing, binding – presents an especially complex and protracted development. This was due partly to the complexity of the operations, but also to plentiful resources of cheap human labour: compositors were a more select group and their sphere was mechanized only in the face of notable resistance from workers, and under the threat of labour being imported from outside the trade. One can say that by 1900 most of the larger binderies would have been substantially mechanized.

Two new processes of this period should also be mentioned: lithography and photography. 'Typography' is here being widely and generously understood, to include much else besides metal types and their effects. But for a long time, and sometimes still,

1. See: N. Pevsner, *Pioneers of modern design*, revised edn, Harmondsworth: Penguin Books, 1960, especially chapter 1.

lithographic and typographic (or letterpress) printing were seen as having nothing essential in common. This conceptual separation corresponded to another distinction, between text and image. The process of lithography was discovered around 1798, but its potential for what might be called 'useful printing' (as against 'artistic') could at first be realized only in small-scale applications: the printing of notices or business cards, or informal publications in limited numbers. For as long as text for lithographic printing had to be written by hand or first set in type, printed by letterpress, and finally transferred photographically to a lithographic printing surface, then lithography could find only special applications, such as the printing of music and of maps. Its progress was speeded with the invention of offset printing on a cylinder press, towards the end of the century. But lithography only really came into its own, as a general method of printing, with the widespread application of photocomposition, from the 1950s onwards. Similarly, photography first came to play an important part in printing some decades after its first stage of development, in producing half-tone blocks for letterpress printing (this process was patented in 1881).

The view that the application of steam and, later, of electrical power to the printing processes led to a fall from grace, in the quality of the product, has often been expressed or implied: it was a prime motive of the 'revival of printing' movement at the end of the century. But any survey of the average products of earlier printing would suggest that the idea of a 'fall' is a myth. Standards of presswork only improved with powered printing. And, while intelligence in composition of text (leaving aside notions of beauty) is a matter that is not open to large-scale generalization, there is much to be said for the 'functional tradition' in nineteenth-century typography (as in engineering and building). If powered presses and mechanical composition divided labour at the expense of overall control of a job, the system whereby a text was divided between workers had been instituted already in the days of hand-composition. At the leading edge of the trade in Britain – in London and other metropolitan centres – compositors were usually paid by a precisely calculated piecework system, rather than by a weekly wage: this tended to encourage cutting corners for quick results, with text treated in units of length rather than of meaning.[2] In other words, it was not technical development as such that caused the loss of control over the product, but rather that the new machines were incorporated into a larger development of quality being trimmed and sacrificed, for the sake of maintaining or improving cash profits for owners. The situation of unruly, dissenting, and exploited workers had always been characteristic of printing. One may cite the observation of a historian of book-production in eighteenth-century France:

> The 'bourgeois' retained most of the power and manipulated it brutally, by hiring and firing, while the workers responded with the few devices at their disposal. They quit, they cheated on their 'voyage'; they collected small advances on the next week's work ('salé') and then disappeared; and sometimes they spied for rival publishers or the police. Although they may have felt some pride in their craft they took shortcuts and compromised on quality where it made labor easier. The results can be seen in any copy of the *Encyclopédie* today – clear, crisp typography for the most part, but margins askew here, pages misnumbered there, uneven register, unsightly spacing, typographical errors, and smudges – all of them testimony to the activity of anonymous artisans two centuries ago.
> (Darnton, *The business of enlightenment*, p. 228.)

New needs, new means

One of the 'complexes' of the nineteenth century was the interaction of demands for new kinds of printing with new means of transmitting information. Thus the need for election posters, railway timetables, manufacturers' catalogues, pictorial papers, and so on, consorted with the development of presses able to print these things, and with the invention of the visual means (processes of pictorial reproduction, typefaces) that could articulate such information adequately. In the field of letterforms, the departure from norms that the modern face represented seemed to open the way to an almost unlimited series of variations, extensions, and exaggerations, in display typefaces. Two categories of letter, which can be

2. Principles of costing a job are explained in the manuals of the period. See, for example: Jacobi, *Printing*, pp. 131–8.

derived from forms that appeared in the first half of the nineteenth
century, were to become essential constituents of the new typography of the twentieth century, and, in this perspective, may be sin-
gled out for special notice. One was to become a new style category
– the sanserif – while the other would become a variation applied to
all styles of letterform: bold type.

Sanserif, as a printing type, made its first appearance in a specimen of 1816 (of William Caslon IV), though it became established
as a recognized style of type only in the 1830s in England. At first its
associations were those of the classical world or of ancient Egypt:
in the 1816 specimen it was termed 'egyptian', and would thus be
grouped with other heavy and more or less monoline types of the
period. But where egyptians proper – as we now identify them – had
slab serifs, this mutation did without any such protusions. Other
early sanserif types were called 'grotesque', and this term has stuck,
to describe (in English and in the German 'Grotesk') nineteenth-
century, anonymously designed sanserifs – before the more formally sophisticated and trade-named typefaces of the twentieth century. In the USA, the name for this letter was and still is 'gothic' (which
in Britain has been used as another name for 'blackletter'). Both the
European 'grotesque' and American 'gothic' suggest the primitive
qualities of the letterform. It was seen as a kind of ur-letter, ancient
and elemental, and thus, in the context of early-nineteenth-century
neo-classicism, it possessed a kind of modernity. These were the letters of the iron steamships or the Euston arch.

An emboldening of letters had begun to be apparent in the
development of the modern face, and was especially evident in the
early English moderns. With the need felt for larger public notices,
and with presses more able to print them, letters had to become
larger and bolder and more various in form.[3] This requirement
seems to be at the root of the proliferation of display typefaces in
this period; but the principle of thickening came to be applied to
all sizes of type. The use of 'heavy' type for emphasis within text of a
normal weight may be seen in examples of English printing from at
least the 1840s onwards: small posters, timetables or other kinds of
essentially informational printing, where the need to articulate content overrode considerations of good taste and the conventions of
book printing.[4] The category of letterform that came to be a stand-

ard for this use was first shown in an English specimen of 1848: the Clarendon, whose tapering or 'bracketed' serifs sorted better with roman letters of normal weight, than did the more square-cut egyptian. Although the first Clarendons were designed by their founder (Besley) to be used with a related type of normal weight, they can be found set with letters of no close stylistic relationship. And, for the printing trade, 'clarendon' came to mean any thickened type used for emphasis.

Historical consciousness

During the 1840s in Britain, Caslon old-face types began to be revived and recut, for what were at first specifically historical uses: the setting of literary or devotional texts for which a period flavour was appropriate. The taste for Caslon spread to the USA, and elsewhere in Europe there were revivals along the same lines. Thus in France, 'Elzévir' types were recut: though here the Didot modern face was to remain the dominant style. In Britain, old face or old style, as it came to be termed, began from the 1860s to be a generic term and on a par with modern face. These were the two major style categories into which types for continuous text were grouped – 'old english' (blackletter) was another, lesser category – before the emergence of individualized typefaces with trade names. Occasionally in Britain, and more often on the Continent, the category of 'old face' was referred to as 'medieval': a usage that dimly and imprecisely suggested that these letters derived from the early years of printing.

The growth of an awareness of the history of printing followed from the larger phenomenon of the emergence of historical consciousness: the progress from informal writings, which retailed and reprocessed anecdotes, to attempts to provide some more objective account. This growing historical awareness is part of the phenomenon of the Enlightenment, and so part also of the modern attitude. Moxon's *Mechanick exercises* set the pattern for the inclusion of a historical component within an essentially practical manual: there

3. See the striking demonstration of this in: Twyman, *Printing 1770–1970*, p. 13.
4. For some evidence of this, see the illustrations in part 2 of Twyman, *Printing 1770–1970*, especially nos. 679, 680.

confined to his brief remarks, in the preface, on the history of the
art. This formula was repeated in the printing manuals, in the major
languages, which began to appear from the late eighteenth century onwards, providing a gradually expanding stock of historical knowledge. Fournier's *Manuel typographique* – as projected in
its four volumes, and even as published (1764–6) – stands out as
a more ambitious combination of theory and practice than was
attempted in the works that succeeded it, in France and elsewhere.
The next equivalent publication would be De Vinne's *The practice
of typography* series (1900–4). But in the manuals and in the occasional purely historical writings (in any language) on printing, the
approach remained antiquarian and anecdotal until at least the
second half of the nineteenth century: William Blades's *Life and
typography of William Caxton* (1861) has been cited as the first work
of 'scientific bibliography' (Morison, *Letter forms*, p. 67).

Composition: mechanization and systematization
While the process of printing is by definition mechanical (the
hand-press is a machine), the process of composing type had always
been one of assembly by hand, with the aid of a simple gauge:
the compositor's stick. With the development of steam-powered
printing and with the advent of machines for casting type (notably
the Bruce machine), mechanization of composition became the
obvious next step for proprietors eager to quicken the flow of work.
Some machines for assembling already cast (thus 'cold') type had
a limited success – from the middle of the nineteenth century – but
the first really effective machines came only in the late 1880s and
the 1890s. The breakthrough was achieved by the incorporation of
matrices into the machine, casting type as it was needed: line for
line (the Linotype) or character for character (the Monotype). The
problem of distributing type after printing was bypassed: softer and
less durable than founders' type, this 'hot metal' type was simply
melted down and reused.

By the later nineteenth century the pace of technical improvement, and of some further systematization of printing, was being
forced in the USA. Mechanical casting had been developed principally by the Bruce foundry in New York. Both the principal composing machines were of American origin: the Linotype was the inven-

tion of a German emigré, Ottmar Mergenthaler; the Monotype, that of Tolbert Lanston of Washington. (Though the Monotype machine was, after its early years, developed primarily by the British branch of the company and took more of the market in Britain than it did in the USA.) An important facilitating device for mechanical composition, a pantographic punchcutting machine, was developed (patented in 1885) by Linn Boyd Benton of Milwaukee: with this machine punches (and thus matrices) could be produced in the numbers necessary for mechanical composition.

It was in the USA also that a standard typographic point was finally agreed and adopted, to become the other principal unit of typographic measurement, beside the Didot point. In 1886 a committee of the US Type Founders' Association adopted the point system (Fournier's of 1764) in place of informal type body nomenclature, but with a unit value that bore no simple relation to any general system of measurement. The unit adopted was that in use in one of the leading foundries, and, as it happened, 996 of these points approximated to 35 cm: an equation, as one commentator remarked, 'of very limited utility' (Tracy, *Letters of credit*, p. 25). One might imagine that the development of composing machines would have encouraged, if not required, standardization of measurement; and this was their eventual consequence, as they spread to become the usual means of setting type. The US Type Founders' Association moved independently of the makers of the machines just then appearing; though the fact that the American foundries had begun to combine and to agree on standards does seem to have been a response to the threat to them from mechanical composition. In Britain, the new American point began to be adopted by the foundries only after a lag of some years, and in the face of some resistance. The Monotype composing machine had at first its own point system, and only later adopted what now became the Anglo-American point system.

With mechanical composition a new realm of exact calculation was introduced into typography. Monotype composition enjoyed a greater degree of precision than Linotype, which incorporated expanding – and thus not precisely calculable – spaces. But in Monotype, each character and each space was assigned a precise width, expressed as a fraction of the 18-unit-square 'em'. Thus, in principle, compositors could work out the exact location of any element in a layout. If hand setting remained an ultimate in intimacy of control – type could be shaved or tissue paper inserted – then the Monotype was its best equivalent. And by taking composition out of the hands of the compositor, Monotype was to offer a new scope for distant control of composition by the typographic designers who were to arrive on the scene in the years to come. Such control, desirable in tabular or other non-prose setting, required that the typographer find out the set widths of characters: information not usually published, but available to the determined enquirer.

Investigation and description

As described in chapter 2, the first recorded attempt to test the legibility of text had been conducted by Jean Anisson in the late eighteenth century. Other early isolated expressions of interest or opinion in the matter have been documented, but sustained investigation of legibility did not begin until the end of the nineteenth century. This research was conducted largely by physiologists or by the then newly emerging psychologists, and they approached the matter without the help or the interest of printers. Their research thus suffered from a persistent unreality in what was tested. Much work was done on testing the recognizability of isolated letters – as on an optician's test card – rather than the legibility of words or passages of text. Here the researchers were merely operating under the normal psychological assumptions of their time, and it was only when the general theoretical climate in psychology had changed that legibility could be accepted as the comprehension of meaning: not recognition, but reading. This new approach began to be evident around 1900, for example in the research of E. B. Huey in the USA. In the 1920s in Britain, enlightened work was carried out by the Medical Research Council, and published as a government (HMSO) document in R. L. Pyke's *Report on the legibility of print* (1926). In its detailed summary of previous research findings and in its official nature, this report has a certain landmark status.

If early legibility research had no effect on the practice of typography, it did nevertheless suggest a possible approach to typography: one that has its own interest, and which would reappear later in the field designated as information design. This may be seen in the work of the ophthalmologist Emil Javal, who published a series of papers on legibility in the 1870s.[5] Javal wrote from clinical experience, though with no reference to quantified tests, and without any of the inherited assumptions and dispositions of a printer or typographer. He was thus led to conclusions about the forms and treatment of text that violated typographic wisdom, but which seemed to follow from reason. The project of legibility research raised the prospect of a typography that could do something more than be beautiful: it might be effective. In Javal's work, as in that of other researchers of his time and later, what is effective receives only a limited definition, in terms of the stop-watch and measuring rule. There was no attempt to investigate reading of extended texts or of non-continuous prose, in the circumstances of everyday life. There has been an obsessively utilitarian emphasis in this research: as in Javal's search for 'une typographie compacte', whereby lines of text would be set with minimal space between them, in characters with shortened, non-projecting ascenders and descenders: saving paper and perhaps even metal. 'Effective' thus comes to mean 'cost-effective', for the printer.

Proposals of a similar eccentricity appeared in the course of James Millington's *Are we to read backwards?* (1883), which included some discussion of Javal's work (see example 6, pp. 194–5). As his title suggested, Millington toyed with the idea of the boustrophedon arrangement for text matter: alternate lines set in reverse, to make use of the eye's return journey, wasted in normal reading. The pamphlet appeared in a series published by the unorthodox and historicizing printer Andrew Tuer, and thus made some marginal connection with the printing trade. But, after a survey of the field, indicating a fairly wide contemporary debate over legibility, Millington came to common-sense and vague conclusions: type must not be too small, lines not too long, paper not too glossy.

Issues of legibility were given extended treatment in *Typographical printing-surfaces: the technology and mechanism of their production* (1916) by L. A. Legros, an engineer, and J. C. Grant, a novelist. This book, together with the four volumes that comprised T. L. De Vinne's *The practice of typography*, provided a summation of the

---

5. These were gathered and expanded on in Javal's *Physiologie de la lecture*, to which reference is here made.

work of ordering and description that was an achievement of the
period (see example 7, pp.196–7). The content of Legros and Grant's
book is fairly indicated by its title. *Typographical printing-surfaces*
was concerned with the description of the current technics of printing type (though not those of making type by hand), and included
extensive historical accounts of machinery. Legibility was treated
in terms of the resemblance between single characters: those styles
of alphabet whose letters least resembled each other were, it was
suggested, most legible. Fraktur alphabets (as a class) were found
to be among the least legible, with different characters showing
marked formal repetition: thus the common perception of the illeg-
ibility of blackletter text was supported by micrometer microscope
readings. Legros and Grant did not attempt to discuss the design
of letters from any but a technical viewpoint, nor did they consider
the design and configuration of text matter. The book thus separated off matters that would have been thought of as aesthetic. This
was not the case with De Vinne, whose work amounted to a total
description of typography, with a scope that had no exact precedent.
Other writings of this time should be mentioned: John Southward's
Modern printing (1898–1900) and the books of C. T. Jacobi. But it was
De Vinne who represented the best of the articulate printing trade at
the end of the nineteenth century: patient description and ordering of work processes in a time of change; a rational approach to
design, which respected the reader and resisted aestheticism.

4   Reaction and rebellion

News from nowhere

The paradoxes of William Morris's 'typographical adventure' are well known: the socialist who had spent his life 'in ministering to the swinish luxury of the rich'; the medievalizing craftsman whose reaction led on to twentieth-century modernism.[1] These contradictions cannot be resolved away into some black or white view of his achievement: no dogmatism, neither modernist nor traditionalist, can claim Morris entirely.

In view of the significances and theories that have been attached to Morris's typography, it is as well to establish some of the essential facts of the operation. The Kelmscott Press came at the end of Morris's life, after a time of great political engagement (in the 1880s) and after years of intense activity in designing and making. The first Kelmscott book was published in 1891, and the project was drawn to an end after his death in 1896: 62 years old and worn out. The Press produced 52 books in 66 volumes, ranging from a 16-page pamphlet to the folio *Works of Geoffrey Chaucer*. Morris's first intention may have been to produce editions of favourite texts in small numbers for distribution among his circle. But the enterprise grew, from the first book, into a substantial business: though its finances are hard to pin down and evaluate comparatively, the total turnover over seven years has been given as £50,000 (Cave, *The private press*, p. 136). The paper copy Kelmscott books were within reach of those who could afford to buy serious works: two guineas was a standard Kelmscott price, the same as a three-volume edition of Milton issued in 1890 (this was also around the level of the lowest 'comfortable' weekly income). The texts issued included several previously unpublished and amounted to a programme of greater interest and substance than was provided by the presses that followed it. If it was a 'private press', in the sense of the work being done for love rather

1. Both phrases quoted are Morris's: the first from a letter to William Bowden, 3 January 1891; the second is reported by W. R. Lethaby in his *Philip Webb and his work*, London: Oxford University Press, 1935, pp. 94–5.

than profit (though costs were covered), it was also a peculiarly public venture. It was by public demand, after the news had spread, that
the first book was printed in an edition for sale. Kelmscott books,
and their reputation, were broadcast rapidly throughout the world:
so that their effect began to be seen within months of their first appearance. It may be worth pointing out that the Press worked from
Hammersmith in London and used iron hand-presses, then still in
common use. If Morris showed no interest in the newest machines,
neither did he retreat into the country with medieval tools.

   Much of the force of the Kelmscott Press products derived from
their anachronism. Or, more exactly: not simple retreats or re-crea-
tions, the books were out of time. The types that were cut for the
press did look back towards early models, but they created something new. So too the Kelmscott book had the qualities of a dream:
an imagined typography of the past, but one that, in its physical
richness, was very much there in the present as an active statement.
The books were thus of a piece with Morris's utopianism: backward-
looking and forward-looking in one moment. Thus also they had the
quality of splendid indifference to their immediate neighbours, the
ordinary products of trade printing and publishing in Britain in the
late nineteenth century. They were the products of a vision pursued,
with no pains spared in finding good materials, especially paper
and ink. A place can be found for them in the context of the revival
of Caslon and other old-face types: here they may be seen as an extreme and emphatic fresh blow, following those more timid earlier
revivals. In some of his earlier books Morris had himself used the
Chiswick Press and Caslon, but the differences between Kelmscott
and the old face revivalists are as great as any perceived similarities.

   In their few short writings on typography, William Morris and
his adviser Emery Walker provided the view of printing history that
justified the Kelmscott rebellion, and which was to be passed down
over the years in frequent retellings. It is the view already referred
to, in which 'during the first fifty years after its invention, or until
about the year 1500, most books were works of art'.[2] From this point
there was only decline, reaching a depth of false perfection in the
typography of the Didots and Bodoni, with degeneration under
industrialization.

   Emery Walker, in particular, was the source of two principles commonly accepted since as defining good typography. The first and most fundamental was that text should be set with close word spacing, to avoid what were termed 'rivers of white' forming vertically on the page. Morris's ideal of a black page, achieved through thickened letterforms, very black ink, and a heavy impression, took this argument further, and changed it. But, after the vogue for the black effect had passed (it was only really open to hand-press printing on dampened paper), the ideal of closely spaced words remained as a legacy of the Walker–Morris approach. The second idea was of the 'unity of the book'. The essential unit was a double-page spread: facing pages had to balance and any ornament or illustration had to harmonize with the type. Thus, to take the example so often cited in this connection, the *Hypnerotomachia Poliphili* (1499) is said to succeed because its woodcuts are matched in colour to the areas of type against which they are balanced: a view that leads easily to regarding words and images as no more than areas of visual texture.[3] This theory tended to assume that the means of producing illustrations in books should be by cutting or engraving on wood: an assumption that for traditionalist designers lasted well into the age of process-engraving. There is some irony here in the fact that Emery Walker was himself a process-engraver by profession. Walker had refused the offer of a partnership in Kelmscott Press, 'having some sense of proportion' he explained.[4] It seems that for Walker, the Kelmscott ideals, of the black page and woodcut decoration, were matters separate from his everyday work, and from his deepest preferences in typography.

In the wake of Kelmscott

Emery Walker was to perform the function of 'éminence grise' to the 'revival of printing movement' in Britain, on the Continent and

2. Walker's words, from his 1924 Sandars lectures, are quoted by Franklin, *Emery Walker*, p. 14. The prime source of the Walker–Morris view of typography is their joint essay 'Printing' (1893), reprinted in Morris, *The ideal book*, pp. 59–66.

3. See, for example: Updike, *Printing types*, vol. 1, p. 76; Tschichold, *Die neue Typographie*, p. 17.

4. From an extended autobiographical statement, quoted by Franklin, *Emery Walker*, p. 30.

in the USA, which grew out of the inspiration of Kelmscott Press.
This was symptomatic: for the movement was chiefly conducted by
those coming from outside the printing trade, and a sympathetic
source of practical knowledge was important. Beyond his role as
informal adviser to several aspiring printers, Walker entered into a
partnership in one of these ventures: with Thomas Cobden-Sanderson in the Doves Press (1900–16); though the capital was provided
by Cobden-Sanderson's wife. While the other private presses of
this period were, to varying degrees, imitations of Kelmscott, or
were otherwise without any clear direction beyond the wish to do
beautiful printing, Doves Press books stand out as the products of a
clear vision. It used an interpretation of a Jenson type, without the
amateur qualities (in the worst sense) that characterized the types
of the other presses. Illustration was renounced: Doves Press books
were exercises in pure typography; Renaissance and Romantic literary texts were used for the most part. Cobden-Sanderson espoused
a quasi-mystical notion of 'the book beautiful'. Like Morris on occasions, he regarded printing as a fall from the ideal of calligraphy. At
the least, the practice of calligraphy was proposed as essential to the
printer. 'Such practice would keep Type alive under the influence of
an ever living and fluent prototype.' (Cobden-Sanderson, *The ideal
book*, p. 2.)

Cobden-Sanderson – who, from a career as a lawyer, had taken
up bookbinding as a living – went to Edward Johnston's writing
classes at the Central School of Arts & Crafts, and Johnston and his
pupils were employed to draw the initial letters that were the only
decorations of Doves Press books.

The other private presses of this time in Britain may be passed
over without much comment. C. R. Ashbee's Essex House Press
is of interest within the context of that interesting man's life and
work, but made no contribution to typography. The latter part of
this judgement may be fairly applied to the other presses, whose
operations were directed by lesser designers than Ashbee: Ash-
endene, Eragny, Golden Cockerel. In the Vale Press (1896–1903) one
encounters the work of Charles Ricketts. He may stand as one of the
clearest representatives of a new figure who appears in printing and
publishing at this time: the book designer. Ricketts worked in this
capacity for commercial publishers both before and after the life of

the Vale Press, attempting to take control of the design and decoration (the two aspects were nearly synonymous) of the whole book, especially its binding and displayed elements. Before the appearance of the book designer, 'designer' had, in the context of publishing, meant essentially 'illustrator'. The work of Ricketts, and other designers for commercial publishers of the late nineteenth century, represents the incursion of art into machine production; and even Vale Press books were printed on powered presses at the Ballantyne Press. Though sharing some stylistic resemblances with Kelmscott books, the work of these designers was without qualms about 'the machine', was without any social impulse, and participated in the satanic-erotic spirit of the 1890s. Though Morris's products (outside typography) had been commandeered by the earlier aesthetic movement, his work shared nothing in intention or in practice with the culmination of aestheticism at the close of the century.

The revival of formal writing

An investigation of writing was entailed by the Arts & Crafts rebellion: printing, as an early form of mass-production, was seen as inevitably sharing some of the taint cast on mechanization, and formal writing thus possessed a pre-lapsarian glow. Ruskin collected manuscripts; so too did William Morris, who characteristically made the next step and took to writing and illuminating his own. The academic, palaeographic interest of this time was thus joined by the desire to revive the practice of writing. A central, mediating figure here was W. R. Lethaby, who had deep historical knowledge of building and culture in classical antiquity and the medieval period, and was able to connect this with a strong concern for the regeneration of contemporary culture. It was Lethaby who recognized in Edward Johnston the capacity to take on the work of reinventing formal writing, with only the lead given by Morris (and one or two other early investigators) to follow. Within a year of his being directed by Lethaby to take up the practice, Johnston started (in 1899) to teach his first class in writing, at the Central School of Arts & Crafts.

In view of the insipid nature of much of the 'calligraphy' that has followed it, this term seems inappropriate for Johnston's activity (see example 11, pp. 204–5). His formal writing and his teaching show the Arts & Crafts movement at its most vital. This work was

at first bound to be experimental: there were no rules or models
to follow, except those that could be discovered from manuscripts
and which could be rediscovered in the act of writing by Johnston
and his pupils, whom he regarded as partners in the exploration.
The models were certainly old ones: his first 'foundational hand' (a
half-uncial) derived from a manuscript from around the year 700;
his later basic model was that of a tenth-century Winchester Psalter.
Johnston's concern, however, was always with fresh creation. This
was the point of hand-work: mere copying of these or other models
was not contemplated; mistakes were crossed through and left to
stand; writing for reproduction – which inevitably led to touch-
ing up and fudging – was resisted. Thus, for example, the idea of
freedom ('as having skilled and unaffected boldness') was essential
to him, as was that of constraint: 'True spontaneity, however, seems
to come from *working by rule, but not being bound by it*.' (Johnston,
Writing & illuminating, & lettering, pp. 203, 333 [Johnston's empha-
sis].) And, in a letter of 1903, he wrote: 'Set no limit to your hopes
(which may contemplate Eternity) but *every limit of the moment to
your work*.' (P. Johnston, *Edward Johnston*, p. 135 [Johnston's empha-
sis].) Despite chronic slowness and apparent indirection – entailed
by his seriousness and inability to compromise – Johnston did (with
the help of his pupils) complete one book: *Writing & illuminating, &
lettering* (1906). And, with this work, which has stayed continuously
in print, and through his teaching and the teaching of his pupils
– and of their pupils – the revival of formal writing was effected.

   Johnston himself resisted much involvement in printing: apart
from his moral doubts about mechanical reproduction, the project
of formal writing was already a fully demanding task. He had only
marginal dealings with the design of letterforms for printing. His
one real involvement with the designing of a typeface for text printing was the italic type for Kessler's Cranach Press. But, far from
being confined to memorial scrolls and certificates, the revival of
writing did have a pervasive effect on typography. Most fundamentally, it was a means of raising awareness of letters, and of developing skills in their handling. Anyone who had learned formal writing
at school would from this have access to principles of the construction of letters and of their combination as text: lessons that could
be transferred to typography. One might plausibly argue that, for

its best standards, the theory and practice of typography has always looked to – or perhaps held at the back of its mind – the practice of formal writing in the design of letters and in their disposition as text.

Trade aesthetics

The return to pre-modern sources for letterforms was in part a reaction to what was felt – by Lethaby, especially – as the degenerations of aestheticism. The aesthetic impulse had in the 1870s and 1880s been a high-minded reforming movement in the USA and in Britain. It was an attempt to infuse art into every aspect of comfortable lives, through considered, simplified decoration, which replaced the stylistically promiscuous overload of ornament that had then become normal. In typography, this intellectual aestheticism was best represented by James McNeill Whistler's experiments in asymmetry (in his own books). Another side of this phenomenon appeared in the printing trade in the USA and Britain, becoming known as 'artistic printing'. Where Whistler and other leaders of taste largely confined their experiments to books, artistic printing found its application in jobbing work.

The characteristics of artistic printing can be simply summarized: an absence of any rules or obvious logic in the disposition of visual elements; the simulation of 'freedom' in the patterns made from these elements; the use of letters and ornaments that defy ideas of normative construction; the use of several colours, often in soft, pastel shades. Artistic printing was taken up by letterpress printers, and a large part of their motivation was a wish to outdo in decorative freedom the lithographic printers who were beginning to provide significant competition. Aestheticism could lend intellectual sanction to a style that was commercially motivated. In Britain, uniquely – as Nicolete Gray suggested – artistic printing occurred at the moment when a change in taste became apparent: between highbrow and lowbrow, between a minority and a mass-market (Gray, *Nineteenth century ornamented typefaces*, pp. 108–9). Thus, in the 1890s, while the intellectual minority was aligned with Kelmscott Press and Arts & Crafts values, artistic printing had reached its degenerate extreme. The pattern persisted into the new century, and artistic printing became the style of the trade. Where the reformers of printing cultivated restraint, appropriateness, sensitivity to meaning, the trade prized technical ingenuity and ostentation. This can be seen most clearly – even now – in the printing that the trade does to advertise its own achievements: as in the printers' calendar, where images of exquisite bad taste show off immaculate technique.

Design for print

In the publishing trade, at least, there was some recognition of Arts & Crafts aspirations. This manifested itself superficially in pale imitations of Kelmscott style, as in the Everyman series of books of J. M. Dent (from 1905, and into the 1930s). The deeper and more lasting repercussion came with the appearance of the typographer. Morris prepared the ground here, setting the pattern of an outsider to the trade, with strong historical interests, and a concern for the whole product. Morris, however, never sought to work through the trade. The typographer came into existence when the attempt to raise standards, and to rediscover the lost aesthetic factor, began to be conducted within trade printing and publishing. For the young men and women who took up typography under the spell of Kelmscott, printing was at first predominantly a matter of aesthetics: the wish to make beautiful books. If they had not the means to start their own press, then it had to be done through the trade; and, for those who were socially motivated, this was the proper course. But, in any case, the perils of aimless luxury printing had soon become apparent in the hands of those less committed and less visually sure than Morris.

Reading accounts of the typography of this period, written by anyone under the Kelmscott influence, one receives the impression that the printing trade had entirely lost its standards of good work, having sunk under the dross of novelty display letters and emaciated text types printed on shiny paper. This is an essentially stylistic view of the matter, and one that leaves out of account the element of rationality that was still then present within the trade. This rational element may be seen in the moves to reform Anglo-American typographic measurement, in the handbooks of printing that appeared in these years, and in the output of a solid core of the trade carrying out the ordinary jobs of printing for information and instruction and pleasure.

For a representative of the best trade values, one may turn again to T. L. De Vinne. At a printers' convention in August 1892, De Vinne proposed the ideal of 'masculine printing', in opposition to the 'feminine' variety that he saw as a weakening of standards. This latter was an approach interested in ornamental effects and especially in a cultivation of hair-line delicacy, as if in imitation of lithography: he seems to have been describing artistic printing. By contrast:

> The object of the masculine style is the instruction of the reader. To do this, the printer tries to show the intent of the writer by the simplest methods. He does it by selecting easily read types of good cut, and of the plainest form. He does not refuse the aid of the headband or initial, or any device that helps the reader to a better understanding of the subject, but he does discard every ornament that needlessly diverts his attention. He does not try to show his skill, nor his fads, nor his employer's wealth of types. He keeps himself and his notions in the background. He tries to make his work readable by its simplicity and its honest workmanship, and he succeeds perfectly when the reader finds it a pleasure to read his work, without thinking at all of the means by which this pleasure is had.[5]

De Vinne acknowledged the William Morris ideal – 'masculine printing' summons up the black, heavily impressed Kelmscott pages – and that he should do so within months of the first appearance of Kelmscott books is a testimony to the rapidity of their effect. But he distanced himself from any uncritical adulation of that typography, sensing perhaps the dangers of its strongly formal motivation. His view was a more open one than Morris's, and it gave room in the pantheon to Didot as well as to Jenson. De Vinne represented the possibility of a proper typography coming from within the trade. But he was to prove an exceptional voice, and the future would lie with the typographer.

5. De Vinne, 'Masculine printing', *United Typothetae of America*, 6th Annual Convention, 1892, pp. 163–4.

5 Traditional values in a new world

In the nineteenth century, apart from its woodletter display typography, the distinctive American contribution came in the form of mechanical improvements. In the fields of punchcutting and type-casting and in the composition of type, the important mechanical advances had all been made in the USA. So too, American powered printing presses – those of Robert Hoe, above all – had gained an international reputation. But, despite this technological success, for the visual substance of their work American printers and type-founders looked to, or followed unthinkingly, European models. American typography, up to 1900, consisted essentially of regional variations on European themes. Its most enduring contributions came from the scholar-printers, who wrote from a mastery of their trade: Isiah Thomas, the early historian of American printing, Joel Munsell and Theodore Low De Vinne. De Vinne's work was a culmination of the nineteenth-century tradition of sound practice and sound writing about that practice and its history, with a common-sense rationalism that was little tempted by aesthetic experiment.

The relative visual stagnation of American typography was markedly and rapidly affected by the phenomenon of the Kelmscott Press books. The extent and force of this reaction to Morris's typography was more noticeable than in Britain or on the continent of Europe, and this suggests the degree of hunger for aesthetic elements in printing. The Kelmscott style was taken up most eagerly by the 'literary' and 'artistic' book publishers in Boston, Chicago, and New York. It was here, in the trade editions of publishers such as Copeland & Day, Houghton Mifflin, Stone & Kimball, that the impetus provided by Kelmscott encouraged the best and least slavishly imitative results. Private presses were set up in the wake of Kelmscott, but were as inconsequential as they were in Europe in their achievements. It was a strength of American typography that ways were found of applying craft ideals to commercial work that used machine composition and powered printing. The presence of beneficent institutional patrons – universities, museums, foundations – requiring quality printing of serious intellectual content, provided staple work for several of the presses that led the American 'revival of printing' (though the term 'revival' has no real meaning in the American context).

Practice and history

Of the typographers who started work around the time of Kelmscott, and who were notably – if briefly – affected by it, Daniel Berkeley Updike stands out. Updike began with the Boston publisher Houghton Mifflin, moving after some years to work at their Riverside Press in Cambridge Massachusetts, and thus learning the rudiments of printing at first hand. In 1892 he completed the design of *The book of common prayer*, a freelance commission. This comprised the 'chilly but workmanlike' text typography of the De Vinne Press with surrounding decorations designed by Bertram Goodhue and Updike himself (Updike, *Notes on the Merrymount Press*, p. 9). It was an unsatisfactory conjunction which seemed to epitomize the state of cultivated American typography at that moment. With the offer of a second major freelance job – the design of an altar book – he was able to leave the Riverside Press (in 1893) and set up on his own as a designer. According to Updike's own account of his career, the establishment of his press was an accident, based on ignorance, rather than the result of any long-held vision. 'In no exact sense was the Press ever founded – it only began; and as to its progress – it merely continued.' (Updike, *Notes on the Merrymount Press*, p. 56.) The move was made, however, in the wish to get what he wanted: as with all such decisions by typographers to acquire their own equipment, before and since.

Updike's early work followed the pattern of the small presses of the time; and, as was obligatory in those circles, he too made the pilgrimage to Kelmscott House, shortly after Morris's death. He had two typefaces cut for his own use, both loose variations on the Jenson model. The first, Merrymount, was designed principally by Bertram Goodhue, around 1895 and at the height of Updike's Kelmscott phase, as the 'black' quality of the letters suggest. An architect by profession, Goodhue was then active also as a book decorator, and was responsible for the design of another typeface of the period, which was to become widely available in its large set of variant forms. This was Cheltenham, first issued by the American

Type Founders Company in 1904: a typeface that seemed to rest on the 'bad' side of the divide in taste that separated the trade from the printing revivalists. The Press's second type was Montallegro, designed by the Englishman Herbert Horne: first in use in 1905, and an index of Updike's move away from the Kelmscott style, towards a lighter, more Italianate style of printing.

The success of the Merrymount Press, both commercially and in the character of its output, followed from the quality of its work, in all departments, and from finding steady customers who wanted distinguished printing, especially among the academic institutions of New England and the literary publishers. Updike made a point of accepting work of all kinds: visiting cards as well as university calendars and books. The size of the firm was deliberately limited, and Updike or John Bianchi (his business partner from 1915) could oversee every job in detail. In the 1920s it was described as employing fifteen compositors, four pressmen and two readers.[1] As well as the powered cylinder presses that it used from early on, Monotype composing machines were acquired, after much deliberation.[2] The Merrymount Press was thus a fully commercial operation of some size. But Updike found himself becoming a printer, diffidently, and he never showed any great interest in the mechanics of composition or presswork, such as was displayed by the other American printer-typographers – De Vinne above all.

In a similar manner, Updike found himself doing history and writing about the practice of typography. His writings on practice were occasional essays and, as was consistent with his common-sense traditionalist approach (decisions should more or less decide themselves), they offered very little detailed commentary: they do however express, at a more general level, and with considerable grace and moral force, what the work of typography entails. His single work of history was published first in 1922: the two volumes of *Printing types*. The book derived from lectures on 'The technique of printing' given at the Graduate School of Business Administration at Harvard between 1911 and 1916. The demands of this first audience for Updike's history can be discerned in its published form. The book has the subtitle 'A study in survivals', and it was intended 'to show what types have survived for modern use' (Updike, *Printing types*, vol. 1, p. xii). The utilitarian justification came in its penultimate chapter, 'The choice of types for a composing room', which addressed the decisions to be made when setting up a printing establishment, and thus touched most directly the concerns of 'business administration'. So too the last chapter, on 'Industrial conditions of the past and their relation to the printer's problem to-day' had a business rationale, as well as serving Updike's larger purpose of arguing that there had been no 'golden age', and thus no fall, and that good work was still possible in the modern world. 'The outlook for typography is as good as ever it was – and much the same. Its future depends largely on the knowledge and taste of educated men.' (Updike, *Printing types*, vol. 2, p. 275.)

But the major achievement of Updike's book was its history, extending over 500 pages, of the types used in Western printing. His account proceeds first by time (1450–1500; 1500–1800; the nineteenth century and after) and then by place. As well as discussing types as shown in specimens, he took representative books, focussing on the types used in them. But there was no strict method employed, and his tone was informal. The book was a product of lightly-worn knowledge, much of it acquired through observation of artefacts rather than from authorities. His opinions were not hidden: his prejudice against German culture and against extreme neo-classicism; his feeling for warmer, less formal products; his special interest in Spanish typography. Though it stands at the head of a line of professional historical research into typography, *Printing types* was essentially the product of a widely cultivated working typographer. This explains its qualities and why the book has not been surpassed, although a good deal of its content requires revision.

Designer typography

D. B. Updike was the oldest of the generation of typographers that produced the American 'revival of printing'. He also stood rather apart from the others in running his own printing company, rather than working as a freelance typographic designer. The other leading

1. W. A. Dwiggins, 'D. B. Updike and the Merrymount Press', *The Fleuron*, no. 3, 1924, pp. 1–8.
2. The final decision to install Monotype equipment was made in 1927. See: Morison & Updike, *Selected correspondence*, and Nicolas Barker's discussion in his introduction to that book (p. xxvi).

figures of this group – Bruce Rogers, Frederic Goudy, W. A. Dwiggins, Will Ransom, T. M. Cleland, Frederic Warde – all worked for most of their careers as freelance designers. Some others worked for large publishing or printing houses, such as Carl P. Rollins at Yale University Press. High standards of design and production were achieved notably by the university presses, which could provide ideal conditions for good work: serious books with real problems of design to be resolved, in conditions free of the more extreme demands of the market place.

The patterns of work of these typographers were eclectic, perhaps more so than their counterparts in the reform of printing movement in Britain, and this was a reflection of the younger and more open society in which they operated. The move from 'commercial art' – advertising or magazine illustration – into book or typeface design work was a typical feature of their careers. Thus the doyen of the book designers, Bruce Rogers, started out doing commercial art and illustration in Indianapolis before moving to Boston and there falling into the orbit of the literary publishers. He too was among the young men who had been astonished by the sight of Kelmscott books. Following in Updike's path, Rogers joined Houghton Mifflin at their Riverside Press in 1896. After some years there, he was given what seems to have been a very free hand in designing books in limited editions, published by Houghton Mifflin as a form of self-advertisement. This set the pattern for Rogers's subsequent career, which was devoted to the design of exclusive books in a highly-wrought decorative manner whose historical references were adjusted to the period of the text. He became renowned for the infinite pains devoted especially to the design of title pages: labour was still cheap enough for him and other such typographers to work through rough sketches and successive stages of proofing, rather than by precise first-time instructions on a measured layout. The results were books designed for collectors, who bought a 'Bruce Rogers' rather than any particular text.

Rogers made two extended working visits to Britain (1916–19, 1926–32). The first, as discussed in chapter 6, was of some importance to the just nascent British revival. By then he could represent a distinctively American combination of an exquisitely worked decorative typography and an untroubled acceptance of machine composition. This conjunction was also evident in the two typefaces that he designed. Both were exercises in the style of the Jenson roman. The first, Montaigne, cut in 1901 for the Riverside Press, was not commercially issued; the second, Centaur, after limited initial application as a founder's type, was eventually adapted for Monotype composition. Centaur embodied the characteristic qualities of Rogers's work: exquisite refinement and judicious historical reference, finding its place in the modern world only in the luxury market.

Trade relations

Other, more popular and trade-oriented applications of the growth of typographic consciousness can be seen in the work of Will Bradley and Frederic Goudy. Like Rogers, they had their beginnings in commercial art, were drawn to typography under the spell of Kelmscott, and, after starting their typographic careers in Chicago, eventually moved east. Bradley was essentially a graphic artist and a designer of display typefaces and ornaments, having a long association with the American Type Founders Company. His work belongs as much to the history of graphic design as to that of typography.

After unsuccessful attempts at making a living as a printer, Goudy was principally active as a designer of typefaces. His Village Press carried on production until 1938, but it was not a commercial operation; its continuation and, he suggested, its achievements were due to Bertha Goudy, his wife and co-worker. Frederic Goudy was prolific as a designer of typefaces: the bulk of these were display faces, for use in advertising, but he also designed text faces and, from 1920, was employed as a consultant designer by the American Monotype company. Although much attached to historical models, he took no part in the attempts at exact recreation of these models: his typefaces were, rather, free variations on historical themes. This approach was in marked contrast to the policy of the British Monotype company and its consultant, Stanley Morison; Goudy came to be one of Morison's anti-figures. Thus Morison was concerned to produce a typeface – such as Times New Roman – which 'has the merit of not looking as if it had been designed by somebody in particular – Mr Goudy for instance, who has designed a whole century of peculiar looking types …' (Letter of 15 September 1937: Morison & Updike, *Selected correspondence*, p. 185.) Goudy's work suffered from a certain lack of taste, in the eyes of Morison and of European-minded, historically sensitive typographers such as Updike.

Goudy was also productive as writer about lettering and as an editor of the journals *Typographica* and *Ars Typographica*. In his writings, as in his typefaces, the subject of his exposition became, inevitably, his own work. His chief book had the title *Typologia*.

Craft and experiment

Among the work of those typographers commonly included with the traditionalists, that of W. A. Dwiggins represents the most interesting application of traditional values to tasks newly defined by modern conditions. Younger than Goudy (by fifteen years) and Rogers (by ten years), his early career followed the pattern of theirs: a start in commercial art and then moving – under the Arts & Crafts spell – to work more directly in printing. Dwiggins came to know Goudy as a student in the latter's lettering classes in Chicago. After a short-lived attempt to run his own printing business, he worked briefly at Goudy's Village Press in Hingham, Massachusetts, where he was to live for the rest of his life. With the commercial failure of Goudy's press, Dwiggins turned to doing advertising work for agencies and for customers directly.

It was during this extended period of producing press and direct-mail advertisements that Dwiggins was able to develop his calligraphic skills. He became a strong advocate of the pen as an essential shaping agent underlying good letterforms for printing. Though there might seem to be a theoretical resemblance, Dwiggins's formal writing was in practice and appearance very different from that of his near contemporary, Edward Johnston. While Johnston adopted the broad pen and returned to ancient models, Dwiggins belonged to a continuous American tradition that used the pointed, flexing ('copperplate') pen. His formal writing, developed as it was in strictly commercial conditions, thus took on an aspect entirely different to that of the tradition re-created by Johnston. Beyond obvious visual differences, the more essential difference was that Dwiggins worked for reproduction, while Johnston's writing was 'in itself' and in opposition to processes of replication.

Dwiggins gave up advertising work in the mid-1920s, turning to book design and then also to the design of typefaces. This change of direction followed from his dislike of contemporary developments. At the end of his manual of technique, *Layout in advertising* (1928), which summarized the lessons of twenty years of this kind of work, he made a distinction between 'honorable merchandizing, without taint' and exploitative work: 'a kind of leverage that no person with a rudimentary sense of social values is willing to help apply' (Dwiggins, *Layout in advertising*, p.194; see example 13, pp.208–9). He left the field just at the time of the rise of this second class of advertising, with its dependence on photography and machine-produced letterforms, in which there would be less place for his hand skills.

Dwiggins was a prolific and a lively writer, though *Layout in advertising* was his only full-length work. The book testifies to his complete engagement with the techniques and materials of his trade, as well as to his down-to-earth approach to design. He was concerned to dispute any fake-psychological theory of layout and good proportion, to which commercial art was then especially prone. What was good, he argued, was what could be demonstrated to work, in the copious examples that illustrated his text. And on the larger question of a philosophy of design – and, in particular, of modernism – he showed the same pragmatism: '"Modernist" printing design? "Modernism" is not a system of design – it is a state of mind. It is a natural and wholesome reaction against an overdose of traditionalism ... Most masquerading quasi-modernist printing is revived 1840. Actual modernism is a state of mind that says: "Let's forget (for the sake of experiment) about Aldus, and Baskerville, and William Morris (and the Masters of the 'forties) and take these types and machines and see what we can do with them on our own. Now." The graphic results of this state of mind are extraordinary, often highly stimulating, sometimes deplorable. The game is worth the risk ...' (Dwiggins, *Layout in advertising*, p.193.)

Dwiggins was by this time beginning to conduct his own experiments in book design. He had announced his disgust with the standards of trade publishing in a pseudonymous pamphlet of 1919: 'An investigation into the physical properties of books', written in the form of the transcript of a committee of inquiry. His craftsman's emphasis on material qualities – rather than just image – was characteristic, and it was to be borne out in his own book design work. Dwiggins attempted to apply the belief in good

materials to the trade editions with which he became principally
concerned. His long association with Alfred A. Knopf, a publisher
alert to the possibilities of design, allowed him the right conditions,
in an ordinary commercial context, for experiment in the decoration of boards and spines, and in display typography. His stencil
decorations, in particular, were an attempt to devise a kind of ornament appropriate, by the method of their generation and in their
forms, to the conditions of industrial production. Dwiggins was also
concerned with the smallest aspects of text typography, and he was
rare among typographers in writing in detail about such matters as
contents pages and indexes.

Dwiggins's approach to typeface design had these same qualities of experiment and of a concern with a clearly defined problem,
in all its details. His long association with the Mergenthaler Linotype company started (in 1929) with the design of a sanserif that was
intended to get beyond the aesthetic impoverishment of the grotesques that were then the only available types of this category. The
result was Metro, a typeface that was less successful, commercially
as well as in its design, than its European counterparts (notably
Futura and Gill Sans).

From the considerable number of experimental projects of
Dwiggins's collaboration with Linotype, two thoroughly successful
typefaces resulted: Electra (issued in 1935) and Caledonia (issued
in 1938). The latter was a fairly close adaptation, to the constraints
of line composition, of a generic 'Scotch roman' model. Electra
showed no obvious allegiance to any style model: its forms follow rather from Dwiggins's own formal writing. The typeface was
distinguished especially by its 'sloped roman', in place of a cursive
partner to the upright forms. Dwiggins was here directly prompted
by Stanley Morison's essay 'Towards an ideal italic' of 1926. The
result was one of the more satisfactory realizations of this idea, certainly more so than Morison's own efforts with Eric Gill's Perpetua.
Among the other projects of this collaboration were the design of an
upright cursive letter; of a typeface incorporating a revised English
orthography; and a long-term and ultimately fruitless attempt to
design a newspaper typeface that would rise above the minimal
aesthetic content of that class of typeface. In this latter project,
Dwiggins was attempting to enter the most difficult but also the

most ubiquitous application of typography, and to infuse it with the ideals of design. Mergenthaler Linotype had, however, a number of typefaces (Ionic, Excelsior, Corona, and others) that at least satisfied technical demands and those of legibility. The company, already dominating the market for newspaper composition, had little impulse to attempt what were seen as merely visual improvements.

A finale

In the conditions of economic depression of the 1930s, the private presses and limited edition publishers, and their patrons, were forced into cutbacks. This had been the base from which had been generated traditionalist typography in the USA, at its most traditional and exclusive. The pressures of the modern world became more compelling. So too did the presence of modernist designers from Europe, at first by reputation and then in their physical presence. Writing to Stanley Morison in 1937, D. B. Updike caught this moment exactly: 'About world conditions one can't be very cheerful. The way things are going nowadays is not at all my way, and the world I liked – while not gone – is shattered … As to printing, it is discouraging to see changes for the worse, but after all it "goes" neatly with jazz, and its equivalent in books and decorations. One strives for an ordered severity – one gets sloppy exhibitionism!' (Letter of 8 March 1937: Morison & Updike, *Selected correspondence*, p. 180.) Traditionalist typography in the USA would survive, and still does; but as one element in a repertoire of possible approaches.

6 New traditionalism

The 'reform of printing movement', which began to gather momentum in Britain in the years immediately before the First World War, can be most simply characterized through its relation to William Morris, whose typography had been a first stage of 'revival'. The movement took up Morris's fight for high standards and for an awareness of aesthetic qualities in printing: as at least one of its leading members reported, the sight of a Kelmscott book had provided the shock of excitement that started a life-long engagement with typography (Simon, *Printer and playground*, p. 8). But the reformers dissented from Morris on the question of the machine. Besides the further spread and development of powered presses, Linotype and Monotype composition machines were now in quite widespread use in Britain, and the quality of typography evident in the printing trade at large seemed (to the reformers) as undistinguished as that which had provoked Morris's rebellion. Furthermore, the legacy of Kelmscott as taken up by the private presses had there become ossified in the cult of the 'book beautiful' or had degenerated in weak imitations of the original conception. The advent of Art Nouveau, and its degeneration, had brought further confusion, especially to a trade printer trying to keep up with fashion.

In the face of this situation of decline, the compromise made by the reformers was to accept the machine and provide it with good typefaces. For the book-centred reformers, 'the machine' meant above all the Lanston Monotype composing machine, which in Britain was dominant in the sphere of book-printing; line-composing machines predominated in newspaper production. At this first stage of the movement's development (and, for many of its members, throughout its history) style was not seen as much of an issue. The main impulse was rather the avoidance of any gross stylism: the 'medievalism' of Morris or the 'sentimentalism' of Art Nouveau (Jackson, *The printing of books*, p. 217).

The Imprint

The first rallying point of the reforming movement was *The Imprint*, published between January and November 1913. The journal was founded and co-edited by a group of four men of different backgrounds and specialisms, though all with strong attachments to the Arts & Crafts movement and, in the case of three of them, to the Central School of Arts & Crafts. Gerard Meynell had been running the Westminster Press since 1899, as one of a few enlightened trade printers attempting standards higher than were normal: by the time of *The Imprint*, which it printed, it was perhaps in the league of the Arden Press and the Chiswick Press. J. H. Mason had trained as a compositor at the Ballantyne Press, worked at the Doves Press, and then joined the Central School as a teacher of typography. Edward Johnston had worked with the Doves Press and had taught at the Central School in its early days (from 1899). F. Ernest Jackson, the fourth editor, was an artist and a specialist in lithography, which he taught at the Central School.

Although an independent venture, the journal can be seen as representing exactly the position of the Arts & Crafts movement as it had by then developed. Thus the first number led off with a short text by W. R. Lethaby on 'Art and workmanship'. While aligning himself with Morris on the question of good work ('a work of art is a well-made thing, that is all'), Lethaby stated the one clear difference with Morris: 'Although a machine-made thing can never be a work of art in the proper sense, there is no reason why it should not be good in a secondary order – shapely, smooth, strong, well fitting, useful; in fact, like a machine itself. Machine-work should show quite frankly that it is the child of the machine; it is the pretence and subterfuge of most machine-made things which make them disgusting.' But against any suggestion of the 'style of the machine age', Lethaby went on to propose that: 'usually the best method of designing has been to improve on an existing model by bettering it at a point in time; a perfect table or chair or book has to be very well bred'.[1]

This philosophy of immaculate breeding was borne out in the

1. W. R. Lethaby, 'Art and workmanship', *The Imprint*, no. 1, January 1913, pp. 2, 3.

design of the typeface commissioned for the setting of the journal itself. As reported by J. H. Mason, the typeface, which was given the name 'Imprint Old Face' (it is now known just as Monotype Imprint), issued out of exchanges between himself and Gerard Meynell.[2] Mason, true to his education, proposed Caslon, then available only in founder's type for hand-setting; the Westminster Press had a Monotype composing machine and Meynell wanted to use it for the journal. The project of a typeface using Caslon as a starting point, but designed for Monotype composition, was thus conceived as a compromise, and carried out very quickly. The result does not bear any close relation to the founder's Caslon: rather, it achieved an unusual quality of anonymity or self-effacement. One suspects that it was the people in the Monotype drawing office – more than either Mason or Meynell – who played the most significant part in this achievement. Monotype Imprint seems now to be the very 'type' of a seriffed typeface: in this it was an exemplary instance of the ideals of the journal's editors and inspirers.

The contents of *The Imprint* do suggest a concerted attempt to speak with the printing trade. For example, there were articles on recent printing machinery, trade education, costing practices, and – though this proportion was to diminish – a quarter of the first issue was given over to largely trade advertisements. Thus, although the journal is remembered by historians as looking forward to the historical-aesthetic typographic journals that followed in the 1920s and 1930s, it hoped to reach beyond a merely bibliophile readership.

The strains of compromise with trade values can be sensed in its attitude towards pictorial reproduction. In a review of the new *Penrose's Pictorial Annual*, the show-piece of the trade, J. H. Mason could not refrain from making what amounted to an objection to process-engraving as such: 'But I come back to the joyless ingenuity that has gone to the making of this dull volume, and think of the destruction of the real art of book illustration, which the half tone process has brought about'.[3]

Edward Johnston was persuaded to contribute a series of articles, extending to seven parts, on 'Decoration and its uses' (in calligraphic work),[4] but he never gave up his objections to reproduction and reduction of hand-work by mechanical means. His illustrations for these pieces – as well as a calligraphic masthead for the journal – were mechanically reproduced (by line blocks), but to the same size as his drawings. In support of these attitudes, a heavy emphasis was laid on the woodcut and wood-engraving in the historical component of the journal.

The Imprint came to an unexpected and unannounced end after nine issues. Financial difficulties and disagreements within the editorial group have been cited as reasons for this, but in any case it would have found a monthly schedule difficult to maintain in conditions of war.

The typographer

If *The Imprint* was a premature flourish, another kind of preface to the post-war reforming movement was provided by the activity of Bruce Rogers at Cambridge University Press. Rogers had come to England in 1916 to work for a time at the Mall Press with Emery Walker. In 1917 he was invited by Cambridge University Press to act as their 'printing adviser'. This was a new post (though a temporary one) and without obvious precedent in Britain. It was a recognition of factors in printing and book production that were then beyond the grasp of the printer – even a press with as long and distinguished a tradition as Cambridge. At this date it was only at Cambridge that the decline of standards could be recognized and a remedy proposed. The presence on the Press's governing body (the Syndics) of Sydney Cockerell – who had been William Morris's secretary – provided a confirming link with Arts & Crafts ideals.

In December 1917, Rogers submitted to the Syndics a 'Report on the typography of the Cambridge University Press', which addressed the problem of how to attain 'a distinctive style in book-making'. Rogers evaluated the materials already possessed by the Press and recommended new acquisitions, and in particular an expansion of the Monotype plant, with certain typefaces, especially Imprint and Plantin: 'hand-work should be brought to an irreducible minimum,

2. See: 'The Imprint: fifty years on', *Monotype Newsletter*, no. 71, October 1963, pp. 1–5; also: Owens, *J. H. Mason*.

3. J. H. Mason, 'Biblion a-biblion', *The Imprint*, no. 3, March 1913, p. 210.

4. These were later reprinted in: Edward Johnston, *Formal penmanship and other papers*, London: Lund Humphries, 1971.

while machine-work should be correspondingly developed'. In his concluding section on future policy, Rogers recommended the appointment of a permanent 'adviser'.[5]

The post-war reformation was to be largely the creation of such 'advisers', bringing to the printing trade the elements of design. 'Design', that is, both in the sense of an aesthetic awareness and in the sense of rational co-ordination of production. (How much these two considerations connected and overlapped is perhaps the great question to be addressed to any such movement.) The function of design in printing might not have changed, but the functionary had: design would now become embodied in the emerging figure of the typographer. This person was no longer the master printer, but in Britain was typically the educated (or self-educated) amateur, with an aesthetic sense and a passion for the history of books and printing.

The role of typographer can be seen clearly worked out in the career of Francis Meynell (a cousin of Gerard Meynell). His first experience was in directing book design and production at his father's publishing company of Burns & Oates (1911–13). Then, passing on to journalism and socialist and anti-war agitation, he started the Pelican Press in 1916. This was essentially a design office with hand-composition facilities, using the printing capacity of the political press to which it was an adjunct. The work that issued from the Pelican Press showed a strong aesthetic interest; for example, in the decorated typography of sixteenth-century France. This sorted oddly with the left-socialist content of the products.

The career of another typographer, Stanley Morison, intertwined with Meynell's, both at Burns & Oates and then at the Pelican Press. Morison, though slightly older than Meynell, was without the family advantages of the other: he had worked his way through clerks' jobs to an induction into the world of enlightened printing as a junior assistant on *The Imprint*. As well as their common printing-historical enthusiasm, Morison shared both Roman Catholicism and socialism with Meynell. He had been in prison as a conscientious objector, but now, after the war, began to work as a typographer.

Morison's blend of practice and history, each activity informing the other, showed itself already during his short spell at the Pelican

Press, taking over during Meynell's absence (1919–21). His first substantial historical essay, *The craft of printing: notes on the history of type forms* (1921), was published by the Pelican Press. It served as publicity and as a contribution to knowledge: the first of many such publications from Morison.

Typefaces: the work of revival

In the post-war period, with the days of cheap hand-labour gone, any lingering doubts over the benefits of mechanized type-setting could hardly be sustained. The question was simply one of quality of typeface design. The diet of undistinguished 'old faces' and 'moderns' with which the Monotype and Linotype systems were equipped was felt to be inadequate. After their largely successful experience with Imprint, Lanston Monotype had continued with the idea of adapting historical faces for machine composition. There had followed a Plantin (1913), a Caslon (1915), a Scotch Roman (1920), and a Bodoni (from 1921). The British Linotype company (Linotype & Machinery) had as yet taken no steps in this direction, but in September 1921 appointed a 'printing adviser', as if in recognition of the need to remedy deficiencies in typographic quality. Their consultant, George W. Jones, was a master printer with historical interests: he now concerned himself with the design of the company's publications, and with the quest for better typefaces.

In the search for a typeface for modern-day composition that could emulate the products of what was seen as a (or the) golden period of printing history – the French sixteenth century – the running was being made in the USA. The American Type Founders Company had started work before the war on a Garamond typeface for handcomposition. The typographic reformers in Britain began to hear of this, and to see samples, and some quantities of the type were ordered in 1920 by C. W. Hobson for his Cloister Press. This was the context in which the Lanston Monotype Corporation then started on designing a Garamond for its machines, and in which Linotype & Machinery began (slightly later) to work on the typeface that was issued as Linotype Granjon.

5. The report was only published much later, on the occasion of his eightieth birthday: Rogers, *Report on the typography of the Cambridge University Press*, pp. 1, 31.

The story of these various attempts to recreate a Garamond typeface is a complex one, and it has been the subject of some dispute.[6] Rather than engage in an estimation of precedence and influence, the point to observe here is that the leading machine typesetting companies in the USA and in Britain, as well as some founders of type for hand-composition, began to produce typefaces that were based on historical models, and that this now became their pattern of operation: replacing the previous almost unconscious production of 'old face' or 'modern' variants, or the commissioning of 'original' or 'artistic' designs. Typographic quality was to be found by scouring the past. The revolution brought to the trade by the typographers was to be a historical (or historicist) one: the best old typefaces, machine composed, and used in a historically-conscious manner.

This effort of revival was considerably enabled by the appearance of D. B. Updike's *Printing types* in 1922. For the emerging band of typographers, history was now given a clear outline, and provided with much more factual and also visual substance than had previously been available. For those working on the history of typefaces, contributions could now be fairly described as 'before' and 'after' Updike.

With his appointment as 'typographic adviser' to the Lanston Monotype Corporation in Britain, Stanley Morison became the principal figure in the revival of historical typefaces. The date of this appointment has been disputed: on various occasions Morison suggested that it had come in 1922, and that he therefore had some major responsibility for the cutting of Monotype Garamond. The balance of evidence now published suggests that Morison played an informal, agitating role in the production of this typeface, and that his formal appointment as consultant to the company came only 'in the early part of 1923' (Barker, *Stanley Morison*, p.123).

In the 1920s and 1930s, the typeface production of the Monotype Corporation – 'Lanston' was dropped from the company name in 1931 – was to become the central achievement of the British reforming movement, providing the essential materials for its design work. In his retrospective survey of these typefaces (1950), Morison ran through the production of the company before his appointment as 'adviser': 'Such was the type-cutting performance of the Lanston

Monotype Corporation, showing very little originality, up to 1922, when a plan was laid before the managing director. It was intended as a programme of typographical design, rational, systematic, and corresponding effectively with the forseeable needs of printing.' (Morison, *A tally of types*, p. 32.)

The problem with this claim has been its stress on the rationality and foresight of the operation, which, when viewed dispassionately, seems to have been marked by a good deal of improvisation, if not muddle. Thus, as Morison's chief revisionist critic observed, the typefaces that followed from this 'plan' or 'programme' (of which no contemporary documentation exists) were the results of events that he could not have foreseen in 1922 or 1923 (Moran, *Stanley Morison*, p. 76). The case is rather one of Morison joining the company with the proposition of reviving typefaces, discovering models as he went along (fired especially by current historical enthusiasms), and then – later in his life – casting his characteristic aura of rationality over the whole operation.

In his retrospective commentary, Morison touched on a chief difficulty in this 'plan': the obstinacy and independence of the 'works'. While the typographical adviser was based in London, along with the sales department and administration of the company, the actual work of drawing and production was in the hands of the draughtsmen (mainly women, in fact) and engineers at Salfords, Surrey. This distance and division of labour certainly affected the processes of design: while Morison could make proposals and then urge corrections, the final forms of a typeface were in the hands of the people at the works. This would account for what one can discern as a common Monotype style, evident in many of the company's typefaces, especially in numerals and other characters beyond the primary interest of the consultant designer. Thus, even with the typefaces in whose design Morison was most deeply involved (such as Times New Roman), one should hesitate before attributing them to him without qualification.

In Morison's account, the Monotype works showed resistance

6. See the works of Moran and Barker. The classic work on the sources is by Beatrice Warde, as: Paul Beaujon, 'The "Garamond" types', *The Fleuron*, no. 5, 1926, pp. 131–79.

to 'the ideas of outside experts with theoretical learning but of un-
proved utility': they would rather wait for trade demand to suggest
new typefaces (Morison, *A tally of types*, p. 34). He then admitted
the good fortune of the other major consultancy of his early years
with the Monotype Corporation: as typographical adviser to Cambridge University Press (the position created first for Bruce Rogers).
Through this post, as later with *The Times*, Morison was able to
direct a large and influential customer to purchase Monotype equipment and thus to stimulate demand for Monotype products more
widely in the trade.

The typographic club

During the 1920s, a network of enterprises and associations, re-
inforcing each other, came to define the reform of printing movement, and to aid its progress: *The Fleuron* (1923–30); the Double
Crown Club (from 1924); the reinvigorated Curwen Press; the
Nonesuch Press (from 1923); the Monotype Corporation. In different areas of work, each of these enterprises developed the themes
of the movement: the belief in machine composition and machine
printing; the revival of historical typefaces (and the cautious admit-
tance of some 'original' faces); a historically sanctioned approach to
design. These aims were to be entrusted to the figure, newly perceived, of the typographer. All this was felt to be 'new' and 'modern':
thus Holbrook Jackson, a participant in the movement and an early
chronicler of it, could apply both of these words to its typography
and its typographers, with no hint of awareness of the contempora-
neous Continental new typography (Jackson, *The printing of books*,
pp. 33, 47, 226). The difference was between the merely modern,
seen against a backward trade or ossified bibliophile context, and
the consciously modern or the modernist.

The movement worked by example and by propaganda. In the
first category one would place the output of the Nonesuch Press,
run by Francis Meynell, as a demonstration that good qualities in
book design were attainable under ordinary trade conditions, if
the operation was directed by a designer. Nonesuch books mixed
limited editions (up to around 1500 copies) with unlimited ones,
each painstakingly designed. The venture ran profitably, finding
success with intelligent collectors (those who read books too), until
the recession of the 1930s.

The Curwen Press was the best advertisement for the movement among trade printers: its management had been taken over before the war by Harold Curwen (grandson of the founder), who instituted a policy of good relations within the workforce and good quality in its products. Curwen had been strongly affected by Arts & Crafts ideals (joining Edward Johnston's class at the Central School) and was a founder member of the Design and Industries Association. After the war, and particularly after it had taken on the services of a typographer (Oliver Simon), the Curwen Press developed a distinctive style or manner. As well as book production, the press engaged in jobbing and advertising work, and to some considerable extent it functioned as a design studio. It built up an informal stable of artist-illustrators and its own repertoire of typefaces and decorative elements. So 'Curwen' came to denote a world of gentle refinement: literate but not too serious, it was associated particularly with good food and wine.

This hedonist, self-deflating aspect of the movement was enshrined in the Double Crown Club: the occasional dining club in London at which papers on typography were delivered, followed by discussion. A more serious forum was provided by *The Fleuron*, the journal published in seven numbers between 1923 and 1930. Edited first by Oliver Simon and then by Stanley Morison, *The Fleuron* continued the project that had been suggested by *The Imprint*: a combination of historical articles and reviews, with discussions of contemporary work. And while it had no obvious ambition to speak to the printing trade, *The Fleuron* did serve as a vehicle for discussion within the movement – or club – which was now becoming an international one. A consistent feature of the journal was its surveys of work from abroad: thus there were contributions from and about D. B. Updike, and surveys of contemporary traditionalist work in the USA and on the Continent.

For Stanley Morison, these were years of intense production, with historical research going hand-in-hand with consultancy work. His historical work issued in articles and short texts – introductions and annotating pieces – rather than in anything of the scale of Updike's *Printing types*. Given the multiplicity of his interests, this was perhaps inevitable. As a historian, Morison's achievement now resides chiefly in works compiled after his death: the two volumes of

Selected essays and what was to have been a 'summa' of his investigations into the history of letterforms, *Politics and script*. For several generations of typographers and graphic designers, Morison's history was communicated through *Four centuries of fine printing*, the anthology of reproductions of pages from books, with a survey introduction, published first as a large folio in 1924 and subsequently in reduced and revised editions.

It was Morison who provided the movement with a summary of its design philosophy, *First principles of typography*. This short text started life as the entry on 'typography' in the *Encyclopaedia Britannica* (1929), was rewritten and published in the last number of *The Fleuron* (1930), and in later years republished separately in further editions, including several foreign-language ones. The text was concerned to assert the inviolability of certain governing values: 'reason', 'convention', 'the reader's comprehension of the text'. Having offered a definition of typography in these heavily charged terms, Morison ran through the elements of book design and production.

The *First principles* served to emphasize that, for this movement, typography was almost always book typography (and books consisting of continuous text, with no mention of tables or even footnotes). The constraints and traditions of book typography were the bases from which Morison generalized a theory that might be taken to apply to the whole field. Outside books, Morison did elsewhere recognize 'advertisement setting', where novelty and play were allowed.[7] But he never admitted the possibility of other areas of typography (or, at least, thought it worth discussing them in print), and thus he polarized the field into the area of strict obedience to convention and that where no rules obtained. His own ventures in publicity typography (for example, the celebrated dust jackets for Gollancz) demonstrated the burdens of designing without principles. In a postscript to this essay, written in the 1960s, Morison referred to modernist approaches to typography (as at the Bauhaus), but brushed them aside, as making an art out of something that should essentially be a service, and as violating tradition, convention, orthodoxy.[8]

Dissident presences and new letterforms

Though the British reforming movement advanced by way of historical revival, the process could reveal new things. This double aspect is clear in Edward Johnston's formal writing, which set out to discover lost practices and forms, but which put its faith in making 'the thing itself', rather than its reproduction or recreation (see chapter 4). Pre-eminent among Johnston's new things was the London Underground Railway alphabet. Johnston's alphabet was a product of the moment of *The Imprint*: the project was conceived in 1913, and his working drawings for the first set of letters were done in 1915–16. The alphabet was grounded in the forms of classical Roman and Renaissance humanist letters, but as a sanserif and 'elemental', it had the right qualities and associations for its purpose of a letterform for public spaces, for a company then renewing its visual identity. Johnston's Arts & Crafts scruples and his natural diffidence obstructed any collaboration with the world of machine production: he never developed the alphabet as a typeface (i.e. in a range of sizes, with variant forms) for a typefounder, still less for machine composition. And, apart from his involvement with *The Imprint* – he seems to have played an observer's part in the design of its typeface – this was his only sustained contact with the printing reformers in Britain.

Although he started as a pupil of Johnston at the Central School, and was soon his revering friend and associate, Eric Gill's relations with the printing reformation were more involved. Gill's liberation from the drudgery of apprenticeship in an architect's office had come through taking jobs of inscriptional letter-cutting. From this time (1903), he was a 'workman', with 'a workman's rights, the right to design what he made; and a workman's duties, the duty to make what he designed' (Gill, *Autobiography*, p.115). Gill belonged to the tradition of Morris and Lethaby, but with qualifications and differences: an attachment to anarchist rather than Marxist (let alone

7. See Morison's manifesto 'The 2 kinds of effectiveness' (1928), reproduced in: Moran, *Stanley Morison*, p.119; and also his 'On advertisement settings', *Signature*, old series, no.3, 1936, pp.1–6; *Rationalism and novelty appropriate in display advertising*, London: The Times, 1954.
8. See also the remarks on typographic modernism in Morison's *The typographic arts*, pp.50–1, 97.

Fabian) socialism, and to a radical Roman Catholicism (he had had an early conversion, from a non-conformist upbringing). He thus stood at some distance both from the Arts & Crafts movement as it had developed after Morris, and from those (in the Design and Industries Association, most notably) prepared to give succour to the world of industrial production. Gill did come to make pacts with the twin devils of industrialism and capitalism: but on his own terms, and while never ceasing to pour reasoned abuse on them in lectures, essays, and letters to the press.

The start of Gill's engagement with typography proper – letter-forms for composition and printing, rather than cut in stone – can be dated at 1925. He was asked by Stanley Morison to draw alphabets that could be reproduced as a printing type for Monotype composition. Gill's inscribed letterforms – which by then had become a stable and immediately identifiable set of forms – seemed to provide a suitable model for a typeface for printing. Morison was then developing the theory that quality in typeface design was inseparable from the operation of engraving or inscribing, and that something had been lost with the introduction of the pantograph punchcutting machine. He therefore commissioned one of the surviving punchcutters (Charles Malin in Paris) to work from Gill's drawings; the Monotype draughtsmen would then work from smoke-proofs of these punches. This process of design proved to be a muddle, and the result – Monotype Perpetua – was long in the making. Writing years after the event, even Morison, at his most ponderous, admitted that 'the question whether the sizes 8 point to 14 point fully realize the ambition with which they were begun, i.e, to create an original type serviceable for all kinds of books, does not permit of an answer in the unqualified affirmative' (Morison, *A tally of types*, p. 103).

The unsatisfactory experiences of Perpetua may well have stimulated Gill to a greater interest in typography. He became fully engaged in the activity with the production of the typeface that became known as Gill Sans. The clear precedent for this letterform was the Johnston Underground alphabet, and Gill had been around during its design: both men were living in Ditchling, Sussex, at the time. Monotype Gill Sans followed from some painted signs that Gill had recently designed, using a 'block' (sanserif) letterform;

and perhaps Morison and Monotype were then becoming aware of the burgeoning production of sanserif typefaces in Germany (see chapter 9). Gill's first informal drawings for the typeface were done in 1926; the first drawings for production went to Monotype in 1927.

In a paper delivered to the Double Crown Club in April 1926, just before the General Strike ('I feel like a miner before a court of mandarins'), Gill had represented his world of the workman-artist as unreconcilable with that of the book-producers. He could not accept the attempt to bridge it by 'men of taste' (the typographers of the printing reform), if this meant machine-made decoration: 'what I ask of machine-made books is that they shall *look* machine-made'.[9] By entering fully into the process of design for machine-tool execution (and then for machine composition and powered printing presses), Gill now became thoroughly implicated in the world of industrial production. In confirmation of this, in 1928, the Monotype Corporation started to pay him retaining fees.

For Morison, Gill Sans represented a deal with modernism. The need for an improved and refined sanserif had been accepted, but its place was clearly defined: as a display letter (usually in all-capital setting) in public contexts, or perhaps in ephemeral literature, but not in books, and there was no 'spirit of the age' talk. When, very soon after the first matrices became available, it was adopted by the London & North-Eastern Railway company as their standard letterform, Gill Sans became, for the Monotype Corporation, the railway letter: equally at home on an engine name-plate and in a timetable.[10]

Gill's other major typeface – Joanna – soon followed, in 1930. This was designed for the use of the printing press that his son-in-law René Hague set up at Piggots, Buckinghamshire, and which they ran in partnership as 'Hague & Gill' (see example 12, pp. 206–7). This press, Gill took pains to point out, was not a private press but a printing business (with a powered press) and, as such, endeavoured to achieve 'a good reasonable commonplace', without excessive aes-

9. The text was not published in Gill's lifetime, but as: 'The artist & book production', *Fine Print*, vol. 8, no. 3, 1982, pp. 96–7, 111.
10. Among the contemporary literature, see especially the 'Modern typography number' of the *Monotype Recorder*, vol. 32, no. 4, 1933.

thetic or moralizing scruples.[11] Hague & Gill undertook a good deal
of jobbing work for local customers, as well as book production. In
a short text entitled 'Reason and typography' (1936), Hague outlined
his credo: 'There is only one sort of hope, and that is in establishing a new tradition, but not a new academicism, in keeping everything plain, trying not to remember the —teenth century (filling in
whatever is the fashionable number) when you are struggling with a
newspaper in a tube, remembering that, finally, printing will have to
be judged as printing and not as advertisement or fine art.'[12]

An early production of this press was Gill's own *Essay on typography*, published first by Sheed & Ward in an edition limited to
500 copies. Gill discussed typography – both letterforms and their
composition as printed text – in his present context of England in
1931, suffering under a rampant, inhuman 'industrialism'. In such
conditions, he argued, undecorated plainness was all one could de-
cently hope for (thus Gill Sans) and, in the face of the sentimentality
of machine-produced ornamentation, it was perhaps a noble aspiration. Gill's rationalism also led him to argue for unjustified setting:
'even spacing is of more importance typographically than equal
length. Even spacing is a great assistance to easy reading …' (Gill,
Essay on typography, p. 91). The *Essay* is thus much more radical, in
all senses, than any document produced from within the orthodoxy
of the printing reform movement. It compares interestingly with
the *First principles of typography*: where Morison is sententious,
attempting timelessness, Gill is down-to-earth and pointed, in his
illustrations as in his language.

The hegemony of invisibility

The period of most intense activity for the reforming movement
came to an end around 1930. There are obvious economic explana-
tions for the slackening of pace then: recession and cutbacks meant
less demand for printing and thus for enlightened typography. The
change from a time of rather feverish discovery to one of steadier
consolidation is also a reflection of the fact that the stock of typographic history that fuelled the movement had limits. By the 1930s,
the reformers were provided with sufficient materials, in the form
of typefaces, easily available reproductions of historical examples,
and a literature of the subject (Updike's *Printing types*, *The Fleuron*,
Monotype publications).

The typeface 'programme' (if such it was) of the Monotype Corporation seems to come to an end with Bembo (cut in 1929) and Bell (cut in 1930). After this, apart from some new faces, the revivals were the less celebrated Ehrhardt and Van Dijck (both 1937–8). Times New Roman (cut in 1931) was a special case: designed very specifically for *The Times*, it was not intended as a historical revival, though it does nevertheless refer, via Monotype Plantin, to an existing (French sixteenth-century) model.[13] Morison's historical bent of mind (and, one might add, his lack of drawing skills) thus informed this 'new roman' designed for the most demanding production conditions of the modern world. (It is interesting that his first proposal to *The Times* included the suggestion of a modified Perpetua: a typeface with stronger claims to being a 'new roman', though hardly robust enough for newspaper printing.) With his appointment in 1929 as its 'typographical adviser', Morison became increasingly absorbed in the affairs of *The Times*. As well as becoming its consultant on typography, in charge of the major redesign that required the cutting of Times New Roman, he became its official historian (his five-volume work came out between 1935 and 1952) and was an unofficial policy adviser to a succession of editors.

While Morison turned to major historical projects, his dicta began to spread through the world of typography in Britain and abroad, both directly through his writings (*First principles of typography* achieved gospel status) and indirectly through the work of

11. 'A letter from Mr Eric Gill', *Monotype Recorder*, vol. 32, no. 3, 1933, p. 32.

12. René Hague, 'Reason and typography', *Typography*, no. 1, 1936, p. 9.

13. See: Barker, *Stanley Morison*, pp. 291–3; Allen Hutt, 'Times New Roman: a reassessment', *Journal of Typographic Research*, vol. 4, no. 3, 1970, pp. 259–70; John Dreyfus, 'The evolution of Times New Roman', *Penrose Annual*, vol. 66, 1973, pp. 165–74; Tracy, *Letters of credit*, pp. 194–210. A later round of discussion was started by Mike Parker with his theory that Times Roman followed the model of a typeface designed by Starling Burgess, around 1904: 'Starling Burgess, type designer?', *Printing History*, no. 31/32, 1994, pp. 52–108. Replies by Harold Berliner, Nicolas Barker, Jim Rimmer and John Dreyfus were published in *Printing History*, no. 37, 1998. Barker's rebuttal, 'Starling Burgess, no type designer', was reprinted in his *Form and meaning in the history of the book*, pp. 371–89 – in its section of essays on forgery.

associates and acolytes. At the Monotype Corporation, the active work of propaganda was in the hands of Beatrice Warde. She had entered the world of typography through a job in the library of the American Typefounders Company, before coming to Europe and the principal centres of typographic history. Following the success of her demonstration of the real sources of the 'Garamond' revivals, and a substantial historical article in the *Monotype Recorder*, she had been asked to join the company in 1927, as editor of the *Recorder* and in charge of publicity. In the years of her association with the company (into the 1960s), the Monotype Corporation became a model of enlightened self-interest. Its publications and its exhibitions were a powerful source of education. Monotype became the medium through which several generations of printers and typographers learned about the practice and (to some considerable extent) the history of their subject. Other companies – Linotype, Intertype, Stephenson Blake – were by comparison very quiet. Beatrice Warde had the popular touch (as Morison hardly had) and was able to make links with the world of printing education and the trade at large. Her lecture of 1932, 'Printing should be invisible' (later published as 'The crystal goblet') recapitulated the Morisonian doctrine of self-effacement and obedience, but in the terms of an after-dinner speech.

Thus it was through the Monotype Corporation that the printing reformers could exert a hegemonic influence over the printing trade. The vulgar extremes of 'printer's typography' were eroded by the teachings of the printing reform: typefaces had a historical pedigree and should not be illegitimately (ahistorically) combined, nor used in too many sizes, nor with too much bold type; the nineteenth century was a dark period typographically (the enthusiasm, towards the end of the 1930s, for its display typography was to come rather from architects); typography should not get in the way of the reader and the text, but should (like Beatrice Warde's crystal goblet) be a transparent and civilizing container. This apparently invincible philosophy was bestowed on and accepted by all sectors of the printing world: the trade and its publications; printing education in the technical colleges and design education (so far as it existed) in the art schools; the newly emerging sphere of the 'typographic designer'. This latter had its own society from 1928, seeking to represent not the gentlemanly book typographers, but rather those working in advertising and the 'commercial' field. The Society of Typographic Designers was a marginal, if persistent, organization, without the scope or the forum of discussion necessary to work out any independent approaches. The potential source of criticism of the doctrines of the printing reformation was the new typography, as it was being developed on the Continent: a spectre that in the 1930s was easily held at bay or domesticated.

7 Cultures of printing: Germany

The aesthetic cul-de-sac

Germany too had its 'revival of printing', but the pattern of this development, and its scale, were different from smaller and more marginal countries (Belgium or Denmark, for example). Germany could claim to be the first home of printing; and by the nineteenth century the phenomenon of Gutenberg had become a key in what one may call the culture of printing in that country. This rested on a large and fairly dispersed trade and a network of typefoundries, over and above which there existed a consciousness of the history of printing and the seeds of an appreciation of aesthetic factors among people with tangential interests (in literature and art). The private press movement in Britain and the USA may have acted as a stimulus for these circles in Germany, but indigenous elements played their part too. And, over the earlier part of the twentieth century, rapid industrialization and economic and political developments gave German typography a particular character.

Although Germany was felt by its reformers to have suffered a decline of typographic standards in the nineteenth century, the Anglo-American revival was used by them to combat not this but the recent efflorescence of Art Nouveau. It is some indication of the marginal nature of Art Nouveau for Britain and the USA that there was no English-language term for the phenomenon. But in German-language countries it enjoyed a significant life and had acquired the label 'Jugendstil', derived perhaps from the cultural weekly *Jugend*, published in Munich (1896–1914). This and other magazines became principal carriers of the style, and through such channels Jugendstil made its impact on the design of all categories of printing.

The main passage out of Jugendstil was through a simpler, less decorated approach that would meet the requirements of the new age and especially those demands posed by industrial production. For the aesthetic minority, for whom art had become life, the further development from Jugendstil could also be towards a greater simplicity. A notable instance here was that of Stefan George, whose interest in typography and book design was a natural consequence of a total approach to literature and to life. His earlier books and his journal *Blätter für die Kunst* were designed by Melchior Lechter in small editions and in the full aesthetic dress of the time. But, especially in the later larger-run editions of his works, George's typography shed its decorations. In the early 1900s he had a founder's grotesque (sanserif) typeface adapted to his own orthography, which incorporated a simplified system of punctuation, the use of some uncial letters and capital letters only at the start of sentences and lines of verse; this typeface became known as the 'Stefan-George-Schrift' (see example 9, pp. 200–1).[1] It stands as a precursor of the new typographers' adoption of sanserif and of their interest in language reform; but George's experiments were without any of the industrializing and standardizing motives of the new typography.

Werkbund attitudes

The more significant way out of the stylistic cul-de-sac of Jugendstil was found by those who accepted the Arts & Crafts impulse from Britain and transformed it in application to the domain of mass-production. This approach was given concrete embodiment in the Deutscher Werkbund, the association of (proto-)designers and manufacturers that was founded in Munich in 1907. Among the founding members were the publisher Eugen Diederichs and the architect Peter Behrens, both of whom contributed to the revival of German typography. In its specific connections with the worlds of publishing and printing, and in the attitudes that it embodied, the Deutscher Werkbund provided an important focus for German typography in the years before 1914 and – in a changed context – in the years between the two world wars.

Werkbund values were centred on the idea of quality ('Qualität'). The organization stood for the application of the highest craft standards to industrial production. The virtues it prized were those of good workmanship, good materials, solidity. Though there were always internal conflicts and arguments, the leading spirits within

1. The origins and development of the 'Stefan-George-Schrift' are discussed in Roland Reuß's essay 'Industrielle Manufaktur', in: Doris Kern & Michel Leiner (ed.), *Stardust*, Frankfurt a.M: Stroemfeld, 2003, pp.166–91.

the Werkbund fully accepted industry, and in this it differed essentially from the British Arts & Crafts and even the later Design and Industry movements, which were much more troubled by 'the machine'. The Werkbund wanted exceptional standards of workmanship and of production and a certain plainness and ordinariness. The striving for simplicity was partly moral (a simpler, nobler life) and partly practical: it wanted forms that could be easily produced by industrial processes and that could attain the status of 'types'. A strong presence in these beliefs was national sentiment: the idea that the way forward for Germany lay through improved manufacture and victories in export battles. There was thus a strong conservative, nationalist tenor to Werkbund ideals, especially before 1914; and this led to differences with aesthetically and politically more radical views, of the kind that emerged after 1918.

The impulse towards simplification and modernity, and the demands of nationalism, were strongly evident in the typography of Peter Behrens. Between 1902 and 1914 Behrens designed four typefaces for the Klingspor typefoundry at Offenbach, which, in sequence, seem to constitute a series of steps away from the phase of Jugendstil – in which he participated fully – towards some classical standard. The other, more difficult dialogue was with German typography: the traditions of the broken letterform ('Textura', 'Fraktur', 'Schwabacher'), which is here termed 'blackletter'. Explaining his first typeface, the Behrens-Schrift (1902), he wrote: 'I took the technical principle of gothic script, the stroke of the quill pen. Also, in order to achieve an even more German character, gothic letters were a decisive influence on me for the proportions, the height and width of the letters and the thickness of the strokes. Therefore, having omitted all extraneous features so that the constructional principle of the diagonally-held pen might be clearly expressed, I hoped, above all, that the letter would hold together well and that I might capture the aesthetic factor which would make the type suitable for all kinds of text: for text requiring dignity as well as for popular material and advertising.'[2]

The relation to blackletter was one of proportion and 'Duktus' (stroke width, as modulated by the angle of a real or imagined pen). The dialogue with Jugendstil can be seen by contrasting the Behrens-Schrift with the Eckmann-Schrift, designed by Otto Eckmann

– a friend and colleague of Behrens – also for the Klingspor type-foundry, and which appeared in 1901. The typefaces share certain formal properties and might be broadly lumped together as 'unser-iffed', but whereas the Eckmann-Schrift exhibited painted, flowing forms, the Behrens-Schrift submitted to the discipline of the pen. Jugendstil might flourish in display lettering, but the demands of text typography proved too great for it: the Eckmann-Schrift was among the most plausible decorative incursions into the field of continuous text, but was ultimately unsuccessful there. The 'Kur-siv' partner to the Behrens-Schrift followed in 1907: as an italic, the reminiscence of blackletter was necessarily diminished and that of Jugendstil increased.

In 1907 Behrens began his employment as a consultant de-signer ('Künstlerischer Beirat') to the Allgemeine Elektrizitäts Gesellschaft (AEG) in Berlin. He was concerned with every aspect and every application of design within the firm: the products, the company's own installations, its publications and printed mat-ter. This total engagement of the artist or designer with industrial production provides the best example of the Werkbund project in its earliest years.

Before Behrens started this work, the company had used the services of artists and designers without co-ordination, and so found its printed matter designed in the style of the moment. Otto Eckmann was among the artists thus employed. From 1907, the visual identity of the company began to show a sober, classical face, felt to be the appropriate one for a leader of modern industry. The Behrens-Antiqua, which first appeared in 1908, was the typeface generally used in AEG publications, and, within the line of Beh-rens's typefaces, it represented a further move towards some more neutral – less gothic – roman norm. Behrens designed a display alphabet, in capitals only, for the company's exclusive use, and this provided the forms for the new AEG logotype; but it was not cut as a

2. Behrens, 'Von der Entwicklung der Schrift', in his *Schriften, Initialen und Schmuck*, Offenbach: Rudhard'sche Giesserei, 1902, pp. 9–10; the translation here is modified from that made by Christopher Burke in his 'Peter Behrens and the German letter', *Journal of Design History*, vol. 5, no. 1, 1992, pp. 19–37.

typeface and seems to have been drawn freshly for each use in company literature. These letters, even more than his Antiqua, were an attempt at a neutral and modern letterform, without national associations. A drawing for sanserif letters has survived among the AEG documents: but this further step along the path of modernity seems not to have been given any extensive development or application.[3]

Behrens left contractual employment with AEG in 1913 and this marked the end of his active involvement with typography. The last of his typefaces, the Behrens-Mediaeval, was produced by Klingspor in 1914. That he should have entered this field of design, as a matter of course, was characteristic of a totalizing approach that was to come to the fore again after 1919, most famously at the Bauhaus. And Behrens had also been active in the movement to reform art and design education, as director of the Kunstgewerbeschule at Düsseldorf (1903–7). One of his innovations there was the teaching of calligraphy on summer courses for college teachers.

The reform of printing design

The Germany private presses followed in the wake of British and American examples; and, like their Anglo-American counterparts, the German private presses occupied a marginal position in relation to the trade. However, several of its participants were notably involved in design or in printing for the trade – C. E. Poeschel, Walter Tiemann, F. H. Ehmcke – and, certainly in comparison with the English private printers, there was less of the spirit of the cultivated amateur in their work. But the reform of typography, and the communication of this to the trade at large, was made not through limited editions, but in the sphere of trade and commerce. For this reason, the German private presses can be largely passed over here.

The practical implications of the spirit of reform were articulated in a text by the printer C. E. Poeschel, *Zeitgemäße Buchdruckkunst*, published in 1904 and originally given as a lecture to an audience of printers.[4] As he made clear, Poeschel took some initial inspiration from Morris and the Arts & Crafts movement, which he encountered at first hand on a visit to England in 1904. (He had also, earlier, made a trip to the USA.) His working-out of Arts & Crafts principles, in this text and in his later practice, went some considerable way beyond the limits of Kelmscott or Doves Press typography. Thus, as well as the familiar calls for simplicity and unity, he entered into discussion of issues in setting text. His attitudes were largely those of Morris and Walker's essay on 'Printing' – in favour of close word-spacing, for example – but elaborated in more detail, as would have befitted his educational context. In pursuit of 'technical exactness in setting', Poeschel discussed such matters as footnotes, the indication of paragraphs, and the position of page numbers – for which he enumerated eleven possibilities. In all this his approach was very much that of a trade printer, though a reflective one. And he was without the anguish over the machine and industrial production, which was so strong a feature of English attitudes.

Poeschel worked all his life as a printer in the Leipzig firm of Poeschel & Trepte, of which his father had been a joint founder. As in the case of other enlightened printers, the work of this firm became larger than the just the work of its director: principles were diffused into the practice of compositors and press-men. These principles would have been largely verbally instructed and tacitly embodied. They were applied to a range of material: the books of several publishers, as well as to smaller, more ephemeral items. In this way the master-printers had a more pervasive effect, though enjoyed less celebration, than freelance designers of single items. Leipzig, above all other places, became the centre of reformed printing in Germany. Here were concentrated several large firms, each depending on high standards of production and design for their success. Leipzig was also the location of the main national library collection devoted to printing, at the Deutsche Bücherei, and of the Staatliche Akademie für Graphische Kunst und Buchgewerbe. These were among the constituents of the culture of printing that has come to distinguish German typography: a serious concern with every aspect of the printed word. This cultural effort received its first public consummation in 1914, on the eve of the First World War, at the 'Bugra' exhibition for book design and graphic art ('Ausstellung für Buchgewerbe und Graphik') in Leipzig.

---

3. See the reproductions in: Buddensieg, *Industriekultur*, p. D210; Windsor, *Peter Behrens*, p. 47.
4. Reprinted in Sichowsky, *Typographie und Bibliophilie*, pp. 124–52.

The book as object

The German culture of printing was to some considerable extent
the physical expression of a flourishing literary and artistic culture. The publishers contributing to this culture were those who
sought distinction both in the content and the form of their books:
both aspects were seen as closely connected. The most celebrated
instance of this attitude has been the Insel Verlag. The publishing
house had its origins in *Die Insel* (subtitled a 'monthly periodical
with decorations and illustrations'), which ran from 1899 to 1902, at
the Jugendstil high-point. And in its early phase the Insel Verlag was
devoted to the publication of exclusive, highly-wrought books. But
its distinction from the other leaders of book-taste of the period was
to begin the publication of large-run editions designed in small-
size, uniform formats. The first of these series was the Großherzog
Wilhelm Ernst edition of German classics, which appeared from
1905 (see example 8, pp.198–9). Significantly for the thesis of
English influence on the German reform, Emery Walker acted as a
consultant on the production of these books, and he arranged for
the involvement of Douglas Cockerell (for the binding covers) and
Edward Johnston and Eric Gill (for internal lettering). The roman
hand-lettering and the old-style text typeface would, in their predominantly blackletter context, have been felt as distinctly new and
foreign. The contact with Emery Walker was probably made by C. E.
Poeschel – they met during the latter's visit to Britain of 1904 – and,
both as adviser and as printer, Poeschel played a considerable part
in the early Insel Verlag production. The idea of the cheap but well-
made small-format popular book received its first full exploration in
the Insel Bücherei (founded in 1912, and, in altered circumstances,
still continuing). The physical form of this series was characterized
by certain standard elements – a single format, boards covered with
decorated paper, pasted labels – but free play was exercised in the
choice of typeface for text-setting and in the patterned papers.

For the newly enlightened publishers, even the plainest, least
decorated books became proper objects for design. The ideal of
'Qualitätsarbeit', of the well-made, encouraged attention to the
whole book. German books commonly had a physical distinction
that would have been exceptional in British or American books of
the period. This phenomenon persists still.

The rich and extensive book production of the first three decades of the twentieth century in Germany can only be hinted at here, by instances. The most severe and least ornamented mode was best represented by the editor, publisher and printer Jakob Hegner. He worked first from the garden city community at Hellerau, a centre of Werkbund values, though with a conservative and, in Hegner's case, strongly religious inflection. After winding up his company at Hellerau, in the economic crisis of 1930, he moved to Leipzig, continuing to publish in association with the printers Oscar Brandstetter. Hegner was a forerunner in the adoption of roman typography in Germany; especially in his Leipzig years – now in mutual contact with the ordinary trade – his books came to constitute models for the mass-production of serious texts.

More differentiated approaches to book design came from the freelance designers who emerged in the first decades of the century. They would typically span the fields of illustration, print-making, calligraphy – and the teaching of these subjects – and would thus come to design every aspect of a book, following the ideal of unity of effect. Notable achievements followed from long-term collaborations of designer and publisher: F. H. Ehmcke with Eugen Diederichs; Paul Renner with Georg Müller. Here too, in both these collaborations, the Werkbund spirit can be found. Diederichs, as well as being a founding member of the Werkbund, actively supported its ideals through the books he published; both Ehmcke and Renner became prominent members and prolific writers in its cause.

The doyen of the freelance designers was E. R. Weiß: a painter and illustrator, but equally able as a book designer (both ornamentation and text typography) and designer of type ornaments and typefaces. Weiß designed a roman and three variations of blackletter for the Bauer foundry, and he worked for the leading literary publishers of his day, particularly the Insel Verlag and the S. Fischer Verlag. With the Werkbund designers he shared the concern for good materials and for the whole book, but his highly worked, decorative approach was personal, rather than referring to some common ideal; his reference points were historical forms, especially of the eighteenth century. Weiß stood at the furthest distance from the 'English' and 'Puritanical' plain typography, as he characterized it in a text entitled – with some point – 'Das Buch als Gegendstand'

('The book as object').[5] In addition to his more purely visual activity, Weiß wrote and translated. He thus joined the visual and literary cultures in a way that was peculiarly German.

Though it may fall outside German national boundaries, one instance of mediation between the world of the private press and that of ordinary commerce should be mentioned here: the Officina Bodoni of Giovanni (originally Hans) Mardersteig, which operated first from Montagnola in Switzerland (1922–7) and then from Verona in Italy (1927–77). From his beginnings at a centre of German artistic and literary culture (with the publisher Kurt Wolff in Leipzig) Mardersteig left Germany for reasons of health and to start a hand press. He was also drawn south intellectually, by his interests in Renaissance culture; and he went on to make some notable contributions to the history of letterforms and printing.

In the 1920s and even into the 1930s it was possible for Mardersteig to run this press as a commercial operation (perhaps taking advantage of cheaper living conditions in Italy). His uncompromising attitude towards standards of editing and production as well as an assured visual sense – rare in such an operation – attracted a faithful group of patrons and customers. With increasing pressure to take on more lucrative work, and with the recognition of the achievements of the press, Mardersteig did make the transition into work for mass-production: typefaces that had been cut for hand-composition were adapted for Monotype setting, and he acted as consultant to an early paperback venture (Albatross Books) and to the Collins Cleartype Press in Glasgow. This expansion into the wider world of European typography was enabled especially by the fact of Mardersteig having left behind German – blackletter – typography: to be roman was to be potentially international.

German letters

The interplay of tradition and modernity in German typography was, until about 1950, conditioned by the blackletter heritage and the debate over 'Fraktur' and 'Antiqua'. This fact of cultural life presented German-language typographers with a context that was essentially different from that for those working in any other Western language. The modern typefaces (of Walbaum, most notably) that had been made and used in Germany in the eighteenth and early

nineteenth centuries, and their unsatisfactory derivatives, constituted the only significant precedent for roman typography. To summarize rather crudely German attitudes on the matter in the twentieth
century: to prefer roman over blackletter was to be modern, and,
especially after 1918, to prefer sanserif roman letters to those with
serifs was to be more modern still. The issue of national character
intersected with but did not always confirm this polarity. Thus the
Behrens-Schrift represented an attempt to resolve conflicting demands: a letterform that was both German (blackletter) and modern
(simplified). In the further development of traditionalist typography
in the first three decades of the century, one sees typeface designers
alternating between the two forms. Not with equal facility, for – to
roman-conditioned eyes, at least – the new German romans of this
period seem to come from designers not quite easy with the norms
for these letterforms. Then, after some twists of ideology within
the National-Socialist Party, the decree of 1941 signalled the end of
blackletter as the German standard letterform (see chapter 10).

This special context figures in attitudes to the letters of Jugendstil. Having no real tradition of roman letterforms, and with
its blackletter forms increasingly degraded and under attack, the
German situation around 1900 was a more open one than that in
the English-language countries. The criticism of blackletter centred
around the complaint that its individual letters were too similar to
each other and that this lack of differentiation impeded recognition.
Blackletter was also felt to be too complicated: a factor that began to
be significant for aesthetic and social reformers, for whom formal
simplicity implied moral virtue.

Insufficiency of differentiation and over-complexity were main
charges against blackletter put forward by Rudolf von Larisch in
his *Über Leserlichkeit von ornamentalen Schriften* ('On the legibility of ornamental lettering') of 1904. This pamphlet opened with
a discussion of general issues of legibility, and included a report
of an informal but clock-measured experiment on the legibility of
words, conducted by Larisch with his pupils. But once the issue of
blackletter had been raised, all other matters were put aside, and

5. Published in the *Fischer-Almanach*, no. 25, 1911; reprinted in
Sichowsky, *Typographie und Bibliophilie*, pp. 153–61.

the writer's tone became increasingly urgent: German printing op-
pressed its readers, overloading them with the horrific complexity
and sameness of its letters. The way out was obscure and apocalyptic: 'No reform can help in this situation of need; something
new must replace the old. Only a genius can help us!' (Larisch, *Über
Leserlichkeit*, p. 47.)

Larisch was an Austrian: a civil servant and a self-taught callig-
rapher who only in his forties took up serious practice of 'ornamental lettering' (the direct and best translation of his description of
his practice). This was in the late 1890s, when he also began to teach
and to publish on the subject. The essential elements of Larisch's
approach were present already in his first publication on lettering:
Über Zierschriften im Dienste der Kunst ('On ornamental letters applied to works of art') of 1899. Primary emphasis was placed not on
the forms of letters, but on the space between them: this should be
optically equal and not equal by linear measure. The question of individual letters and their forms was hardly raised: Larisch leaves his
reader with the impression that all forms are acceptable, provided
that they are properly spaced and that a satisfactory overall effect is
thus achieved. This openness was the main feature of his anthologies, *Beispiele künstlerischer Schrift* ('Examples of artistic lettering'),
which published work from several countries and achieved some
international circulation: any approach was welcomed and included. It was a permissive, liberal view and in this, one might add, a
characteristically Austrian one.

Larisch explained his approach fully in *Unterricht in ornamentaler Schrift* ('Instruction in ornamental lettering'), published first
in 1905 and reaching its eleventh edition in 1934 (see example 10,
pp. 202–3). The book was addressed to beginners, and, as the first
means of writing, Larisch advocated what he termed the 'Quellstift':
'a stick of wood, dipped in ink or paint, which runs off during the
drawing or writing and so makes a very strong stroke of equal thickness and which demands an agile, decisive and sure hand' (Larisch,
Unterricht, 4th edn, 1913, p. 22). And though pens were mentioned,
it was this more primary means that formed the foundations: the
crucial factor was spacing between letters and the subordination of
detail to the total effect.

The methods and views of Larisch have often been seen, with

justice, to stand at an opposite pole to those of Edward Johnston. As well as Larisch's distrust of the pen (which for Johnston was the 'source instrument'), he was indifferent to historical forms (in which Johnston was passionately interested) and his approach was well tuned to the commercial artist's need to work for reduction and reproduction (methods that Johnston abhorred). Johnston's formal writing had entered the typographic culture of Germany as one element in the importation of the English reform. In 1909 he was persuaded to come to give a lecture in Dresden, and, more importantly, a German edition of *Writing & illuminating, & lettering* appeared in the next year. The translation was made by Anna Simons, who had been a pupil of Johnston's at the Royal College of Art and became a principal advocate in Germany of the broad-pen approach to writing and lettering.

Calligraphy was to become a strong presence in German traditionalist typography: important both in its own right – within education and as an element of graphic design (especially on book covers and jackets) – and as a basis for typeface design. If Larisch, through his writings, was the chief teacher of lettering, the lack of any strict style or method in his approach helped to make the situation an open one: unlike that in Britain, where Johnston's much more definite principles dominated. German calligraphy was developed, above all, by a number of practitioners who did not write manuals but who spread the art through personal teaching and through the example of their work. A prominent example of such a practitioner-teacher would be F. H. Ernst Schneidler, head of the graphic department of the Kunstgewerbeschule (later Akademie) at Stuttgart from 1920 to 1948, from which a 'Stuttgart school' of calligraphy can be seen to have emerged. These were all-round graphic artists who painted, illustrated, practised typography and calligraphy, and designed typefaces (most notably Georg Trump, Rudo Spemann, Walter Brudi, Imre Reiner, Albert Kapr). Another 'school' emerged from the Leipzig Akademie, where Hermann Delitsch was an exponent of Larisch's methods; and, especially under the direction (from 1920) of Walter Tiemann, the Akademie became a centre for the practice of calligraphy. F. H. Ehmcke was one practitioner who did write about calligraphy, though usually as one element of the larger theme of typography. He learned from both Larisch and Johnston

and entered the teaching of the subject at the Düsseldorf Kunstgewerbeschule under Peter Behrens; another teacher at Düsseldorf
was Anna Simons. Ehmcke later taught for an extended period
at Munich and among his pupils were Schneidler and Spemann:
through such interconnections did German calligraphy develop. In
Ehmcke's writings one finds articulated the view that was implicit
in traditionalist typography in all countries and which explains the
importance it accorded to calligraphy: this was the theory that writing or (more generally) hand-produced forms should be at the root
of all letters for printing. To ignore written forms, as the 'elemental'
or new typographers tried to do, was thus to discard the very foundations of civilized practice.[6]

If Johnston and Larisch were opposites, it may be reasonable to
see Rudolf Koch's position as occupying some third point, equidis-
tant from each of them. After conventional Jugendstil beginnings,
Koch came to stand for 'German letters' at an extreme of intensity:
heavily charged with Protestant religious significance. His work was
thus entirely different in spirit and appearance from that of Larisch,
who was Catholic in religion as well as catholic in taste and whose
passions were confined to dislike of blackletter. Koch was most
deeply occupied by blackletter and did in superficial respects parallel the nationalist exploitation of these forms, but his religion and
his spirit of 'making it new' removed his work from any taint of the
cynical motives of National Socialism.[7] He died in 1934.

Though emphatically a hand-worker, Koch – unlike Johnston –
had no scruples about designing typefaces. He would have been
helped here by the intimacy of his relations with the Klingspor typefoundry. Koch joined the firm in 1906 and the first of his many typefaces for the company was issued in 1910. He also taught writing
and lettering at the Offenbach Kunst- und Handwerkschule (from
1908) and thus began to establish the conditions for the 'Werkge-
meinschaft' of pupils and collaborators that he presided over and
which developed especially after 1918.

The major part of Koch's typeface production was formed by
blackletter faces, and through these new contributions the Klingspor typefoundry was to become a prominent voice in the advocacy
of blackletter. These letters were seen at their most charming and
benign in the many items that the firm printed for its own purposes:

limited editions, calendars, ephemera. This policy was maintained in the face of the political storms in which the issue became surrounded in the 1930s and 1940s; and as late as 1949, in his *Über Schönheit von Schrift und Druck*, Karl Klingspor made a last-ditch call for the continued use of blackletter as the German standard. As well as his blackletter typefaces, Koch designed a quasi-geometrical sanserif (Kabel), an all-capital 'expressionist' sanserif (Neuland), and two romans. The range and extent of his work with typefaces was thus wider than the image of the intense hand-worker would suggest.

Traditional and modern

Mechanical composition came to Germany with the Linotype machine, from the USA. The American Mergenthaler-Linotype company opened a factory in Berlin for the manufacture of its machines. The typefaces at first available on these machines were American in origin, but Linotype began to acquire rights to matrices of typefaces from German typefoundries. In 1900, a contract with the Stempel typefoundry was signed, giving them rights to certain faces, and this set the pattern for the future development of Linotype in Germany. The other significant line-composition firm, Intertype, bought rights for typefaces from the Bauer typefoundry, though it achieved only a minor share of the German market. Monotype was represented by the British branch of the company, and it found only a modest acceptance. Some of the explanation for this could be the immediate difficulties of establishing a sales and servicing presence in the country, and slowness in providing the alternative and additional characters necessary to German-language typography. But the larger problem was one of policy and attitude: the company did not provide sufficiently for German tastes, and its revivals aroused no particular interest from German traditionalists, whose traditions were largely different ones. The role that Monotype played for English-language typography, as a rallying focus for a new tradi-

6. See: Ehmcke, *Ziele des Schriftunterrichts*, p. iv.

7. The moral-aesthetic cynicism of blackletter types designed in the Nazi spirit is clearly shown by Hans Peter Willberg in his contribution to: Typographische Gesellschaft München, *Hundert Jahre Typographie*.

tionalism, could not extend to Germany (though the company was relatively more successful in Switzerland). At the top of the trade, in book production, hand composition seems to have persisted longer in Germany than in Britain or the USA. The survival rate of typefoundries suggests this: even in 1959 there were still seven in commercial operation.[8] This persistence may have been due to imperfections in Linotype composition, which were overcome in time. When – by at least 1930 – the Linotype machine had been fully developed and was equipped with sound typefaces, there was then little inhibition or ideological difficulty among the traditionally minded in using machine composition: it was not an issue, as it was still in Britain.

After 1918, the politics of German typography became overtaken by the larger politics of the country. Traditionalism and modernism became effectively polarized (though not absolutely) between right and left. To call for a 'German' style or 'German' letters became a narrowly political endeavour, or was seen as such, and traditional values were thus undermined. Some voices, that of F. H. Ehmcke for example, held out for these values, in the face of their politicization. Others, while remaining within the broad ethos of the Werkbund, went over to modernism: notably Paul Renner. This involved a different set of formal principles, and their justification by reference to the conditions of the modern age.

8. See: Schauer, *Deutsche Buchkunst*, pp. 134ff.

8 Cultures of printing: the Low Countries

It may be the fate of small countries to exist in the margins between their larger neighbours. The cultures of the Low Countries might seem to depend for their definition on those of France and Germany and, more distantly, Britain. And certainly within what has become Belgium there is a marginal situation: two language-communities, each looking towards a neighbour – France or the Netherlands – as an external source of cultural production. But, even to an outside observer, it is clear that the Low Countries have always had their own authentic printing cultures. To disabuse notions of the cultural inferiority of these countries, it should be enough to mention the names of Plantin, Elzévier, Enschedé, and the fact that England's first printer learned the skills of the trade in Bruges.

The truer and more surprising case of marginality in twentieth-century typography is that of France. In both broad streams – traditional and modern – it is hard to find more than isolated contributions from France. Perhaps the most notable of these is the typeface classification system proposed by Maximilien Vox (in its first version) in 1954. This system, which crystalized contemporary discussion of the issue, proved – despite a certain whimsy in its nomenclature – to be a more workable tool than anything that had been conceived of before. It was then taken up, in adapted versions, by the German and British national standardization bodies. Vox – writer, editor, and graphic designer – had emerged as one of the strongest voices in French typography in the mid-century. Another central figure, Charles Peignot, worked through the family firm of typefounders, and also as an editor (founding the magazine *Arts et Métiers Graphiques* in 1927). In 1957, Peignot was the dominant voice in the establishment of the Association Typographique Internationale (ATypI) at a meeting in Lausanne, Switzerland. Founded as an organization within which type producers could resolve amicably questions of copyright and licensing, it was to add a cultural and educational superstructure, and thus act as an international meeting place for typographers and manufacturers.

But for most of the twentieth century in France, aesthetic interest was channelled into the 'livre d'artiste' – large-sized art objects in scanty editions – while everyday printing used approaches and conventions little changed since the eighteenth century. Lack of invention or of the impulse to experiment may be a consequence of an early and successful revolution in civil organization and in taste; while industrialization in France had been, in comparison with Britain, rather retarded. France had no real craft-revival movement of its own and was little affected by the British one – as if such a thing was simply not needed – and so, in the field of typography, it escaped the common pattern of revival and reform.

Belgium

French attitudes extended to include those sections of Belgian cultural life that looked towards France; but, taken as a whole, Belgium was significantly affected by the Arts & Crafts movement. In brief sketches of small countries, it may be permissible to rely on a dominant individual case: the dominating figure here was Henry van de Velde. His career provides a link between several of the central preceding phenomena of modernist design: Art Nouveau in Belgium and Paris, Jugendstil in Germany, the Werkbund before 1914, the pre-Bauhaus at Weimar. Starting as a painter, his turn to design and architecture followed the pattern of the time, motivated by the wish to apply art to life, for social and moral reasons. The Arts & Crafts movement provided the focus for these aspirations: Van de Velde began to lecture and to publish on its themes, while pursuing visual approaches independent from those of the British movement.

This literary activity led to involvement with publishing and thus (from 1892) to the decoration and design of books. Van de Velde's book design work was confined to small-circulation works of literature. His most celebrated achievements were two editions of texts by Nietzsche (*Zarathustra*, *Ecce homo*, both of 1908) for the Insel Verlag: splendid and useless monuments, though use was beside their point. His more modest work could have played some part in disseminating a sense of aesthetic quality to the wider world of printing. But, as his contributions to the Werkbund debates made clear, Van de Velde stood for the individual artist, ungoverned by any norms, and in opposition to the standardizing tendencies inherent in the full development of industrial production. The importance of Van de Velde's work for the modern was symbolic and indirect. In Belgium, the involvement of such a designer in this field helped to open the way for a culture of printing to develop there: within design education, around libraries and museums, in literary and bibliophile circles.

After an extended period in Germany and then Switzerland and the Netherlands, Van de Velde returned to Belgium in 1925, to set up the Institut Supérieur des Arts Décoratifs (ISAD), on the model of the reformed art school that he had directed at Weimar. A printing workshop was established at the ISAD and a number of small-edition books produced. Van de Velde's use of Futura – fonts of the typeface were acquired soon after they were first available – again suggests an idiosyncratic approach, at some distance from any orthodoxy.

The Netherlands

The Dutch revival of printing was stronger and based more broadly in the trade than that of Belgium. The Netherlands had had its own movement of cultural reform in the nineteenth century, and the work of Ruskin and Morris was recognized as confirming indigenous developments. In book production, Kelmscott typography provided the point of departure for what would become Dutch new traditionalist typography. The leading figure here was S. H. de Roos, who followed the path from drawing and illustration into text typography. The first book designed by De Roos was, appropriately, an edition of essays by William Morris (*Kunst en maatschappij*, 1903), though its appearance showed Art Nouveau rather than Kelmscott allegiances. This was a temporary phase: he soon began to work out a plainer typography, which could provide a pattern for the production of books by enlightened trade printers; and a 'school' of adherents can be said to have developed from the example of De Roos (notably Charles Nypels, A. A. M. Stols). De Roos was a socialist and disposed to working within industry, though not at the cost of good standards.

De Roos's breakthrough into the world of printing came in 1907, with his appointment as designer at a typefoundry, the Lettergieterij 'Amsterdam'. The first typeface for which he was responsible was the Hollandse Mediaeval (1912): it became the standard roman typeface of quality for Dutch printing. There followed a series of romans, including typefaces for the private presses that were established in the course of the Dutch printing revival; De Roos ran his own small press (De Heuvel) from 1926. His last typeface was issued after the Second World War (appearing first in 1947): the De Roos Romein, a more refined set of forms, without the 'private press' peculiarities that had marked his previous typefaces.

The attitude of working in industry but reserving a sphere of limited, non-commercial production for some higher design aspiration was shared with De Roos by J. F. van Royen. From 1904 until the Second World War, Van Royen worked for the PTT (the Dutch post, telegraph and telephone service), becoming its secretary-general and with responsibilities for design policy. His work for the PTT was enlightened; artists and designers were employed to work on every aspect and artefact of the company. This patronage did not follow any exclusive stylistic or ideological line: designers of all persuasions, modern and traditional, were given work. Van Royen's main typographic commitment was, however, to his private press work: social ideals (the day-time job) were split from aesthetic ones (the spare-time production of limited editions). He collaborated in the Zilverdistel press, for which De Roos designed a typeface, and later set up his own Kunera Press.

The importance of Jan van Krimpen's work lay in the attempt to resolve this split between industrial and private production. Fifteen years younger than De Roos and Van Royen, he was able to join a typographic culture already in formation. Though he had trained at the Hague academy of art, his entry to this culture came through literature as much as through design: freelance work (especially lettering) for publishers and acting both as designer and publisher of some small-edition books. Van Krimpen's breakthrough came in 1923 when he was asked by the printers and typefounders Joh. Enschedé en Zonen to design a typeface for them. He had come to their notice as the designer of lettering on a stamp (a commission from Van Royen) which Enschedé had printed. The success of this typeface – Lutetia, issued in 1925 – led to the lifelong association between this firm and Van Krimpen, working both as a designer of typefaces and of printed matter. Though the firm was then in a state of some stagnation, Enschedé was the principal bearer of tradition

in Dutch typography: founded in 1704, it had gathered a considerable stock of the best typefaces.

Both in the design of typefaces and in designing books, Van
Krimpen developed an approach that stayed firmly within the
traditions of European typography, while eschewing pastiche or
revivalism. In his work, as in his personal temperament, he differed
from the rougher, more robust De Roos: Van Krimpen stood for
the Calvinist virtues of outer reticence and severity, with fastidious
attention to detail. The typefaces for Enschedé were on a level of sophistication some way above those of De Roos, though both worked
on variations within the same genre. Van Krimpen's achievements
were enabled by his own drawing skills and by the skills of the
firm's punchcutter (P. H. Rädisch). Three of the four principal typefaces from this collaboration (Lutetia, Romulus, Spectrum) were
adapted for the Monotype machine. This application of his work
was in line with Van Krimpen's willingness to work with the means
of industry. He did, however, have reservations about, and some
quarrels with, the policies of the Monotype Corporation's typographic consultant, Stanley Morison. These came to a head over the
adaptation of one of the historical Dutch types for Monotype (Van
Dijck): Van Krimpen collaborated, while advancing grave objections. He believed that such resuscitations were invalid and that
new typefaces should take new forms, while observing traditional
norms. In this his attitude lay quite close to that of Eric Gill (Johnston's work lay behind both), as did the level of his hand skills – Van
Krimpen's letter draughtsmanship was perhaps even more assured
than Gill's. Van Krimpen became racked by doubts about the ethics
of the mechanical cutting of punches and expressed these in the
writings of his last years.[1]

Van Krimpen's feeling for the plain and ordinary mass-produced item became evident in his design of the set of definitive
Dutch stamps (after the Second World War) and in his book design
work for trade publishers (an encylopaedia and a dictionary, as well
as literary texts). This work became the progenitor of an approach
to typography that still flourishes in the Netherlands in the field

1. See: Van Krimpen, *On designing and devising type*, pp. 42, 44. See also
his *A letter to Philip Hofer*.

of book design. The other Dutch tradition, of modernism, existed
largely outside book typography, and was developed rather by
people from architecture and industrial design. Though the two
approaches might occasionally coexist (as at the PTT), there was no
contact or exchange between them.

9   New typography

Modernism in twentieth-century typography was, in its 'heroic' period from the end of the First World War to the National-Socialist seizure of power in Germany in 1933, a phenomenon of the European continent. Britain played no part in it, and the USA was significant mainly as a distant emblem of modern life. Germany was the centre, and the meeting ground for an international exchange of experiments and ideas. A full analysis would entail the separate examination of contributions from post-revolutionary Russia. It would also take up the special case of the Netherlands, and also more distant and obscure developments in Poland and Czechoslovakia, as well as contributions from Austria, Switzerland, and Italy. France would be rapidly passed over even in a more detailed account of new typography. Just as the country lacked any revival of printing movement, so France was very little affected by Central European modernism in typography: its typographic modernism was largely confined to stylistic expression, as an aspect of 'l'art décoratif'.

The phrase 'new typography' is adopted here as the descriptive term for the phenomenon, following contemporary usage, most notably in Jan Tschichold's handbook of the movement, *Die neue Typographie* (1928). In this book the historical perspective of new typography was outlined: what came before the new was dealt with in one chapter, entitled 'The old typography (1440–1914)' (Tschichold, *Die neue Typographie* [also English-language edition], pp. 15–29). Tschichold found some sense of confirmation for new typography in the work of the earliest German printers (the practice of setting in two columns, a sense of contrast rather than balance) and in the 'modern' printers of the eighteenth century (especially the Didots). But he was otherwise prepared to consider the history of typography up to 1914 as just a pre-history. Signs of change had begun to be evident in the nineteenth century, when typography escaped from the book, new letterforms were developed (sanserif especially) and new means of reproduction introduced (lithography, photography). William Morris's reaction to the degradations of nineteenth-cen-

tury typography was a false one, in its rejection of the machine. The
Jugendstil designers did at least attempt some harmonization of art
and life, but, in choosing to imitate natural forms, they went up a
blind alley. The 'book artists', as Tschichold described them (often
in ironic quotation marks), who had taken their initial inspiration
from English private press printing, had also become stultified.
At their simplest and best (in the case of C. E. Poeschel) their work
was a kind of zero point between the old decorated typography and
the designing ('gestaltend') new typography.

Tschichold then went on to provide a history of new typography,
turning first to the 'new art', 'for the laws of this kind of typographic
design represent nothing other than the practical application of the
laws of design discovered by the new painters' (Tschichold, *Die neue
Typographie*, p. 30). Abstract art was an art no longer dependent on
imitation and private sentiment; rather it was constructive and belonged to a collective sphere. The old era emphasized individuality
and uniqueness; the new era was one of reproducibility and of the
dissolution of art into architecture and publicly available forms. The
immediate steps leading to the present new typography were then
outlined: the interest in sanserif early in the century; the Futurist
manifesto of 1909 ('Les mots en liberté futuristes'); Dada; De Stijl;
Russian elementarism. The ideas and approaches of these movements coalesced around 1923 into what then became the new typography. This account of the origins of new typography, as essentially
artistic, has become orthodox; and by extension, the movement
itself as it developed during the 1920s and early 1930s has been
regarded as also an artistic phenomenon.

It is clearly true that much of the impulse for the new typography came from people outside the printing trade and from outside
the larger world of typography. It is also true, and less often noticed,
that if these people were 'artists' they were also intent on undermining or demolishing the very notion of art as then conceived. That
is the common link between the otherwise disparate motivations
of the Italian Futurists, the Russian Constructivists, the Dutch Stijl
group, the international Dadaists. Rejecting the bourgeois confine-
ment of art to the framed easel painting, the drawing room and the
sale room, they looked for forms of production that escaped those
shackles. The more positive or utopian elements – the Constructiv-

ists and the Stijl group – went beyond rejection, producing models for a new art, in which distinctions between art and life had been dissolved. Their interest in graphic and typographic design thus took its place as part of a concern with the whole of the humanly constructed world. Also, having strong ideas, they were led to publication – typically, little magazines – and, being visually oriented, they wanted the form of these publications to correspond to their content. This is the most immediate explanation for the interest taken in typography by these artists.

The formulation of some of the leading ideas of the new typography can be traced in the manifestos and articles published by, most notably, El Lissitzky and László Moholy-Nagy, and, less centrally, Kurt Schwitters. Between 1923 and 1925 they published summarizing statements on the nature and aims of a new typography, each one picking up ideas formulated by the other. The statement 'Topographie der Typographie' by Lissitzky, from 1923, may stand as a representative of this early, visionary phase of new typography, in which every convention was open to question:

1   The words on the printed surface are taken in by seeing, not by hearing.

2   One communicates meanings through the convention of words; meaning attains form through letters.

3   Economy of expression: optics not phonetics.

4   The design of the book-space, set according to the constraints of printing mechanics, must correspond to the tensions and pressures of content.

5   The design of the book-space using process blocks which issue from the new optics. The supernatural reality of the perfected eye.

6   The continuous sequence of pages: the bioscopic book.

7   The new book demands the new writer. Ink-pot and quill-pen are dead.

8   The printed surface transcends space and time. The printed surface, the infinity of books, must be transcended. The electro-library.[1]

1. Originally published in *Merz*, no. 4, 1923; reprinted in Lissitzky-Küppers, *El Lissitzky*, p. 356 (English-language edition p. 355, whose translation is here modified).

By 1925, the essential theory of the movement had been articulated. In this year the first summarizing anthology appeared:
'Elementare Typographie', a special issue of *Typographische Mitteilungen*, the magazine of the Bildungsverband der Deutschen Buchdrucker (educational organization of the German printing trade
union). The guest-editor of this issue was Jan Tschichold, who thus,
with this his first publication, embarked on a mission to explain
and diffuse avant-garde ideas in the world of everyday printing. The
issue reproduced a selection of work by those who had emerged as
practitioners of the approach, and it contained explanatory and programmatic texts, including the following statement by Tschichold:

> *Elemental typography*
> 1   The new typography is oriented towards purpose.
> 2   The purpose of any piece of typography is communication
> (the means of which it displays). The communication must ap-
> pear in the briefest, simplest, most urgent form.
> 3   In order to make typography serviceable to social ends, it
> requires the *inner organization* of its materials (the ordering of
> content) and their *outer organization* (the means of typography
> configured in relation to one another).
> 4   *Inner organization* is the limitation to the elemental means
> of typography: letters, numbers, signs, rules – from the typecase
> and the composing machine.
> In the present, visually-attuned world, the exact image –
> photography – also belongs to the elemental means of typo-
> graphy.
> The elemental letterform is the sanserif, in all variations:
> light, medium, bold, and from condensed to expanded.
> Letterforms that belong to particular style-categories or
> which bear definite national characteristics (Gothic, Fraktur,
> Kirchen-Slavisch) are not elementally designed, and to some ex-
> tent limit the possibilities of being understood internationally.
> Mediaeval-Antiqua [roman] is the most usual form of typeface
> for the majority of people. For the setting of continuous text, it
> still – without being elementally designed – has the advantage of
> better legibility over many sanserifs.
> As long as there exists no thoroughly elemental form that is

also legible in text setting, it is appropriate to prefer (against a sanserif) the least obtrusive form of Mediaeval-Antiqua [roman] – one in which period or personal characteristics are least evident.

An extraordinary economy could be achieved through the exclusive use of small letters – the elimination of all capital letters; a form of writing and setting that is recommended as a new script by all innovators in the field. See the book *Sprache und Schrift* by Dr Porstmann (Beuth-Verlag, Berlin sw19, Beuthstraße 8. Price: 5.25 Marks). our script loses nothing through writing in small letters only – but becomes, rather, more legible, easier to learn, essentially more economical. for one sound, for example 'a', why two signs: A and a? one sound, one sign. why two alfabets for one word, why double the quantity of signs, when a half achieves the same?

Through the use of strongly differentiated sizes and forms, and without consideration for previous aesthetic attitudes, the logical arrangement of printed text is made visually perceptible.

The unprinted areas of the paper are as much a means of design as are the visually appearing forms.

5   *Outer organization* is the forming of the strongest contrast (simultaneity) through the use of differentiated shapes, sizes, weights (which must correspond to the value of their content) and the creation of the relation between the positive (coloured) formal values and the (white) negative values of the unprinted paper.

6   Elemental typographic design is the creation of the logical and visual relation between the letters, words, and text, which are given by the job in hand.

7   In order to increase the sense of urgency of new typography, vertical and diagonal lines can also be employed as a means of inner organization.

8   Elemental designing excludes the use of any *ornament* (also 'swelled' and other ornamental rules). The use of rules and inherently elemental forms (squares, circles, triangles) must be convincingly grounded in the total construction.

The *decorative-artistic-fanciful* use of essentially elemental forms is not in keeping with elemental designing.

9   Ordering of elements in new typography should in future be
based on the standardized (DIN) paper formats of the Normenausschuß der Deutschen Industrie (NDI), which alone make
possible a comprehensive organization for all typographic
design. (See: Dr Porstmann, *Die Dinformate und ihre Einführung in die Praxis*, Selbstverlag Dinorm, Berlin NW7, Sommer-
straße 4a. 3.00 Marks.)

   In particular the DIN format A4 (210:297 mm) should be
the basis of all business and other letterheadings. The business letterheading has itself also been standardized: DIN 676,
'Geschäftsbrief', obtainable direct from Beuth-Verlag, Berlin
SW19, Beuthstraße 8; 0.40 Mark. The DIN standard 'Papierfor-
mate' is number 476. The DIN formats have only recently been
introduced into practice. In this special issue there is only one
job that is consciously based on a DIN format.

10   Elemental designing is, in typography as in other fields, not
absolute or conclusive. Elements change through discoveries
that create new means of typographic designing – photography,
for example – therefore the concept of elemental designing will
necessarily also change continually.[2]

Reproduced in its entirety, as here, this text provides a convenient
summary of the aspirations of new typography at its first moment
of self-definition. The leading idea is that of purpose ('Zweck'),
which informs both the details of the designed object and the larger
context, of the artefact in society. Thus formal questions, of the use
of space and of the visual elements of typography, are joined with
social considerations. Much of this had been suggested already by
Lissitzky and Moholy-Nagy. But where these artist-typographers
had stressed the element of expression – not personal expression,
but the expression of content through form – Tschichold's emphasis
is much more on order and organization. Contrast is sought not for
its own sake (as in some of the more Dionysiac tendencies within
modernism), but in order to reveal 'the logical arrangement of the
printed text'. This theme leads on to the specific references to the
standards for paper sizes and to the reform of orthography. The
practical information that Tschichold provided here would become
typical of his constant pedagogy (see example 15, pp. 212–3). As

the contrast of this statement with Lissitzky's 'Topographie der Typographie' suggests, Tschichold was patiently precise, where the artist-typographers were vague and prophetic.

Norms and standards

Attempts to devise norms for the manufacture of products had quickened in pace in the conditions of the First World War. The need to co-ordinate production for efficiency now became urgent and governments were able to take greater steps towards the regulation of industry than in peacetime. Thus a German standards organization, the Normenausschuß der Deutschen Industrie, was established in 1917; in a reorganization of 1926 it became the Deutscher Normenausschuß. Although a self-supporting body funded by membership subscriptions, federal grants and through the sales of its literature, the Deutscher Normenausschuß formulated (and continues to do so) standards for units of measurement, symbols, artefacts, both across and within industries. It might thus be seen as representing a kind of national will, and one might connect this with the Werkbund project – as proposed by Muthesius in 1914 – to establish norms or types for German products. But while the Werkbund artists and architects thought in terms of a settled style and of established type-forms for artefacts, the Deutscher Normenausschuß was concerned rather with the standardization of the dimensions of the elements of manufacture: screw threads, but not whole ensembles. In the paradox of standardization, however, the more that elements were 'normed', the more easily and the more variously they could be combined. The Normenausschuß had been set up by the Verein Deutscher Ingenieure and was a body of engineers, with no reference to art or design; but this only increased its attraction to modernist designers who, in the years after 1918, began to adopt an aesthetic of the machine, while disclaiming any interest

2. Originally published in *Typographische Mitteilungen*, no. 10, 1925, pp. 198, 200; reprinted in Fleischmann, *Bauhaus*, p. 333. In making this translation 'elemental' has been preferred to 'elementary', to avoid any suggestion of 'easy' or 'juvenile'. The passage in the fourth section, set in lowercase and with 'phonetic spelling' in the original, is treated correspondingly here. See also p. 260 below, for some remarks on the orthographic conventions adopted in this book.

in aesthetics as then conceived. This was seductively and famously elaborated in the work of Le Corbusier, in the journal *L'Esprit Nouveau* (1920–4) and in his book *Vers une architecture* (1923). It is the Corbusian vision that lies behind the talismanic figure in Tschichold's *Die neue Typographie*: 'the engineer! This engineer is the designer of our epoch. Characteristics of his work: economy, precision, construction with pure forms corresponding to the function of the object.' (Tschichold, *Die neue Typographie*, p.11.)

For new typographers, the role of this aesthetic of industry and mechanical production can be seen by contrasting their attitudes with the new traditionalists. These latter accepted machine composition and powered printing presses, but they made no connection between methods of production and the visual appearance of their work, which followed traditional forms. For modernist typographers, however, visual appearance was to be shaped by new methods of production: this process of manufacture took its place within the totality of the demands of the 'modern age', which would include the new needs of users or readers too. The applications of this theory included both the relatively trivial (the cult of spiral bindings and metallic finishes) and the more complex (arguments in favour of unjustified setting, as more proper to machine composition), but the most fundamental accommodation to 'the machine' was the adoption of standards.

As well as its activities in the domain of heavy industry, the Deutscher Normenausschuß had soon become concerned with the area of business administration and thus impinged on the printing trade and typography. Standards were issued for, among other items, paper formats (1922), business letterheadings (1924), envelopes (1924), newspapers (1924), book formats (1926). These provided a real, concrete embodiment of what might otherwise have remained a merely aesthetic appeal to the 'engineer'. As one could learn from Tschichold's writings, this figure worked from an address in Berlin, issuing directives and publications that could be bought for 3 Marks.

The key standard was that for paper sizes.[3] This scheme, of a system of sizes of constant proportion, had made its first appearance in the eighteenth-century Enlightenment (see chapter 2). And Lichtenberg's proposal of 1796 was commonly cited by twentieth-century proponents of paper standardization. The immediate initiative for the German system seems to have come from the scientist (and theorist of colour) Wilhelm Ostwald who, in 1911, published a proposal for a 'Weltformat' for paper sizes.[4] The starting unit of this system was a rectangle of 1 x 1.41 cm (1:√2), whose lengths were alternately doubled, maintaining a constant proportion. The drawback of this scheme was – in Tschichold's view – the inconvenience of the size it gave for letterheadings: 320 x 226 mm (as against 297 x 210 mm of A4). Ostwald's proposal had certainly raised the issue of a standard system of paper sizes in Germany: it had been published in a journal of the printing trade and had provoked some controversy. When, after the First World War, the Deutscher Normenausschuß issued its standard (DIN 476), it adopted the 1:√2 proportion and the principle of halving, but started from a sheet 1 square metre in area (1189 x 841 mm) and worked down from that. In a standard issued in 1923 (DIN 198) categories of printed item were matched to possible paper sizes: a structure of order was thus made available to the world of printed matter, from posters (A0) to gummed stamps (A13).

Letters of the modern age

New typographers explained their preference for sanserif as following directly from the belief in forms appropriate to the time: the modern age of the machine. This was the essential difference with others who had earlier taken up sanserif in the search for aesthetic simplicity (Stefan George or J. L. M. Lauweriks). The new typographers also made much of the 'elemental' or skeletal nature of sanserif, but went on to add that these letters had advantages beyond the merely formal ones. Though it was sometimes implied that letters without ornaments (serifs) enabled better, less fettered communication, their arguments referred very little to legibility, but rather to 'atmosphere' or association. Sanserif transcended the individual qualities of the artist's typeface; an argument that would have had

3. For a clear account, see: Tschichold, *Die neue Typographie*, pp. 99–109; English-language edition, pp. 96–106.
4. See: W. Ostwald, 'Das einheitliche Weltformat', *Börsenblatt für den Deutschen Buchhandel*, no. 243, 1911, pp. 12330–3.

particular force in the German context, in which traditionalist typography was largely characterized by such typefaces. Sanserif was
without national connotations and provided a complete break: from
blackletter into the world of international exchange.

The purest and clearest expressions of this belief appeared in
attempts at a universal alphabet, in which the design of new sanserif letterforms was combined with an orthography that abolished
capital letters and, in some cases, provided a phonetically more
correct set of signs. Here again impetus came from the engineers,
notably Dr Walter Porstmann, whose book *Sprache und Schrift* had
been published by the Verlag des Vereins Deutscher Ingenieure in
1920. Porstmann had written a dissertation on the construction
and co-ordination of measurement systems and, during the 1920s,
wrote about the new German standards (including the DIN paper
formats) for the Normenausschuß. The main lesson taken by the
typographers from *Sprache und Schrift* was the idea of the simplified
one-alphabet orthography of 'Kleinschreibung', in which 'our letters
lose nothing, but rather become more legible, easier to learn, essentially more scientific'.[5] While in Porstmann's book the advantages
of 'Kleinschreibung' were essentially those of greater efficiency in
business, the idea was given an explicit ideological charge by the
designers who took it up: capital letters were another hierarchy to
be abolished.

The interest in the project of a universal alphabet at the Bauhaus dates from around 1925, the time of its move from Weimar to
Dessau, where a fully equipped typographic workshop was established. The central figure here was László Moholy-Nagy, who had
joined the school in 1923, and had helped to direct policy away
from the initial craft-based assumptions towards a more properly
modernist, industry-oriented approach. In his writings on typography of 1925, Moholy-Nagy discussed the idea of simplified lettering,
quoting Porstmann's proposals. In this year also capital letters were
abolished at the Bauhaus and student exercises in the construction of geometrical alphabets became a staple part of the teaching
programme. The most celebrated result of this interest was Herbert
Bayer's alphabet, published first in 1926 as a research project ('Versuch einer neuen Schrift') and which was used in publicity matter
designed by Bayer; it was never cut as a type. These were purely

geometrical letterforms in one alphabet only, carrying with them the full weight of modernist theory: an international letterform, suitable for all applications (both in type and in handwriting), and in its 'exact' character and as composed of primary forms it corresponded to the demands of the machine: 'to print a hand-produced letterform with a machine is false romanticism'.[6]

There were no fully-fledged typographers at the Bauhaus: even Herbert Bayer, who, of the teachers at Dessau, became the most persistently occupied with typography, remained essentially a designer of images with a less than assured ability to handle words (contrast Renner or Tschichold). The search of the Bauhäusler for a new alphabet was conducted under a vision of industry and the machine that was little touched by the mentality of the actually-existing printing trade. But if no typefaces issued from their research, their work, and the school's effective publicity for itself, did help to create a climate in which typefoundries were encouraged to take up the idea of a new sanserif. The first of these to appear was Erbar, designed by Jakob Erbar and issued by Ludwig & Mayer in 1926; early drawings for the typeface are dated 1922. The idea for a freshly designed sanserif, breaking from the hitherto 'undesigned' grotesque, might in Germany be traced back to the Behrens-Schrift (if that is taken as a hint towards a sanserif). Though the speculation is an attractive one, there is no real evidence of German interest in the Johnston Underground letter playing any part in these new typefaces.[7] Jakob Erbar had been to classes taught by Anna Simons and had designed an earlier sanserif (Feder Grotesk, 1908) rather in the manner of the Behrens-Schrift.[8]

Futura, designed by Paul Renner for the Bauer typefoundry,

5. From the Bauhaus letterheading (1925) designed by Herbert Bayer and reproduced in Tschichold, *Die neue Typographie*, p. 128; English-language edition, p. 124.
6. From Bayer's original presentation in: 'Versuch einer neuen Schrift', *Offset*, no. 7, 1926, pp. 398–400; reprinted in Fleischmann, *Bauhaus*, pp. 25–7.
7. See: Denis Megaw, '20th century sans serif types', *Typography*, no. 7, 1938, pp. 27–35.
8. On Erbar, and on sanserif generally, see: Tracy, *Letters of credit*, pp. 84–98.

became accepted by the new typographers as the most satisfactory
of the new (twentieth-century) sanserifs. Drawings and trial settings
for the typeface date from 1925, and it was first issued commercially in 1927. In the middle 1920s Renner changed – with the times
– from his earlier traditionalist manner to a modernist approach,
though he held throughout his career to what can be summarized as
Werkbund values. In 1925 he had gone to teach at the school of art
at Frankfurt and would there have been in the thick of the atmosphere of socialist modernism that inspired a notable programme
of municipal building. A set of sanserif capitals designed by the
architect Ferdinand Kramer is said to have provided some impetus
for Futura, though early versions of the typeface show eccentrici-
ties that are unlike any other letterform of the time. In 1926 Renner
moved to the Graphische Berufsschule at Munich, where he then
took charge of the establishment of the Meisterschule für Deutschlands Buchdrucker (which opened in 1927). Jan Tschichold came to
teach in Munich (at both schools) from 1926.

The achievement of Futura was of a typeface that satisfied
both the desire for a geometrical typeface, constructed with ruler
and compass, and for a typeface that composed well as text, over
a whole range of sizes. This latter capacity was achieved by subtle
deviations from strict geometry. The quality of Futura can be seen
by contrasting it with a third significant new sanserif from these
years: Kabel, designed by Rudolf Koch for the Klingspor typefoundry. Kabel appears rather as an artist's typeface, easily characterized by its quirks, while Futura consists of a more harmonious set
of forms. With Futura, new typography might have seemed to have
found its ideal letterform: a sanserif that was satisfactory in practice
as well as in theory. But the matter was still open to debate. Thus
Tschichold, in 1928, while welcoming Futura as 'a substantial step
forward' went on to voice a fundamental doubt: 'I myself think that
it cannot be open to one person to create the letterform of our age,
which is something that must be free of any personal traces. It will
be the work of several people, among whom one will probably find
an engineer.' (Tschichold, *Die neue Typographie*, p.76.) The argument was taken up again in Switzerland after the Second World War.

The new book

It was one of the complaints made by the new typographers that
the traditionalists were limited to book typography. If it was not
said at the time, it may be fair to observe that everything designed
by the new traditionalists, whether book or not, tended to look like
a traditional book. The traditionalists, for their part, claimed that
new typography was limited to display and publicity typography,
and was incapable of tackling the more intricate problems of books.
Both of these views were well articulated by Jan Tschichold, before
and after his break with modernism.

The most radical charge against the traditionalist book-artists
was that they were devoted to the production of rarities: 'The
general exaggerated compliance with the pre-war catchword of
"quality materials!" has meant that German books are now the
world's most expensive, and that for someone of even middle-range
income a German book has become a more or less exorbitant luxury
object. Our situation now depends on: (1) finding a contemporary
(i.e. non-historicizing) form of typography; (2) producing cheap
popular books, not expensive luxury items for snobs.' (Tschichold,
Die neue Typographie, pp. 230–1.) Elsewhere, in his programmatic
text 'Was ist und was will die Neue Typografie', concluding a list of
oppositions between new and traditional, Tschichold proclaimed:
'*active literature* not passive leather-bound books'. (Tschichold, *Eine
Stunde Druckgestaltung*, p. 7; reprinted in his *Schriften 1925–1974*,
vol. 1, at p. 90.) Both typographic-visual and social-political activity were implied here. Left-wing publishers were among those who
consistently supported experiments in book design; or, at least,
those socialist publishers whose politics included an espousal of
aesthetic modernism.

Attempts to provide cheap but well-produced editions of serious books were made by a number of progressive bookclubs in
Germany, most notably the Büchergilde Gutenberg and the Bücherkreis. Both were founded in 1924, supported by (respectively) the
Bildungsverband der Deutschen Buchdrucker and the SPD (German
Social-Democratic Party). In the later 1920s and early 1930s, these
clubs – especially the Bücherkreis, for whom Tschichold worked as a
consultant designer – ran publishing programmes that represented
sustained attempts to work out what 'the new book' might be (see
example 14, pp. 210–11).

The utopian-visionary statements of artist-designers looked forward beyond the book as a container of 'grey' continuous text to 'the
coloured picture book ... as a continuous visual design (a coherent
sequence of many individual pages)' (Moholy-Nagy), and further to
'the electro-library' (Lissitzky).[9] In practice, the new typography of
the book was constrained by the techniques of the day – letterpress,
for the most part – and by printing-trade attitudes. The gap between
the ideas of these artists and the reality of their printed products
may be explained by the difficulties that outsiders to typography
would have had in specifying their wishes to printers, as well as the
limited materials that an average printer could provide. But modernist designers with a typographic education did begin to design
books that broke significantly from traditional patterns.

Together with the introduction of standardized formats and
sanserif typefaces, as already discussed, the most important new
element was the photographic image. This broke radically with the
traditionalist dogma that the visual texture of book-illustration
should balance with that of the text (on a facing page), and that the
ideal medium of illustration was the woodcut. Where photographic
images were used, traditionalist and trade practice was to reserve
separate sections of coated paper for these images, printed as half-
tone blocks. New typographers sought to integrate such blocks with
the text, using a smoother paper than was normal for text printing
and renouncing any gesture – which they saw as false – towards
hand-made papers, whether real or imitation. This integration of
photographs, and also drawn images, was to be achieved without
the device of running text around the image: text should be set to
a constant width. Partly for the reason of accommodating illustrations, two-column setting became more common in these new
books: traditionalists objected that this was the manner of magazines and newspapers, which was one of its attractions for modernists. The book was regarded as a device for reading: headings in text
were allowed to stand out; page numbers were set in bold and sometimes in larger sizes, and this, together with the use of rules and
dots to draw attention to and organize passages of text, became a
hallmark of the cruder early new typography. The approach was one
of organization through visual contrast, rather than of balance and
reticence. Content was to shape form, rather than to be poured into

some ancient container (as in the theories of correct page proportion). New typography thus resisted the idea that literature should
enjoy a separate, special status: it was another design problem.
And perhaps more interesting than 'literature' for new typographers
were industrial catalogues and other texts with complex problems
of ordering and configuration to be resolved. Here the contrast with
the traditionalist artist-typographers became complete.

Organization and dissemination

New typography, like all of the activity of the modern movement
in design between the two world wars, was a minority affair. The
sense of a small band of like-minded designers scattered over
continental Europe is conveyed by the lists of names and addresses
that Tschichold published in *Die neue Typographie* (1928) and in a
later book *Eine Stunde Druckgestaltung* (1931). As well as the German designers, who predominated in these lists, there were also
representatives from the Netherlands (Piet Zwart, Paul Schuitema),
Czechoslovakia (Karel Teige), Austria (Lajos Kassák: in fact Hungar-
ian), the Soviet Union (El Lissitzky) and some suggestions for France
(Theo van Doesburg, Hans Arp, Cassandre, Tristan Tzara). Some of
these people were also members of the Ring Neuer Werbegestalter
(circle of new graphic designers), that was formed in 1927, evidently
inspired by the 'Ring' of new architects (founded in 1925). Considerably fuelled by the energy and enthusiasm of Kurt Schwitters, the
group held occasional meetings and organized some exhibitions of
work by members and guests, in Germany and elsewhere in Europe.
These were among a handful of exhibitions held during the period,
which would have served to define the movement to its members, as
well as to raise public awareness.

Tschichold was the most active propagandist and explainer of
the movement. He was the son of a sign-writer in Leipzig and had
had a thorough calligraphic and typographic education, going to the
Akademie in that city. His turn to modernism was, by his own account, a sudden affair: following from a visit to the exhibition of the

9. Moholy-Nagy, 'Zeitgemäße Typografie', *Offset*, no. 7, 1926, pp. 375–85,
reprinted in Fleischmann, *Bauhaus*, pp. 17–20; Lissitzky, 'Topographie
der Typographie' (see note 1 above).

Weimar Bauhaus in 1923. Much more than the other modernist typographers, he could articulate theory in practical terms and could
engage in dialogue with both traditionalist typographers and the
printing trade. From 1925 he wrote prolifically: articles for the trade
and also the design press (such as it was), as well as one full-length
and four lesser books (up to 1933). One other extended consideration of new typography came from Paul Renner (*Mechanisierter
Grafik*, 1930). Other designers contributed just occasional articles
and the examples of work that were reproduced in the anthologies
and special issues of magazines.

   The movement did begin to take root within education, in the
training of both designers and printers. Although the Bauhaus has
been most celebrated among the schools of the period in Germany,
its reputation (over all fields of design) is probably out of true proportion to its real achievements and effects. Student numbers were
small and, in typography, the school lacked any specialist teacher
and had little connection with the printing trade. A more developed interest in new typography came from the Meisterschule für
Deutschlands Buchdrucker in Munich, under Paul Renner and with
Tschichold on the staff. Another teacher there (from 1929 to 1931
and again from 1933) was Georg Trump. Like Renner and Tschichold, he had had a complete education in traditionalist calligraphy
and typography, as well as painting and illustration, before taking
up a modernist approach. Though he designed some printed items,
he was more active as a type designer, and one display typeface
from these years was a real contribution to the movement: City, for
the Berthold typefoundry, which rethought the slab-serif in terms
of machine aesthetics. Trump also taught at Bielefeld (1926–9) and
Berlin (1931–3). Among other teacher-practitioners of the movement, one would mention Max Burchartz (at the Folkwangschule
in Essen, 1926–33) and Walter Dexel (at the Kunstgewerbeschule at
Magdeburg, 1928–33).

   Before the economic crisis of 1929 and the return of political
turmoil in the early 1930s, one can recognize a brief phase, in the
later 1920s, when there was in Germany some greater economic
and political stability. At this moment, in typography, there seemed
to be the prospect of a rational approach that had worked through
an initial, artistic phase. Writing in 1928, Tschichold sensed that

further progress 'will rest less on artistic developments than on changes in the means of reproduction and on the altered needs created by these technical changes and by social relations' (Tschichold, *Die neue Typographie*, p. 65.) But this hope would be defeated in the 1930s. The conclusive event was the National-Socialist seizure of power in January 1933.

For the centres of modernism in Germany, enforced closure or take-over came very rapidly: at the Bauhaus (already severely reduced in its circumstances), in the Werkbund, and in any socialist organization or publication. For some of the proponents of new typography there were overnight changes: Tschichold was detained in custody for six weeks, after which he emigrated to Switzerland; Paul Renner was forced to resign from his post at Munich, after which he went into 'inner emigration'. These two patterns represented the choices facing opponents of the new order. But other modernists adapted to the new regime, and some, no doubt, actively supported it. It would be wrong to suggest a total difference before and after January 1933. New typography had made only limited inroads. The bulk of German printing still showed, it is safe to say, an indifference to the standards raised by typographers, both traditionalist and new. And it would be misleading to represent National-Socialist attitudes as uniform or coherent: certainly in the early years of Nazi power there were debates and differences between modernist and traditionalist factions within that party. But in 1933 conditions at the centre of modernism did change with as drastic a rupture as can occur in human history. From this time, in the years up to and into the Second World War, it was no longer possible to maintain the spirit of hope that is necessary to the life of modern design.

10   Emigration of the modern

Modernism and National Socialism

The forced departure of modernism from Central Europe, from 1933 onwards, served paradoxically to confirm certain tendencies and aspirations of its adherents. Chief among the crimes of those who left was cosmopolitanism or, less pejoratively, internationalism. With the diaspora, this ideal had to take on real substance. If 'Amerika' had been the dream-land of Central European progressive circles in the 1920s, it now became in many cases an everyday reality. And, in the difficult circumstances of emigration, the processes of idealization began to be directed back in time.

To some considerable extent, the idea of the golden cultural era of the Weimar Republic has been fostered by the emigré imagination. For example, the reputation of the Bauhaus rested for many years on the exhibition about it held at the Museum of Modern Art in New York in 1938, and more especially on the book that accompanied the show.[1] In this publication, Walter Gropius and colleagues from his years as the school's director put forward a partial account of the institution, which suppressed internal conflicts and played down the early expressionist phase and the later developments under the direction of Hannes Meyer. The success of this account of the school can be seen in the fact that for many years 'Bauhaus' and 'modern' were, and sometimes still are, synonymous terms. This view neglects the variety and contradictions within the Bauhaus and, more importantly, it excludes the many other elements and institutions that constituted the modern movement of that time.

The retrospective idealization of modernism also meant that, for decades after 1945, the culture of National-Socialism was almost unmentionable. Commentators outside the German-speaking world, either emigrés or those under the sway of emigré modernist thought, were content to dismiss this history as being a time of horror and of horrible bad taste: a time in which the floodgates were opened to kitsch and when modernist achievements were desecrated (the pitched roof that was added to the studio wing of the Dessau Bauhaus). For those who had witnessed National-Socialism at home, the period was passed over in silence. Thus, for example, G. K. Schauer in his extended and detailed account, *Deutsche Buchkunst: 1890 bis 1960*, made only the most fleeting references to the years of National-Socialist power and never addressed the phenomenon directly. This silence, either of disgust or of unease, has meant that there do not exist the secondary materials from which to synthesize an account of typography under National-Socialism.

The one issue here that has been the subject of quite frequent discussion is that of the conflict between 'Fraktur' and 'Antiqua': blackletter and roman. Beyond the professional typographic circles, where it had been a leading theme since the turn of the century, this was a matter of wide cultural interest. The choice between modern-ity (roman) and German-ness (blackletter) was something that informed the design of every newspaper and every shop sign. The temperature of the debate had been raised by modernists with their advocacy of sanserif, and criticism of blackletter (as nationalist and archaic) and even of roman (as not sharing in the spirit of the new age).

National-Socialist beliefs were not consistent. At the time of the seizure of power in 1933, two opposing attitudes in cultural mat-ters were evident. There was a modernizing group within the party, identified with Joseph Goebbels, which wished to adopt a forward-looking attitude and which emphasized technological development. The opposing tendency, identified with Alfred Rosenberg, espoused a backward-looking, anti-urban and 'völkisch' vision. Thus, contrary to the popular idea of a single Teutonic-Nazi visual identity, both reactionary and modern attitudes can be seen in National-Socialist design of the 1930s. One finds a poster in sanserif celebrating the Volkswagen as the 'strength through joy' car.[2] And, by way of dispel-ling myths about Social-Democratic culture too, it has been noted that roman was the standard letterform on German postage stamps before 1919, that blackletter was introduced with the Weimar Re-public and that its use continued until its replacement by roman in

1. Herbert Bayer, Walter Gropius & Ise Gropius (ed.), *Bauhaus 1919–1928*, London: Allen & Unwin, 1939.
2. See: Kenneth Frampton, *Modern architecture*, London: Thames & Hudson, 1980, p. 217.

1941.[3] In this year came the sudden and decisive turning point, announced in a decree of 3 January 1941, signed by Martin Bormann:

> It is false to regard or to describe the so-called gothic script as a German script. In reality the so-called gothic script consists of Schwabacher-Jewish letters. Just as they later took possession of newspapers, so the Jews living in Germany owned the printing offices at the introduction of printing and thus there came about the strong influx into Germany of Schwabacher-Jewish letters.
>
> Today the Führer, in a discussion with Herr Reichsleiter Amann and the printer Herr Adolf Müller, decided that roman is from now on to be designated as the standard letter. All printed products will be progressively changed over to this standard letter. As soon as is feasible, only the standard script will be taught in schools.
>
> The use of Schwabacher-Jewish letters by authorities will in future cease; certificates of appointment for officials, street-name signs, and the like, will in future only be produced in standard lettering.
>
> By order of the Führer, Herr Reichsleiter Amann will first change over to the standard script those newspapers and magazines that already have a foreign distribution or whose foreign circulation is desired.[4]

With this decree, the dilemma of 'German' or 'modern' was resolved. By a fabrication of history, blackletter was declared to be 'Jewish' and condemned; the future would lie with roman. Just as the Führer had adopted a neo-classical style for his public architecture, so the words of the Thousand Year Reich were to be clothed in the timeless and world-wide authority of roman letterforms.

The new policy was rather rapidly and effectively implemented, as it could not have been in a democratic state, and it has since been welcomed by commentators who have otherwise abhorred National-Socialism. In the years immediately after 1945, there was some protest against the deposition of blackletter. Cultural conservatives, such as F. H. Ehmcke and Karl Klingspor, sought to rescue blackletter from all political taint and argued that it was the only

proper means of representing the idiosyncrasies of the German language (for example, the three variants of 's'), as well having greater
potential for variety, charm, and beauty. But, in the aftermath of a
catastrophic war, technical arguments, not to mention an appeal to
'German-ness', could hardly be convincing or attractive. Since that
time, the case for a considered revival of blackletter has sometimes
been formulated, but by typographers cultivating the byways of
their subject, rather than in any concerted programme of action.

Typography in resistance

In conditions of war and of enemy occupation, printing could, in
isolated and tiny cells, take on primary tasks: the production of
forged identity cards and leaflets of opposition. And, in a climate of
oppression, the production of literature, not apparently political in
content but defying cultural fetters, became a political act. Scarcity
of means, as well as the need for secrecy, placed great constraints
on these printers, and this increases the value that one places on
products that, superficially inspected, might seem unremarkable.
The underground printers of the Second World War in the Netherlands and in France have been celebrated, mainly by war historians
and bibliographers, rather than for any contribution to book design,
but their work belongs to typographic history too.

Over 1000 books, mostly small in their extent and in numbers
printed, are known to have been produced illegally in the Netherlands during the years of occupation (1940–5). This suggests that
here, as elsewhere in Europe (including the free countries), literature became a source of consolation and an encouragement in the
struggle. In the Dutch case, the phenomenon of underground literature owed much to the culture of printing that had developed in the
previous decades: the private press now had a real use. Within the

3. See: Erich Stier, 'Fraktur oder Antiqua als Schrift auf deutschen Brief-
marken', in: Plata, *Fraktur, Gotisch, Schwabacher*, pp. 80–1.

4. Translated (with some improvements to its execrable tone) from the
text given in Klingspor, *Über Schönheit von Schrift und Druck*, p. 44. The
typewritten document is also reproduced in: Typographische Gesellschaft München, *Hundert Jahre Typographie*, p. 102. See also the translation and commentary by S. H. Steinberg, *Printing News*, 9 May 1957,
pp. 9, 11.

development of modern typography, most of this printing can be understood as the application of 'fine printing' ideals to literature that had become in some way dangerous: to publish the poetry of Rimbaud in those conditions was a serious provocation. Two small bodies of work stand clearly apart from this generalization: those of H. N. Werkman and Willem Sandberg. In their typographies, experiments of configuration and of technique, in alliance with subversive content, suggested 'an aesthetics of resistance' and of hope kept alive.

Werkman, though culturally and socially isolated in Groningen, in the north of the country, had started his experimental typography in the 1920s. While earning his living as a jobbing provincial printer, he painted, exhibiting with the local group of progressive artists, and began to do experimental printing. His publication, *The Next Call* (this was its title, though comprising mainly Dutch texts), appeared in nine issues between 1923 and 1926; it belongs with the little magazines of the European avant garde of the time, though Werkman's contact with other designers and artists was made almost entirely by post. His non-commercial printing was done on a hand press in very small runs, with single items often differing significantly from each other. It thus lies outside the main stream of modernist typography, which was preoccupied with mass-production and standardization. A superficial inspection might lead to a comparison with the work of another Dutch modernist, Piet Zwart. There are similarities of down-to-earth simplicity and fearless experiment in the use of space, but the differences are absolutely clear: Werkman belonged to the sphere of hand-production, Zwart to the world of mechanized industry. Werkman continued with his experiments during the war years, setting and illustrating oppositional texts. He was arrested in the last days of the occupation for alleged excessive use of paper, and was shot by German military authorities who, it has been suggested, were provoked by his unorthodox typography.

Some synthesis of the opposition of hand against machine, and rough against smooth, appeared in the work of Sandberg, who was an early champion of both Werkman and Zwart. His *Experimenta typographica* comprised eighteen short manuscript books in A5 format, made between 1943 and 1945, while in hiding. Three were published in printed interpretations in 1944–5. These books consisted of quotations and short texts, given typographic and graphic form in sympathy with their meaning. In them appeared the seeds of the approach that Sandberg was to develop in his catalogues for the Stedelijk Museum in Amsterdam, for which he worked as director from 1945 into the 1960s (see example 17, pp. 216–17). Sandberg's typography suggested a way out of the modernist impasse of perfect technique. Conditioned at first by sheer material scarcity, his typography seized the opportunities offered by ordinary materials: characteristically, paper and board normally reserved for wrapping or packing. Roughness and chance were prime qualities of this work, as in the lettering and images produced by torn paper placed in direct contact with lithographic plates. But Sandberg also stuck to DIN formats and to a limited and mundane selection of typefaces. He was also an early user of text set with equal word-spaces (unjustified). This mode of setting synthesized the two aspects: open to exact specification and thus more rational than the approximations of justified setting; but also 'ragged' and informal in appearance. Sandberg's was a typography of open, democratic dialogue, and a continuation of the spirit of resistance into the post-war world.

'Typographic design'

Of those who emigrated from Germany, none can be said to have been 'typical': the progress of each was conditioned by an idiosyncratic interplay of contacts, friendships, family ties, financial constraints. The career of Jan Tschichold in the 1930s and 1940s provides a case of special interest, as that of the chief articulator of the new typography and its most assured exponent. The possibility of emigration was secured by an offer of part-time work with the printing and publishing firm of Benno Schwabe, in Basel, and some teaching at the Allgemeine Gewerbeschule there. On Tschichold's own account, this provided a minimum income. It was supplemented by earnings from other design work, which included adapting typefaces for an early photocomposing machine, the Uhertype; there would also have been some money earned from writing.

Tschichold's first book during this new phase appeared in 1935: *Typographische Gestaltung* was published by Schwabe, though only against the security of pre-publication subscriptions. This book

condensed and developed the material of *Die neue Typographie*, but
without the missionary zeal of the earlier book: Tschichold could no
longer act as the spokesman for a movement that was scattered and
demoralized. *Typographische Gestaltung* was concerned rather with
details of typography and dealt with themes such as 'the word', 'the
line of text', 'emphasis in text', 'tables'. The exposition was calmer
than in the first book, and so too its own design showed the matu-
rity and assurance that Tschichold had gained by this time. The text
was set in Monotype Bodoni, with headings hand-set in Berthold's
City, and the author's name on the title page in a script typeface. As
Tschichold made clear in his text, the doctrinaire belief in sanserif
had been diluted (though not abandoned) and, within specified
limits, typefaces could be mixed for aesthetic effect and without
much regard for their historical provenance. As the title of this book
suggested, Tschichold felt he had now found a typography that was
more than merely 'new' or possessed of some limiting stylistic trait
such as asymmetry; like Le Corbusier's 'architecture' (in *Vers une
architecture*), this was simply 'a typography'.[5] Within a collapsing
world, his mood seemed to be serene, as the book's epigraph from
Goethe suggested:

> There is no past to which one may look back longingly,
>   there is only an eternal new that is formed
>   out of the extended elements of the past,
>   and the pure longing must be continually productive,
>   creating a new better thing.

Danish, Swedish, and Dutch editions of *Typographische Gestaltung*
appeared in the following years. In 1935, Tschichold travelled to
Denmark (to give lectures) and to Britain, where an exhibition of his
work was held in the London offices of the printers and publishers
Lund Humphries. This was Tschichold's first personal encounter
with the English-speaking world, though translations of his writings
had appeared in *Commercial Art*, a magazine of the British advertising business, in 1930–1. Now, in its more mature form, his work
began to make some small impression on typographers in Britain:
Lund Humphries commissioned a redesign of their letterheading
from him, and the design of a volume of the *Penrose Annual* (appear-

ing in 1938), the printing-trade anthology which the firm published. The journal *Typography* (1936–9) took some notice of Tschichold in its break with the limitations of the book-design dominated traditionalists around Stanley Morison. An article by him on 'type mixtures' (the most attractive aspect of his typography to the un-committed) was published there in 1937. However, neither in this journal nor elsewhere in British typographic circles was there any determined exploration of modernism: at best, it was admitted as one element, useful in advertising, in an eclectic and light-hearted plurality of approaches.

There is some evidence to suggest that the contact with Britain played a part in Tschichold's move to a traditional manner, which became evident in the later 1930s. Already in 1935 he had published an article on 'correct' procedures in centred typography, as if flirt-ing with this approach.[6] On another visit to London, in 1937, he gave a talk at the Double Crown Club on 'A new approach to typography'. Thus, just at the time of his change, he was welcomed into the heart of British new traditionalism, which – from a continent running fast towards war – might have seemed to offer an enviable combination of typographic and democratic values. Among the various specula-tions on Tschichold's career – all still based on inadequate evidence – G. K. Schauer's theory of 'Heimatlosigkeit' is of interest: of dis-placed Slavic origin, Tschichold's life and work can be represented as a long search for a home.[7] With the break-up of modernism, he returned to where he started: to a traditional typography, which, this time, had taken on an English inflection.

5. The title of the English-language edition, *Asymmetric typography*, approved by the later Tschichold, is thus a subtle distortion; Le Cor-busier's book was similarly limited by its translation as *Towards a new architecture*.
6. 'Vom richtigen Satz auf Mittelachse', *Typographische Monatsblät-ter*, no. 3, 1935, pp. 113–18; reprinted in his *Schriften 1925–1974*, vol. 1, pp. 178–85; a translation of the article is given by McLean, *Jan Tschi-chold*, pp. 126–31.
7. See: G. K. Schauer, 'Jan Tschichold: Anmerkungen zu einer tragischen Existenz', *Börsenblatt für den Deutschen Buchhandel* (Frankfurt), no. 95, 1978, pp. A421–3; see also the subsequent exchange between Schauer and Kurt Weidemann in this journal, no. 26, 1979, pp. A114–15.

A moral debate

Only in the immediate aftermath of the war did Tschichold first announce and explain his disillusion with the new typography. 'It seems to me no accident that this typography was practised almost exclusively in Germany and hardly found acceptance in other countries. In particular, its intolerant attitude corresponds to the German inclination to the absolute, its military will to order and claim to sole domination correspond to those terrible components of the German character that unleashed the rule of Hitler and the Second World War.'[8] This charge, which Tschichold was to maintain in all his subsequent discussions of the matter, was made in reply to an attack by Max Bill on his change of position. Bill had been a student at the Dessau Bauhaus, and had since adhered to the new typography; though a painter and sculptor, as well as architect, Bill had earned a living mostly from graphic design and was a leader of the then just nascent 'Swiss typography'.

Max Bill's article 'Über Typografie' ('on typography') took Tschichold's apostasy as its starting point, though the antagonist was unnamed and described merely as 'a well-known theoretician of typography'. He then made the assertions that provoked Tschichold's equation of new typography and National-Socialism. For Bill, any retreat from modernism amounted to a political and moral reversion, like the retreat of architects into a 'Heimat' style (vernacular or pseudo-vernacular). Restating the faith of a style to match the 'Zeitgeist', Bill suggested that the 'elemental' typography of the first phase of new typography (up to around 1930) had possessed a decorative impulse, though in functional disguise: bold rules, oversize page numbers, and so on. But this had become transmuted into a typography that was genuinely functional: logically derived from the material being designed and producing a visual harmony that 'clearly corresponds to the technical and artistic possibilities of our age'.[9]

In his response to this, Tschichold made some criticism of the details of this new typography: that it was limited in its range to works about modern art and to industrial literature; that it neglected the traditional wisdom of book typography, for example, in refusing to indent new paragraphs. He was here writing out of his recent more intensive engagement with book design, with the publishers

Birkhäuser and the Holbein Verlag. It was this work, of designing a range of literary and academic texts, that must have contributed most immediately to his change of typographic manner.

Apart from the defence of indentation, Tschichold's argument over typographic matters was largely concerned with stylistic appropriateness. His more radical criticism tackled political and ethical themes. 'Bill's current typography is, just like my own work of between 1924 and around 1935, characterized by a naive overvaluation of so-called technical progress. Those who work like this see in the machine production of consumer goods – certainly a characteristic of our time – something extraordinarily gratifying. Indeed, we cannot escape using and producing these things. Yet there is no need to surround them with an aura, just because they come off a conveyor belt, with the exploitation of the latest "rationalized" methods.' ('Glaube und Wirklichkeit', p. 235.) Tschichold thus mounted a critique of stylistically preoccupied modernism, which makes an aesthetic fetish out of efficiency and machine-production. He went on:

> An artist like Bill probably does not realize what price in blood and tears the application of rationalized production methods costs 'civilized' mankind and every single worker. These new possibilities certainly give scope for play to Bill or some other designer, but not to the 'hand' who day-in day-out has to insert the same screw into a typewriter. … With pride, though sometimes in error, Bill notes in captions to his examples of work that they were set with a machine. He forgets that the hand-compositor, who has to make up and complete the work of the machine-compositor, is no longer granted the satisfaction that even his grandfather could find in the job. Because he must take finished lines of text to work with, he can almost never finish a

8. Jan Tschichold, 'Glaube und Wirklichkeit', *Schweizer Graphische Mitteilungen*, no. 6, 1946, p. 234; the article is reprinted in his *Schriften 1925–1974*, vol. 1, pp. 310–28; a translation of the article is given in *Typography Papers*, no. 4, 2000, pp. 71–86.
9. Max Bill, 'Über Typografie', *Schweizer Graphische Mitteilungen*, no. 4, 1946, p. 200; a translation of the article is given in *Typography Papers*, no. 4, 2000, pp. 62–70.

job with the satisfaction of having made something whole with his own hands.

   For the worker, machine production has thus meant a heavy, almost deadly loss in the value of experience, and it is entirely wrong to put it on a pedestal. That it is 'modern' is by no means the same thing as saying that it has value or even that it is good; much more is it evil. But since we are unable to manage without machine production, we must accept its products simply as facts, without worshipping them on account of their origins.

('Glaube und Wirklichkeit', p. 235.)

The debate between Tschichold and Bill did not continue beyond this exchange, though a wise reflection on it by Paul Renner was published two years later.[10] It was to resurface on occasions, between other antagonists, during the years of the international success of modernist Swiss typography. This may have been a local clash between two verbally aggressive and self-proud contestants, but they had raised profound issues. Tschichold, especially, had put forward arguments that continue to resonate, and with which any continuation of modern typography needs to come to terms.

   Germans in Britain

Traditionalist typographers did not, for the most part, leave Central Europe in the 1930s. One exception was Jakob Hegner, who spent the war years in Britain doing journeyman work, then returning to the Continent to restart as a designer and editor of books. The indifference of the English-speaking world to his typography, despite its roman bias, suggests the width of the gap of understanding between the two versions of typographic traditionalism. However, two younger designers did cross the cultural gulf: Berthold Wolpe and Hans Schmoller.

   Wolpe was born in Offenbach and had been a pupil of Rudolf Koch in the Kunstgewerbeschule there. His first discipline, before coming to do lettering, was that of the silversmith. He thus brought with him a strong and specifically German craft orientation, when he came to settle in Britain in 1935. The passage of emigration was eased by having already (from 1932) started work on the design of a display typeface for the Monotype Corporation. This became

Monotype Albertus, a roman capitals-only typeface (as first issued), whose distinctive wedge forms derived from the techniques of raised-metal inscriptions: it was very much in Koch's spirit, though regularized by English draughtsmen. Wolpe's transition, after emigration, was from his Offenbach roots in craft-work and blackletter to long engagements with book-design in industrial conditions and with roman letterforms. This transition was effected in his years as principal book-designer with Faber & Faber (1941–75), when he also became an exponent of italic formal writing, in the Johnston tradition, and wrote on the history of writing and printing. His background might have been forbiddingly 'German', but through these activities he became eminently assimilated into the world of British typography.

Schmoller's experiences and inclinations would seem to have predisposed him more obviously to Britain. His allegiances, as they showed themselves in his British work, were to the classical, understated typography of Poeschel and also Mardersteig, about both of whom he wrote with great sympathy.[11] Schmoller had finished a compositor's apprenticeship in Berlin in 1937 and then came to Britain. Unable to find work there, he went on to South Africa, running a mission printing office during the war years. Schmoller's British emigration started properly only after the war: as an assistant typographer at the Curwen Press (1947–9), and then as chief typographer at Penguin Books (from 1949), where he continued and developed what was the main – if delayed – legacy of the diaspora to British traditional typography. This was the brief but intense time that Jan Tschichold spent in England (1947–9) at Penguins.

The achievement of Tschichold's work at Penguin Books was the demonstration that good standards of text composition could be obtained from printers who had never had such things expected of them. This situation had been made worse during the war, when Penguins had found an apparently insatiable readership, while the printing trade had suffered a drainage of skills and a shortage of

10. Paul Renner, 'Über moderne Typographie', *Schweizer Graphische Mitteilungen*, no. 3, 1948, pp. 119–20; a translation of the article is given in *Typography Papers*, no. 4, 2000, pp. 87–90.

11. See Schmoller's article 'Carl Ernst Poeschel', *Signature*, new series, no. 11, 1950, pp. 20–36, and a book that he edited, translated, and introduced: Mardersteig, *The Officina Bodoni*.

materials. Developing the lessons of his Birkhäuser work (particularly the multi-volume editions of classic authors), Tschichold's
reform was founded on the list of composition rules that he introduced as guidance to printers: for the spacing of words and punctuation marks, the setting of footnotes and page numbers, and other
fine details of composition. Through this means the typographic
designer was, with the collaboration of thorough copy-editors, able
to win control of the significant ground of book design: practices
that had been incorporated, though hardly consciously, in the work
of the best printing offices, but which were then being lost in the
British printing trade.

Tschichold returned to Switzerland in 1949, at the time of the
devaluation of the British pound (he reported this as a significant factor in his decision to leave), and his job was taken over by
Schmoller. Oliver Simon, the chief typographer at Curwen Press,
was influential both in this appointment and in the earlier one of
Tschichold. Simon was an admirer of German printing culture, and
the qualities that were needed for the Penguin job were 'German'
ones: a relish for detail and persistence in enforcing instructions.
Beyond this, both Tschichold and Schmoller brought with them a
'German' feeling for 'the book as object', tempered by a strong sense
of restraint and propriety. This feeling became clear in their cased
books, in the quiet attention shown to details of binding and finishing. Equally, it was just this self-restraint that allowed them to work
with complete conviction on the mass-production of cheap books
(see example 18, pp. 218–19).

American assimilation

If the few traditionalist typographers who left Central Europe in the
1930s went to Britain, the second axiom of the emigration would be
that the modernists did leave in significant numbers and that they
went to the USA. (That the modernist John Heartfield got stuck in
Britain and was then forced to take up a largely traditionalist manner seems to provide further support for this thesis.) 'Typography'
may be too narrow a description for the fields in which these designers had begun to work on the Continent, and this change of practice
from typography and illustration into graphic design was encouraged by American conditions. Their progress was, characteristically,
from work in advertising and magazine design in the 1930s, to the

work of the freelance consultant designer after the Second World War. The war years provided the ground for this transition: the switching mechanism by which the American economy was lifted out of depression and into full production, from which position the country was able to reap the riches of the post-war recovery in the West.

The roll-call of designers who helped to establish graphic design in the USA is not entirely composed of Europeans: Lester Beall, Alvin Lustig, Paul Rand, were among those American-born. But the emigré presence was notable: Herbert Bayer, Joseph Binder, Will Burtin, Alexey Brodovich, Leo Lionni, László Moholy-Nagy, Ladislav Sutnar, among others. Of these, Sutnar was perhaps the most purely a typographer. He had been a principal exponent of new typography in Czechoslovakia, and now found long-term work in designing technical literature (see example 16, pp. 214–15).

The same phenomenon of emigrés opening up the field of graphic design can be observed on a smaller scale in Britain, where Hans Schleger and F. H. K. Henrion (both of German birth) were among the early consultant designers after the war. For an explanation of this phenomenon, one would examine the assumptions of Continental modernism: that design should infuse every aspect of life; that technological advances should be accepted and explored. A significant factor would also seem to be the greater experience of the emigrés: including the experience of emigration itself, with its challenge of survival in a foreign culture. Often their education had been at a high level, extending beyond a simple art-school training. What was needed by the consultant graphic designer was not so much the skills of the drawing-board artist, but rather abilities in analysis of complex systems and in human dealing.

The new typography was thus fed into the world of American corporate culture, without much effect on existing printing trade practice, nor on the world of the traditionalist typographers. The best attempt at a sympathetic interpretation of European modernism for American typographers was made by Douglas C. McMurtrie, notably in his book *Modern typography and layout*, first published in 1929. Though without a full trade apprenticeship, McMurtrie had come to typographic design through work in printing offices; he was also an extraordinarily prolific writer on the history and practice of printing, and he knew German. His book proposed modernism as a healthy way out of a stultified historicism, and, while critical of what he saw as its machine-worship and its more extreme practices, he developed a local variation of new typography. McMurtrie remained outside the preserves of traditionalist typography in America: his manner, both in his design work and in his writing, lacked refinement. For evidence of the infiltration of modernism into the world of commercial art, and its extreme dilution there, one may cite the book by Frederic Ehrlich, *The new typography and modern layouts* (1934). Without McMurtrie's grasp of underlying principles, this book amounted to no more than a sampler of the 'moderne' style, for use principally in press advertisements. Traditionalists, such as Updike, could be properly contemptuous of modernism thus interpreted.

A more concerted attempt to promote a new typography emerged after the war, in an exhibition and accompanying publication with the title *Books for our time*, produced under the auspices of the American Institute of Graphic Arts and edited by Marshall Lee. This consisted of a conspectus of modern book design, since the 1920s. The thesis of the organizers, as outlined in their statements, was that, contrary to traditionalist notions of the immutability of book typography, books could and should become 'modern', just as architecture had. They suggested that the centre of this new development was, since the emigration of the 1930s, now in the USA.

For this group of designers, a modern book was one that was designed through and through. 'The book designer must now participate actively in the author's attempt to contact the poetic sensibilities of the reader.' (Lee, *Books for our time*, p. 15.) Designers were to become as Toscanini to the Beethoven of the writer, arranging and re-scoring and inevitably leaving very evident signs of their involvement, for example in the complete integration of text and image. This was an opposite from traditionalist ideals of invisibility and unity of materials. It was also opposed to the reticent and self-denying sensibilities of the modernists in Europe who were just then taking up the legacy of new typography. But in the USA, modern typography now had no independent existence; it had been dissolved into something larger and more worldly. 'The vastly expanded resources available to the book designer indicate a fundamental change in his function. He is essentially an art director ...' (Lee, *Books for our time*, p. 18.)

11 Aftermath and renewal

In the years after 1945, the two broad streams of typography were
posed different problems. For those of a traditionalist persuasion,
visual style was a settled matter: the question was, how to maintain
this manner in the circumstances of the new economic and social
order, very different from that of the world they had first known.
With the end of the Second World War, the last remnants of this old
order disappeared: though the case of Britain – still with a monarch
and an aristocracy, and without a written constitution – provides
an exception to this pattern. Western Europe was now open to the
prospect, which unfolded in the 1950s, of a democracy centred on
the production and consumption of mass-produced goods, following the North American pattern. For modernists, this new order was
attractive, at least in its aspect of democratization: the problem was,
how to find forms appropriate to it, and, specifically, how to continue the modernist flourish of the 1920s and early 1930s.

An international club

In 1951, Jan van Krimpen and Giovanni Mardersteig made a joint
appeal to Stanley Morison and the Monotype Corporation 'not to
neglect the needs of a Europe under reconstruction'.[1] Both Van
Krimpen and Mardersteig had continued to work through the war,
and both were then working on the design of new typefaces. Van
Krimpen's Spectrum was designed and produced at Enschedé in the
war years, and in 1950 an agreement had been made for an adaptation of it by Monotype. Mardersteig's Dante was designed and produced for hand-setting in the immediate post-war years. In a letter
of reply to Mardersteig, Morison explained some of the reasons for
the contraction of business at Monotype. In particular, he cited the
rise of non-Latin typography, with the liberation of British colonies.
This letter suggests that for Morison as for most western typogra-

---

1. This is Hans Schmoller's paraphrase in his 'Introduction' to:
Mardersteig, *The Officina Bodoni*, p. xlv; see also: Barker, *Stanley
Morison*, pp. 430–2.

phers (then, if not still) it was enough to characterize non-Latin scripts as 'exotic' and to consider questions of quality of letterform as hardly applicable to them. In 1951, still in the aftermath of the war, Morison saw no possibility of any British typefoundry or composing machine manufacturer cutting a new typeface. He looked back wistfully to the time when he had first met Mardersteig (1924) as 'a golden age' (Barker, *Stanley Morison*, p. 431). The situation for the Monotype Corporation did improve in the 1950s and 1960s: some new typefaces were cut or adapted for Monotype composition, including the Dante of Mardersteig (issued in 1951). But these were the last flourishes of the company's concern with metal typography, and Morison, who gave up his advisory post at Monotype in 1954, was by then largely occupied with historical matters.

Stanley Morison still made occasional forays into the world of practical typography, and his writing never lost its polemical edge. One such episode was his sponsorship of Cyril Burt's work on legibility and readability. Morison, with Beatrice Warde and S. H. Steinberg, provided Burt with information and support in taking the research from its first appearance in the *British Journal of Statistical Psychology* to its publication by Cambridge University Press as *A psychological study of typography* (1959). For Morison, who wrote an introduction to the book, this work must have seemed to fulfil his desire, expressed in his *First principles of typography*, for 'investigation' rather than 'inspiration or revival'. However, Burt's typographic research was later seen to suffer from the doubtful methods of his other work.[2] More than for any contribution it makes to the theory of readability, *A psychological study* has become interesting for the light it throws on British new traditional typography in the 1950s: for example, the way in which Morison seized on the poor showing of sanserif typefaces in continuous text, as empirical proof of their inferiority. And the book, which relied heavily for its test material on the typefaces of the Monotype Corporation, was incidentally a substantial advertisement for that company.

Apart from such excursions, history now became an exclusive matter for Morison – though one pursued outside the academy. In contrast, Van Krimpen and (to a lesser extent) Mardersteig remained rooted in the practice of typography, with historical concerns as a necessary and vital adjunct. The priority of practice had also characterized the work of Updike, who had died in 1941. Morison himself recognized this in a deeply felt tribute to the most senior member of the informal international club of traditionalist typography. He made a comparison with the Victorian scholar-printers, De Vinne above all, but then went on to suggest Updike's difference and distinction, in 'sense of design and power of typographical discrimination'.[3]

Traditionalism was to be chronically circumscribed by its belief in stylistic fixity and by its dependence on the dying technique of letterpress printing. In Morison's case, this condition was further aggravated by his dogma that 'the quality of line obtainable by the hand of a skilled cutter of punches is unobtainable by any other man or means' and that 'engraving by hand is the only means by which typography can come into the possession of a letter-form which is a direct and wholly human product'.[4] Other traditionalists – notably Van Krimpen – took writing to be the more essential forming factor, and they could thus maintain an interest in producing new letterforms. With the full development of photocomposition, the belief in pen-generated forms found a new rationale: metal punches would never be cut again, and types impressed into paper only on rare and obscure occasions. The new technology was a flat one: on paper, film, or screens.

Letters of light

The idea of composing not metal types but images of letters, by photographic means, was the subject of some experiment in the nineteenth century, and there were isolated applications of it in the 1920s and 1930s (notably with the Uhertype machine). But photocomposition began to be seriously developed only after 1945, and to find full commercial development from the later 1950s onwards.

2. See: James Hartley & Donald Rooum, 'Sir Cyril Burt and typography: a re-evaluation', *British Journal of Psychology*, vol. 74, 1983, pp. 203–12.
3. 'Recollections and perspectives of D. B. Updike' (1947) in: Morison, *Selected essays*, p. 397.
4. Quoted by John Dreyfus from a lecture by Morison of 1958, in his 'Introduction and commentary' to: Van Krimpen, *A letter to Philip Hofer*, p. 25. See also chapter 13, note 5, p. 163 below.

Until then, metal composition and letterpress printing were largely adequate to the needs placed on them. Among reasons for the development of photocomposition, the most immediate was the further development of lithographic printing. Metal type, from which 'reproduction pulls' were made and then photographed in order to produce the lithographic plate, then became an unwelcome detour.

Following the familiar pattern of human invention, the first photocomposition machines imitated the principles of the existing technology of metal composition. Thus, among the early machines, the Intertype Fotosetter was an adaptation of the principle of hot-metal line-composition, in which letters were now assembled on film as previously on metal slugs. In the first Monophoto machines, photographic images (as negatives) were substituted for the hot-metal matrices in the matrix case of a Monotype machine. Such technological conservatism helped to ensure a reasonable degree of typographic quality, in the form and fitting of letters; it also resulted, however, in machines that did not improve over their hot-metal competitors in speed of operation. The Monotype Corporation, in particular, throughout the 1950s and 1960s kept faith with the ideal of typographic quality. Resisting the temptation to economize with a single set of images for a typeface, their photocomposition machines were provided with sets of master characters given compensating variations of form for the sizes at which they were to be produced. So too their typefaces took over from their metal equivalents the full armoury of typographic subtleties: ligatures, accents, mathematical sorts, small capitals, and alternative forms of numerals. This policy was made possible by the store of drawings, and of experience, that the company had accumulated; but it led to commercial and financial difficulties. The way ahead in the new technology lay with machines that broke with the mechanical principles of hot-metal composition, and which could thus operate at significantly increased speeds. Here, as in the development of hot-metal composition, the pace was forced by the special demands of the newspaper industry, especially in the USA. The ideal was for the speed of composition to match the rate at which keys were tapped, without the additions of processing and make-up time that were required in the earliest photocomposition machines. With the simplification of the moving parts of machines (the rotating disc of the Photon 200, rather than the cumbersome matrix case of the Monophoto), this ideal came nearer. But major advances in speed of composition and make-up came only with the introduction of cathode ray and digital technologies in the late 1960s, and of laser technology in the 1970s.

New typographies in Britain

Some modernist seeds from Central Europe had travelled to Britain – most notably, those borne by Jan Tschichold in the mid-1930s – and in the immediate post-war situation some native British explorations of new typography began to be evident. The first impulse of the movement had been sapped by political defeats, the diaspora from Central Europe, and the disasters of war. But the conditions of scarcity and disarray in the aftermath of 1945 did provide a proper context for a typography that was guided by considerations of need and use. Such conditions were general in Europe. In Britain, they were the background for visions of the reconstruction of a social order that had so far resisted modernization. Design was recognized as having an important role in presenting this vision, and it was in this context that elements of modernism became incorporated into officially sanctioned architectural and visual production.

The highpoint of this movement of incorporation came in 1951, at the Festival of Britain. Typographically, the event was dominated by the revival of nineteenth-century slab-serif letters – in the specially designed official lettering and elsewhere – and was in this aspect not clearly modern at all. Beneath some modernist trimmings, the spirit of the Festival was essentially that of cheerful revival and especially of an espousal of the late eighteenth-century 'picturesque': an anti-method of eclecticism, irregularity, and charming incident. The philosophy of this approach to design, and its history, had been formulated already before the war, largely in the pages of the *Architectural Review*. This journal cultivated interests in typographic history, in articles and in its own design, and one of its contributors, Nicolete Gray, was the author of a principal source of material for the revivalists. This was the book first published in 1938 as *Nineteenth century ornamented types and title pages*, and reprinted (significantly) in 1951. The journals published by the Shenval Press – *Typography* (1936–9) and *Alphabet and Image* (1946–8) – provided further material for the revival of nineteenth-century typography, with a certain curiosity about modernism sometimes in evidence.

The prevailing spirit of design-conscious typography in Britain was thus one of eclectic inclusion. Any more determined or rigorous attempt at a new typography had to be conducted in the margins of the typographic and printing worlds. The clearest instance of this course was provided by the work of Anthony Froshaug, whose achievement is suggestive beyond the fragmentary and small-scale nature of its material products. Born and educated in England, though with a Norwegian father, Froshaug emerged as a freelance typographer at the end of the Second World War. He had picked up the elements of the Central European new typography from such publications as had come his way in London; crucial among them were some of Tschichold's writings, and especially *Typografische Entwurfstechnik*. He was soon involved in a plan (which came to nothing) to translate and publish this and other texts by Tschichold. This engagement with the original sources of the new typography, rather than with its British dilutions and imitations, was characteristic of an uncompromising attitude, which led Froshaug to set up his own printing workshop. This move was, he later wrote, the way out of the problem of trade compositors failing to follow layouts, however precisely drawn and annotated.[5] Traditionalist typography, as it had existed in the inter-war years in Britain and elsewhere, depended on intelligent compositors who could interpret roughly sketched layouts, and whose labour in implementing revisions could be bought cheaply. New typography, and especially radical versions such as Froshaug was developing, had no such base of understanding and sympathy in the trade, least of all among the cheaper printers, who were its usual producers. And a new typography depended for its success on an exactness of execution that was less necessary for traditional work. For example, one may cite the need for unjustified or 'ragged' setting to be elaborately specified, in terms of a given word-space and treatment of word-breaks; while justified setting can be understood and accomplished without further explanation, or it may even be the norm that needs no instruction.

In 1949, Froshaug set up a one-man printing workshop in Cornwall: he was thus geographically as well as philosophically in the margins of British typography. He survived for two and a half years as a typographer-printer, using only table-top and treadle platen presses. If the conditions for this experiment were those of the craft printer – or perhaps of the earliest presses – Froshaug looked for confirmation to contemporary modernist work from the Continent. The philosophy of the press was essentially that outlined by Lewis Mumford in *Technics and civilization* (1934): acceptance of machine production and of standardization, but under the sanction of human control. In this vision, small decentralized workshops found their place, not just as test-beds for mass-production (as Gropius had envisaged for the Dessau Bauhaus), but as enduring and substantial producers in their own right.

After this brief but intense experience of printing, Froshaug went on to work as a typographer and, increasingly, as a teacher. He was one of the fostering teachers of the graphic designers who began to emerge in Britain in the late 1950s. And, in confirmation of his Continental aspirations, Froshaug also taught in Germany, from 1959 to 1963, at the Hochschule für Gestaltung Ulm. Thus, through teaching, the lessons of the small workshop were spread quite widely into everyday practice.

Another kind of diffusion of new typography in Britain occurred through the work of Herbert Spencer. While Froshaug worked outside or on the edges of the established institutions of British typography, the achievement of Spencer was to work with and through them. The most important such connection was a long consultancy with the printers and publishers Lund Humphries – Tschichold's sponsor in the 1930s. Through such established channels, Spencer's contribution was to introduce into Britain some of the material evidence of Continental modernism in typography. This was effected especially through the journal *Typographica* (1949–67), edited and designed by Spencer for Lund Humphries. A second editorship, of the *Penrose Annual* (1964–73), created a forum of enlightened discussion for the printing trade and for designers equally.

This twofold exercise of importation and diffusion was evident in Spencer's first book, *Design in business printing* (1952). This fol-

---

5. See his statement in: Gerald Woods, Philip Thompson & John Williams (ed.), *Art without boundaries*, Thames & Hudson, 1972, pp. 206–7; reprinted in Kinross, *Anthony Froshaug: Documents of a life*, p. 245.

lowed the model of Tschichold's *Typographische Gestaltung*: a short historical survey that ran through the development of modernist typography, followed by detailed advice. The teachings of Tschichold's typography, of simplification and rationalization in such matters as tabular setting and punctuation of abbreviations, were made accessible to the printing trade and, more speculatively, to the world of business itself. But where Tschichold remained wedded, at all stages of his career, to an aesthetically and ideologically engaged typography, Spencer's advice was without any such components, at least overtly. It was a typography for the mundane world of businessmen, in which simplification of form meant efficiency and cost-saving, but without philosophical overtones.

The idea of proven efficiency was taken up again by Spencer in the late 1960s in work conducted under his direction at the Readability of Print Research Unit at the Royal College of Art. This was the most sustained attempt at research in this field in Britain, and was distinguished in being informed from the outset by design considerations – not merely those of professional psychology. (The design-political concerns of Cyril Burt's work were not integral to its conception, but were applied only to its popular dissemination.) An initial survey of the field, *The visible word* (published in its first form in 1968), was followed by publication of a number of reports of specific research projects. At this time also, Spencer's *Pioneers of modern typography* was published: a survey and anthology that consolidated and expanded on material published in *Typographica*. These concurrent projects – legibility research and the history of modernist typography – were kept largely separate: a policy that mirrored prevailing views and institutional structures, but one that obstructed chances of fruitful interplay between simple printing and aesthetic experiment, or between – to use Spencer's distinction of the 1950s – business and pleasure.

German reconstructions

The legacy of National-Socialism, beyond the sheer material devastation that it left, posed enormous difficulties to cultural reconstruction in Germany. The most fundamental consequence of this immediate past history was that two Germanies came into existence. The culture of typography was resumed in both states, but in uncertain forms: the split, and the presence of occupying forces, added further complications to those of a deeply wounded society. For traditionalists, hope lay in picking up connections that were seen to have been broken in 1933; though it is easy to over-emphasize this break, and in many places the tradition was continued with only small adjustments. Leipzig maintained its position as the centre of typographic culture, but now only for the German Democratic Republic. With the economic recovery – or 'miracle' – in the Federal Republic, the GDR came to be culturally much the more conservative society. Modernism there was welcomed insofar as it echoed the socialist radicalism of the years between the wars. For example, John Heartfield was welcomed back to the East, on his return to Germany in 1950 from emigration in England, and his work was allowed a place and celebrated as a part of history. But no contemporary critical modernism, such as Heartfield's photomontages had represented in Weimar Germany, could be allowed to develop in a society of such all-pervasive constraint. It seems significant that Jan Tschichold should have turned, towards the end of his life, to the GDR and to Leipzig for the publication of his *Leben und Werk*. Here was a stronghold of decent, traditional sobriety, little affected by the onslaughts of capitalist modernization, which had by then so altered the typographic cultures of the German-speaking countries of the West.

Traditionalist typographic culture was resumed in the Federal Republic. As before, it was allied to the literary publishers, to the typefoundries (such of them as still survived), to historical research. The tradition of the new classical typography – of C. E. Poeschel or Jakob Hegner – was picked up again with some vigour. It had never disappeared in the National-Socialist years, though some of its practitioners had suffered for reasons that can hardly be related to principles of typography. Hegner himself went after the war to Italy and then Switzerland, where he revived his imprint, co-publishing in the Federal Republic. Of the generation of typographers who came to prominence after 1945, Hermann Zapf may stand as the most lucid practitioner of an enlightened traditionalist approach: in book typography, but, more importantly, in the design of typefaces. Zapf's production in this latter sphere has been rooted in calligraphy, and specifically in the manner developed before the war (by

Weiß or Schneidler); from this base he was able to tackle a succession of contemporary tasks, in designing typefaces for new systems of text composition and letter generation.

The fate of modernism in the Federal Republic worked itself out very visibly at the Hochschule für Gestaltung Ulm. The school had its beginnings in an effort of social reconstruction after the war: to commemorate, in particular, a movement of anti-Nazi opposition (the 'Weiße Rose' group), through building a new college of progressive and international character. The project materialized, with financial support from US government sources and from German industry, as a school of design. The HfG Ulm took considerable inspiration from the Bauhaus: in the ideals of a total approach to design, as well as in the formulation of its title, and in gathering teaching staff from among old Bauhäusler. The most important of these was Max Bill, the first rector of the school and architect of its buildings.

The Bauhaus legacy provided a focus for an early and formative conflict within the school. This concerned the pattern of teaching that had been adopted, which followed that of the Bauhaus (even in its years at Dessau), where 'master' and pupils gathered in an 'atelier' and engaged in craft pursuits; the alternative prospect was of approaches that were collaborative and without connotations of fine art, but were directed rather to fully industrialized production. With Bill's resignation and departure from the school (in 1957), the latter approach came to the fore. The HfG Ulm then became a focus for advanced work in developing rational approaches to design. Already under Bill, a department of information had been established, with cybernetics as a main interest. As the school then developed, particularly under the guidance of Tomás Maldonado, this theoretical concern came to include information theory, semiotics, methodology: a nexus of interests that helped to provide a radical alternative to an Arts & Crafts oriented view of design. These opposed views were, however, not quite mutually exclusive. They coexisted, for example, in the work of one teacher at the school: Anthony Froshaug, a main contributor to its typographic work in this new phase. Froshaug established a printing workshop there, and also took part in the theoretical work of the school. Another approach – and another synthesis of practical and philosophical-theoretical

concerns – can be seen in the work of Otl Aicher, a co-founder of the
school. But, at the height of its phase of 'methodolatry', there was
raised the vision of a design that could operate by rational analysis,
with intuition and hand skills relegated to insignificance. In such
a view, typography, along with every other area of design activity,
would be dissolved into analytics and industrial production.

The HfG Ulm did in many respects, and especially in certain
phases, correspond sympathetically with the economic reconstruction under way in the Federal Republic in the 1950s and 1960s. The
school was partially dependent for its survival on contracts with
industry; but, in any case, its chosen course was one of connection
with the needs of the society in which it was situated. The conflicts
within the school, and between it and its supporting authorities, followed the larger politics of the time. As if in a replay of Bauhaus history, its closure (in 1968) was enforced and followed long disputes
with the state and 'Land' authorities. The HfG Ulm had by then
moved to a more politically critical position. While maintaining
ideals of rationality, these were now directed against the humanly
and environmentally destructive tendencies of advanced capitalism. Such ideas of a critical design were barely formulated and had
no time to be implemented in the work that issued from the school.
Thus its typographic and graphic design stayed faithfully with the
prevailing modernist patterns of the time. Its manner was 'Swiss':
the accepted clothing for any progressive company or institution in
the West, and especially one with international ambitions.

12 Swiss typography

National peculiarities
In the years of economic expansion – past the aftermath of 1945 – the leading model of modern typography derived from Switzerland: the phenomenon that has become known simply as 'Swiss typography'. Certainly for the emerging first generation of graphic designers in the western countries, it was the style of the moment: though style was something that Swiss typographers disclaimed. For some explanation of the character and strengths of this typography, one may look to its beginnings in the years between the wars and to a salient factor in its development: Switzerland's neutrality in the Second World War. This allowed for a continuity of development that no other country enjoyed. (Sweden might provide another comparative instance, but, with its less developed typographic culture and exclusive language, a much weaker one.)

In the 1930s, in the larger field of graphic art, and in poster design above all, modernist approaches had become well established in Switzerland: simplified images; integration of text and image; the use of photographs, especially as photomontage. In such work, where image was reduced to type-like simplicity, and where type was given a graphic, image-like presence, the categories of 'typography' and 'graphic art' were broken down and fused to produce what then became 'graphic design'.

Certain special characteristics of life and culture lay behind this development: the country's long tradition of direct democracy, in which voting on details of political policy has been a habitual, almost weekly, practice – for male citizens, at least. But, as the other side of this bargain, regulations and limitations have also been deeply ingrained, through custom and law. The acceptance of constraints on individual and corporate liberties has led, for example, to a view of advertising as essentially a medium of information: an idea that has been proposed in other capitalist countries, though with less conviction and less truth. In Switzerland, however, with its widely shared ideals of stability, continuity, equality, it was possible to develop a graphic design that could plausibly aspire to being 'functional', in the sense of being an unobtrusive medium for the communication of useful information, with the demands of competition being correspondingly muted.

The strong craft tradition, carried over into industrial production, provided another special condition of Swiss typography. The characteristic pattern of industry has been of high degrees of craft skill combined with advanced technology in small, self-reliant units: in printing, as elsewhere, this has helped to minimize the split between production and design. Design has also been integrated into the education of printers, just as the education of designers has been grounded in the values of proper techniques in hand and machine production. Evidence of the good relation between printers and designers may be seen in the journal *Typographische Monatsblätter* (founded in 1933), which has catered for both groups equally and facilitated communication between them. Swiss typography has thus had a stronger base than any mere designer's style: printers could be relied on to produce competent (if not inspired) work, without a designer's instructions. This has applied to both modernist and to traditionalist typography. While it is an assumption of traditionalist typography that its manner is available to any practitioner, that this should have been true of modernist typography – the Swiss typography of these years – is an index of how well established modernism had become in places of influence, and especially within printing education.

Formations and distribution

The founding statement of Swiss typography can be seen to have been Max Bill's 'Über Typografie' of 1946, and in that text and in Jan Tschichold's criticisms of it, most of the issues of this typography had been raised (see chapter 10). In the immediate post-war years a 'school' of typographers, following the principles outlined by Bill, then started to form, as a younger generation entered practice. By the mid-1950s Swiss typography had begun to penetrate into international consciousness. This awareness was spread particularly though the magazine *Neue Grafik / New Graphic Design* (1958–65) and the book *Die neue Graphik / The new graphic art* (1959) by Karl Gerstner and Markus Kutter. The magazine *Graphis*, published from Zurich since 1944, and with an international readership, had neglected the phenomenon, being interested in graphic art of a more traditional kind. But in 1959, *Graphis* published a two-page account by Emil Ruder 'of the underlying principles of this new movement', entitled 'The typography of order'.[1] This text was supported by reproductions of work 'for the most part by old students of the author'. Ruder had been teaching typography at the Allgemeine Gewerbeschule Basel since 1942, later becoming head of department there; at his death, in 1970, he was still at the school, as its director. From this long-held position at Basel, and as one of the clearest and sternest practitioners of Swiss typography, Ruder exerted a powerful influence on its development. He was to summarize his approach in the book *Typographie* (1967).

If Ruder at Basel was one of the main disseminators of the Swiss approach, through his students and through their students, the other was his contemporary Josef Müller-Brockmann. Following a period of teaching at the Kunstgewerbeschule Zurich, Müller-Brockmann published his *Gestaltungsprobleme des Grafikers / The graphic artist and his design problems* in 1961. This became a prime document in the international transmission of Swiss typography and its methods; like much of the literature of the movement, the author's German text was supplemented by English and French parallel translations.

After sketching the historical transition from illustration and the 'subjectivist mode of expression' to a typographically oriented 'objective, constructive method' – exemplified by his own turn from illustration to graphic design – Müller-Brockmann then spelled out in some detail the principles of this 'new graphic art' (Müller-Brockmann, *Gestaltungsprobleme des Grafikers*, p. 5). The whole programme is here made explicit: the striving for impersonality and objectivity, through an elimination of decorative or expressive effects ('the paramount requirement is an unadorned typographical form serving purely the needs of communication') and through the application of an ordering grid; restriction of type sizes and typefaces (sanserif is 'the expression of our age' and suitable for 'almost any typographical job'); the use of unjustified text (though the text of the book itself was set justified); the use of photography in preference to illustration, with drawing allowed an important role in diagrams (Müller-Brockmann, *Gestaltungsprobleme des Grafikers*, pp. 16, 25.) All this was exemplified by reproductions of work by Müller-Brockmann and his associates and students.

Müller-Brockmann was one of the co-editors of *Neue Grafik*, with three other graphic designers working in Zurich: Richard Lohse, Hans Neuberg, Carlo Vivarelli. In the first number of the magazine the editors explained that they aimed to 'make a collection of work showing significant trends and gradually to reproduce that work in a periodical for examination and discussion' (*Neue Grafik*, no. 1, 1958, p. 2). In keeping with their hope for it to become an international platform, texts of articles were given in three languages, in the multi-column, square format that became habitual in Swiss typography. Throughout its seven years of publication (in eighteen numbers), the design of the magazine never deviated: as if to exemplify the settled, thoroughly 'objective' nature of its approach. In support of its publication of recent work by this burgeoning new school of graphic designers, *Neue Grafik* included substantial historical articles on modernist graphic and typographic design from between the wars. Leading the way in the rediscovery of this work, the magazine aimed to establish a tradition whose most recent development was Swiss typography. However, neither the name nor the work of Jan Tschichold was mentioned in its pages, while contributions by Max Bill and reproductions of his work appeared with some frequency: a sign of the intensity of party commitment that informed the enterprise.

In confirmation of the arrival of this 'new graphic design', a book of (almost) this title – *Die neue Graphik* – was published soon after the start of the magazine *Neue Grafik*. The book was announced in the second number of the magazine, in an advertisement that took pains to disclaim rivalry and to affirm a common spirit: 'There are some subjects which are very much in the air …' (*Neue Grafik*, no. 2, 1959, p. 63.) The book's authors, Karl Gerstner and Markus Kutter, worked from Basel, where they set up an advertising partnership in 1959. Kutter was a copy-writer (and later published some experimental fiction), while Gerstner had learned typography at the Allgemeine Gewerbeschule Basel under Ruder

1. Emil Ruder, 'The typography of order', *Graphis*, vol. 15, no. 85, 1959, p. 404.

and subsequently worked as a designer for Geigy and as a freelance. Born in 1930, Gerstner represented the generation after that of Max Bill (born in 1908) and most of the *Neue Grafik* group (of whom Vivarelli – born in 1919 – was the youngest).

Gerstner and Kutter's book certainly shared much with *Neue Grafik*, both in form and content: the same almost-square, multi-column format (though with more refinements of configuration than were possible in the design of the magazine), and the same marshalling of historical examples to form a sequence leading to the present 'new graphic design'. In their historical coverage, Gerstner and Kutter cast their net wider than the magazine was to do. According to their account, graphic design had its first seeds in the 'timeless' work of 'primitive' graphic art, and its proper beginning was located in the nineteenth century: the work of anonymous printers and of the poster artists. The 'break-through' came with the modern movement in the twentieth century. After a substantial representation of modernist work up to 1945, the second half of the book was devoted to 'the present' ('the generation of graphic artists which has been at work since the Second World War') and to 'the future'. This last section featured a selection of recent work consisting of planned sets of items (corporate identity work, as it would become known), as if to suggest that this more rigorous approach, where design was considered 'on equal terms with the economic, administrative and editorial aspects of advertising technique', was the way ahead for the new graphic design (Gerstner & Kutter, *Die neue Graphik*, p. 215).

A persistent interest in advertising was a characteristic of *Die neue Graphik*. Gerstner and Kutter were about to enter advertising themselves, while elsewhere the new graphic design was turning away from this sphere of activity. However, as already suggested, advertising in Switzerland was the subject of a marked degree of mutually understood self-constraint on the part of advertisers and their agents, so that it was possible and also necessary to practise an informative and systematic approach, avoiding arbitrariness and fiction. Such an approach was evident in Gerstner and Kutter's work, which was however by no means staid or merely prosaic. As *Die neue Graphik* showed, they looked towards recent work from the USA, in advertising and graphic design, and thus sought to tap sources more vital than those that were available at home.

Renewed debate

In the year of publication of *Die neue Graphik* – 1959 – another declaration of principles of Swiss typography appeared: a special number of *Typographische Monatsblätter*, with the general rubric of 'Integrale Typographie'. This was also the title of Karl Gerstner's extended contribution to the issue. In this text he reaffirmed the thesis of Max Bill in 'Über Typografie', that the new and valid typography was 'functional or organic', without the strain or quasi-decorative effects of the earlier modernist 'elementary' typography. This approach Gerstner now called 'integral', summarizing it thus: 'Integral typography strives for the marriage of language and type resulting in a new unity, in a superior whole. Text and typography are not so much two consecutive processes on different levels as interpenetrating elements.'[2] Among his examples of this integral typography – suggesting a scope more liberal than that of Max Bill's ideals for a functional typography – Gerstner included a recent series of advertisements for the *New York Times*, set in a seriffed typeface and without any strict underpinning from a grid.

In his introduction to the special issue, Rudolf Hostettler, the long-serving editor of *Typographische Monatsblätter*, explained that the present situation 'in many respects corresponds to that which prompted Max Bill to write his essay "Über Typografie"', and he cited an article recently published by Jan Tschichold: 'Zur Typographie der Gegenwart' ('On present-day typography').[3] The special issue was a collective rejoinder to Tschichold's renewed aspersions against typographic modernism: both explicitly in one article and through reproductions of work and statements by leading representatives of Swiss typography.

Tschichold's article had been published first in Germany in 1957 and had subsequently (in 1960) appeared as a pamphlet published by the Monotype Corporation in Berne. His argument was

---

2. Gerstner's text was reprinted in *Programme Entwurfen*; quoted from the English edition (1968), *Designing programmes*, p. 66.

3. Rudolf Hostettler, 'Einführung', *Typographische Monatsblätter*, vol. 78, no. 6/7, 1959, p. 339. Tschichold's 'Zur Typographie der Gegenwart' was first published in *Börsenblatt für den Deutschen Buchhandel*, vol. 13, 1957, pp. 1487–90; quotations here are made from the text given in Tschichold, *Schriften 1925–1974*, vol. 2, pp. 255–65.

accompanied by no pictorial illustration and avoided all specific reference to Swiss typography as a collective phenomenon, still less to any individuals, but his target was unmistakable. Employing his usual free-ranging mixture of technical, aesthetic, and moral argument, Tschichold rounded in turn on each of the central tenets of Swiss typography. He suggested that a preoccupation with the arrangement of blocks of text led to the reduction of words to mere colour and to a denial of their meaning. This pin-pointed one of the most pervasive features of the Swiss approach, inculcated through educational exercises in variations of configuration within a grid. In a series of objections to the cult of sanserif, he asserted that it was not the duty of letterforms to correspond to the spirit of the age, nor to its newest material products (skyscrapers or car bodies); rather 'typography must be itself. It must be adapted to our eyes, and to their well-being'. ('Zur Typographie der Gegenwart', p. 257.) Not so much a modern letterform, the sanserif was a nineteenth-century product, and its original name of 'grotesque' (still current in German) was the correct one: 'it really is a monster' ('Zur Typographie der Gegenwart', p. 258). The lasting letterform was the roman ('Antiqua'), proved over centuries and still maintaining the calligraphic tradition. Other essential features of Swiss typography came in for attack: the refusal to indent first lines of paragraphs (another piece of formalism at the expense of meaning); asymmetrically placed text in book design; DIN paper sizes (lacking in aesthetic quality as well as unpractical); the limitation to a single size of type (leading to a failure to articulate the text); the predilection for large expanses of pure colour or a harsh white paper. Above all, Tschichold suggested, this new typography lacked grace ('Anmut'). By this he meant not prettiness, let alone kitsch, but the quality that follows from work done with love and attention to the smallest details.

Of the group contributing to the special 'Integrale Typographie' issue of *Typographische Monatsblätter*, it was Emil Ruder – perhaps the clearest object of Tschichold's attack – who undertook the task of a direct reply to these severe charges.[4] Though Ruder's article took the form of a point-by-point rebuttal, he tended to shift the issues rather than deal with and refute the charges directly. Thus he discussed the question of relations between compositor and designer: an issue of importance and – as himself a compositor turned

designer – one close to his heart, but something raised only tangen-
tially by Tschichold (in the criticism of the formalist view of text as
no more than an area of colour or tone). On the question of sym-
metry, he defended unjustified or ragged setting (not mentioned by
Tschichold) as obviously the correct way to compose text. While taking pains to distinguish between different kinds of sanserif (some
were better than others), Ruder was prepared to defend the category
as suitable for any kind of text and as having advantages over roman
in its greater possibilities for development as 'families' of related
variant forms. In conclusion, Ruder suggested that Tschichold's po-
lemics were unhelpful: Swiss typography stood out for quality too;
he did not want to reject modernism now, just because bad things
were done in its name; the age of manifestos was over, and the task
was now to refine and build on what had been achieved so far.

Univers and Helvetica

In his advocacy of sanserif, Ruder was now able to call upon what he
seemed to see as a trump-card in the argument: Univers. Together
with its contemporaries Folio (from the Bauer foundry in Germany)
and Helvetica (from Haas in Switzerland), Univers represented an
attempt to provide a sanserif that improved both on the nineteenth-
century grotesques and on the more geometrically designed sanserifs from between the wars (Futura, Erbar). Of the former category,
Berthold Akzidenz Grotesk, available for hand-setting and line-composition machines, was then still the standard in German-speaking
countries (and for the English-speaking market it was given the
name 'Standard'). Gill Sans was available only for Monotype composition and had thus found limited adoption on the Continent: it was
not favoured by the most influential Swiss typographers (Bill and
the *Neue Grafik* group). Rather, where this form of composition was
available, Swiss modernists used Monotype Grot 215 in preference
to Gill; like Akzidenz Grotesk it could be seen to bear the stamp of
anonymous, vernacular authenticity. The calligraphic, Renaissance-
humanist tradition evident in Gill Sans – despite the Monotype

4. Emil Ruder, 'Zur Typographie der Gegenwart', *Typographische
Monatsblätter*, vol. 78, no. 6/7, 1959, pp. 363–71.

Corporation's concession of alternative characters for lowercase 'a' and 'g' – was no recommendation to hard-line Swiss typographers.

Though produced in Paris, initially for the Lumitype photo-composing machine, Univers can be said to have had origins in Switzerland. Its designer was Adrian Frutiger, Swiss by birth and the beneficiary of a thoroughly Swiss education: a compositor's apprenticeship and then the Kunstgewerbeschule Zurich. The most distinctive feature of Univers was that it comprised a family of twenty-one variants. This was conceived at the outset, and the typeface was designed within a programme that was demonstrated by a matrix presentation, each variant bearing an index number.

If all this gave off an air of scientificity, attractive to typographers interested in possibilities of logically determined design, the considerable sophistications of Univers depended on old-fashioned drawing skills and patient small adjustments: it was an exemplary product of the Swiss craft tradition. Though it anticipated the possibilities of computer-aided typeface design, this was done quite innocently.

Although Univers was designed initially for photocomposition, neither this technology in general, nor Lumitype in particular, had made much commercial impact in Europe at that time. An important boost was thus given to the typeface when the Monotype Corporation bought rights to adapt it for their machines. In Switzerland, Emil Ruder led the way in welcoming this development: first in *Neue Grafik*, and then in a special issue of *Typographische Monatsblätter*, in which the Monotype cutting made its first appearance.[5] Matrices became commercially available at the end of 1961. It was clear to Ruder that with this typeface, modernist typography at last had the sanserif that it had previously only been able to postulate. And though the claim was made neither by Ruder, still less by Frutiger (who took care in his writings to resist dogma), the name given to the typeface suggested the grandest ambitions. It did certainly have a more realistic claim to being a 'universal' typeface than the alphabets attempted by Bayer, Schwitters and other between-the-wars modernists: not least because it was manufactured by companies with world-wide markets. As to universal features of its design, the publicists explained that different languages set in the typeface produced blocks of text of the same colour, because of the relatively small size of its capital letters. Thus, for example, French and German (with its high incidence of capitals) produced the same visual effect when set in parallel columns. This was among the features of the typeface of special attraction, in multilingual Switzerland, to typographers interested in the 'Satzbild': the text-image. In due course, following the success of the typeface in the West, non-Latin equivalents of Univers were produced: Cyrillic and Japanese among them.

The other new sanserif of this time associated particularly with Swiss typography was Neue Haas Grotesk, designed within the Haas foundry in Münchenstein. Taking advantage of the reputation of its country of origin, the typeface was named 'Helvetica' for its issue by the Stempel foundry (based in Frankfurt). This was the name by which the typeface became generally known, especially in North America, where it was sold (in innumerable adaptations) more widely than Univers. As its first name suggested, the typeface was an attempt to improve on the model of the nineteenth-century grotesque. Although a more homogenous set of forms than the previous Haas Grotesk, Helvetica retained an air of the reliable but ungainly work-horse, while Univers aspired rather to the race-course.

Both Univers and Helvetica came in for some criticism from Karl Gerstner: as being too smooth and producing too even a colour. If this was a 'graphic' advantage, it was not a 'functional' one: 'what has ocular clarity may appear monotonous when read' (Gerstner, *Designing programmes*, p. 32). Thus he suggested that the old grotesques were still valid models, and, taking Berthold Akzidenz Grotesk as a basis, proposed his own development of the category. The result – which achieved very limited application, on the Berthold Diatype machine – was perhaps more interesting as a case study in programmatic design than it was successful as a working typeface. And, as such, Gerstner included the essay in his book *Programme entwerfen* (*Designing programmes*) of 1963 (see example 19, pp. 220–1).

5. Emil Ruder, 'Univers', *Neue Grafik*, no. 2, 1959, p. 56; 'Die Univers in der Typographie', *Typographische Monatsblätter*, vol. 80, no. 1, 1961, pp. 18– 20.

Out of the straightjacket
Although still working firmly within the Swiss tradition, one may
cite Gerstner as the theorist-practitioner who was best able to point
ways out of what, during the 1960s, became a situation of stagnation in Swiss typographic culture. This impasse was the unwelcome
counterpart of the urge for methods, standards, objectivity, which
was so strong a feature of the work of the leaders of the school
(Ruder, Müller-Brockmann).

To take the example of a fundamental typographic detail: the
consensus among Swiss typographers, at the high point of the
phenomenon, ruled out indentation of first lines of paragraphs. But
gradually – one can see this in the design of *Typographische Monatsblätter* – indentation was rediscovered, and with it a greater freedom
of configuration and a greater sensitivity to the meaning of the text
being designed. Karl Gerstner's major contribution to this loosen-
ing of design dogmas (including much play with indentation) came
in 1972, with the publication of his *Kompendium für Alphabeten*, appearing in English as *Compendium for literates* (1974). This was very
much a book for designers, important for its spirit of experimenta-
tion (small square format, Chinese-folded page leaves bound at
their heads), rather than for any particular design feature or for its
content. It seems, in retrospect, to have signalled the end of Swiss
typography as an internationally understood method or style. By
this time the older generation of typographers was no longer active.
Gerstner had retired from his advertising and design work in 1970,
and then turned increasingly to fine art.

In Gerstner's wake, and under the leadership of Wolfgang
Weingart at the Allgemeine Gewerbeschule Basel, the generation of
designers emerging in the 1970s began to break with some of the essential principles of Swiss typography. This served to confirm that,
like any generally accepted approach to design, Swiss typography
had been a manifestation fitted to its time and place: the years of recovery and prosperity in the western world. Either as a style or as an
attempt at an objective and impersonal method, it represented con-
fidence in technical progress in a successfully modernizing world.

The fundamentally aesthetic approach of Swiss typography,
lying behind its claim to functional effectiveness, becomes evident
enough when viewed historically. Its functional aspirations might

be further doubted by pointing to the fact that several of its leading figures were also professional abstract artists (notably Bill, Lohse, Gerstner) and also to the abstract-art basis of Swiss graphic design education: thus one might imply that Swiss typography was simply art in the guise of useful design. Certainly Swiss typographers' obsession with the grid and the 'Satzbild' meshed perfectly with their geometrical, abstract-art interests. The grid found its functional justification in the frequent need in Switzerland to publish text with illustrations in two or three languages; thus the development of the multi-column, square-format book. Beyond these motivations for Swiss typography, there was also a social impulse that can be seen in at least some of this work. Such an impulse could be there as long as it existed in its original Swiss context. But, in its translation into the everyday style of the West, aesthetic refinements were lost, leaving only the rationale that it was efficient and saved money. In Switzerland, the idea that life might really be improved by infusing it with purifying abstract art did perhaps have some reality, as it did not in other less constrained societies. The strong moral content of this vision of abstract art was clearest in Max Bill's book *Form* of 1952: here 'good form' (abstract form) becomes the principle that might save civilization from the onslaughts of North American streamlining and kitsch.[6] Western civilization – or, at least, western capitalism – allowed Bill's good form to develop in only a partial embodiment. This was the moment of the Swiss ascendancy, in which (even as late as 1967), typography could be serenely described as 'an expression of technology, precision and good order' (Ruder, *Typographie*, p. 14). But, with the years of crisis and recession in the 1970s, the context changed. Technology was no longer an unambiguous blessing; order and precision were in doubt.

6. Max Bill, *Form*, Basel: Karl Werner, 1952; see especially p. 46.

13   Modernity after modernism

The 1950s and 1960s had been a period in which a dream of 'the modern' could come true, on the cushion of material comfort and a settled state in international relations (the Cold War). It was a tamed and safe modernism, with its spiritual centre in neutral Switzerland; it was not the utopian adventure that the European pioneers had briefly imagined in the years between two world wars. And, indeed, it was only in the post-1945 period that the term 'modernism' (at least in its English form) began to be thoroughly filled out, retrospectively. The avant-garde of the interwar period did not think of itself as 'modernist', but conceived rather of discrete movements – 'constructivist', 'suprematist', 'surrealist', and so on. By the time that the term came to be contemporary with the work it described, something different was going on.

The events of 1968 – uprisings and political unrest in Western Europe and North America, as in parts of the Soviet bloc – can be seen, in historical perspective, as a warning sign.[1] The comfortable years certainly came to an end in 1973, with the sudden jump in the price of oil implemented by the OPEC producers. A principal support of the prosperity was removed and, across the world, national economies were thrown into a different gear. At the same time, the process of transnational commercial incorporation was hastened. Thus in 1979 the Linotype company (based principally in Germany and the USA) was bought by Allied Chemical. Already in 1973, the Monotype Corporation (based principally in the UK) had been acquired by a property investment company. For Monotype this was the first of a succession of take-overs through the 1970s and 1980s. These culminated in 1997, with the acquisition by the photochemical company Agfa of Monotype Typography (as it had then become), to form Agfa Monotype. At that time Agfa was itself part of the yet larger Bayer group. The rise of the chemical companies in typography followed the change from metal type and letterpress to photocomposition and offset printing.

After Swiss typography

The coming of this moment of crisis – the end of the years of comfort – can be seen embodied in the learning years of the typographer Wolfgang Weingart, now touchingly described in his book on 'my way to typography'.[2] Weingart was born (in 1941) and raised in southern Germany. After training as an artist at the Merz Academy in Stuttgart and then as a compositor's apprentice, in 1964 Weingart found his way to Basel, the Mecca of Swiss Typography. In his account, he had to confront the Basel vision of typography, as enunciated by its main typography teacher, Emil Ruder. His attempt was to work through it – with the same craft skills that were prized at Basel – to another kind of typography, more fitting to the new times. So Weingart broke from the serene sense of order, making patterns of displacement and disturbance in configuration of the visual materials. It seemed to be a more complete break than was being made then in Zurich, especially by Karl Gerstner, whose work had never carried the formal burdens of Emil Ruder's. A comparison with Gestner's meaning-directed typography shows the limits of Weingart, whose production remained as form-bound as the work from which he dissented. He showed little interest in new typefaces, sticking largely to a hardline German diet of Akzidenz Grotesk, and avoiding Univers, for which Ruder had been a great champion. What was different in Weingart was the way in which, in his small repertoire of typefaces, he attacked the image of letters by cutting or other means of visual distortion. Though not new – almost every kind of violation or elaboration of letters can be seen already in the nineteenth century – it was suggestive for the type designers who would follow in the years to come.

In 1968, after Ruder's retirement, Wolfgang Weingart began to teach at Basel. As in Ruder's day, the school was a focus for students from all over the world. One can explain the spread of Weingartian

1. This is Eric Hobsbawm's view of 1968 in his *Age of extremes: the short twentieth century, 1914–1991* (London: Michael Joseph, 1994, at p. 284).
2. Weingart, *Wege zur Typographie*. The cover and the title-pages suggest that the book's title is also *Typography*. But the word is shown only in fragments: as if acting out Weingart's critique of his Swiss fathers. In 1967 Emil Ruder had published his summarizing book, *Typographie*. In several respects, Weingart's book is a response to Ruder's.

and other 'post-Swiss' ideas of typography by the route of international students coming to Basel and then spreading the message
at home. A prize case would be April Greiman (a student there in
1970–1), who went on to become the key figure of the Californian
post-Swiss typography of the 1980s. Through the 1970s and 1980s,
Weingart undertook a heavy programme of lecture tours, especially
in the USA. There was also the route of publication in magazines:
his sets of text-rich cover designs for *Typographische Monatsblätter*
(1972, 1973, 1974) were formative.

Do-it-yourself graphics

As the years of crisis wore on, other kinds of dissent and attack
emerged. From around 1976 the eruption of punk in music, and
the graphics associated with this music, was important in showing
that anyone could do it. As Piet Schreuders, the Dutch writer, editor,
and designer, wrote in 1977, in an echo of the slogan of that music,
the procedure for graphic design was as follows: '1. Take a piece of
paper. 2. Start making layouts.'[3] The most concentrated work of this
kind emerged from England. And if one has to take one name from
among the designers of the punk culture, it would be that of Neville
Brody, who – more clearly than Weingart – brings us to the theme of
typeface design, which would now become once more a leading sec-
tor within the larger field of typography.

Neville Brody, though he trained for three years at the London
College of Printing, had no education in typeface design (which,
at that time, was confined to informal apprenticeship learning).
Working at first largely in graphic design for the independent music
business, he fell into drawing alphabets that he could use in his own
design work. Brody's fonts were strongly graphic, often strongly
geometric, and this was also their limitation. Beyond the widely influential style of his work, it was this spirit of do-it-yourself that was
its more enduring quality for the many young people who would enter graphic design by way of their commitment to the music. Neville
Brody's ascent reached its highest point in 1988 with his one-man
show at the Victoria & Albert Museum: a remarkable public relations coup, after which 'typography' was put on the agenda for the
cultural establishment in Britain, at least for a while, until the next
star might come along.

When the Apple Macintosh was launched in January 1984, Brody was an early adopter, using the computer for font design as well as for page layouts. But the chronology is clear: he had been working in the do-it-yourself spirit for a few years before this device became available. The same goes for his contemporaries Rudy VanderLans and Zuzana Licko, both born and educated in Europe but by the early 1980s living in California. The first issues of their magazine *Emigre* (published from 1984) were produced by the conventional methods of the time, of paste-up for the reproduction camera. In 1985–6 Licko began to use an Apple Macintosh for making fonts – typefaces that took formal bearings from the constraints of this computer and its accompanying laser printer. In 1989, with the establishment in Berlin of FontShop, a step towards a new way of publishing and distribution of typefaces was taken. This was a company inspired and partly run by designers (principally Erik Spiekermann with Joan Spiekermann, joined by Neville Brody) and organized with designers' needs in mind: the quick and easy provision of fonts from the widest range of sources. FontShop became a channel for typeface designers just breaking into the field to publish their work: doing most of the development work themselves, and receiving a higher royalty than was then paid by the established manufacturers. The FontShop catalogue soon became a central index of available typefaces, including some very usable and long-lasting items (for example Scala, Meta, Quadraat) as well as, inevitably, much dross.

A Dutch voice

These conditions, in which type designers could – as part of the processes of design – become type manufacturers too, were to prove a liberation for older practitioners with strong hand skills and some competence with the new machines. In the Netherlands, the prime case of this liberation was Gerrit Noordzij: a designer and maker with deep roots in the Dutch traditions of writing, lettering, and typography. From the start of his practice, in the 1950s, he had written and made lettering for photographic reproduction, as well

3. Piet Schreuders, *Lay in, lay out*, Amsterdam: Gerrit Jan Thiemefonds, 1977, p. 51; and reprinted within his collection *Lay in – Lay out*, Amsterdam: De Buitenkant, 1997 (at p. 43).

as worked as a typographic designer, mainly for book publishers. He
had also, since 1960, taught classes in writing and typography at the
Koninklijke Academie van Beeldende Kunsten in The Hague. But
he hardly ventured into the sphere of designing typefaces until the
means arrived by which he could do it himself: first on strips of film,
for a simple photosetting apparatus, then from the late 1980s with
an Apple Macintosh computer. It was this second development that
allowed Noordzij to realize in practice some of the theoretical work
that he had long been engaged with.

In 1970 Gerrit Noordzij had burst into the world of international typographic discussion with an article on 'Broken scripts and the
classification of typefaces'.[4] Starting out as a review of Walter Plata's
book *Schätze der Typographie: gebrochene Schriften*, the piece moved
on to consider the classification of any typeface or letterform, and
then, by way of the special question of 'broken scripts', Noordzij
presented his theory of letters. By assuming that written forms un-
derlay all typographic letterforms, and by presenting a simple set of
binary categories, he was able to sweep away the usual categories of
typeface classification and to escape from a rigidly historicist view
of the matter. In this scheme, letters show the properties of 'translation' (as if written with a broad-nibbed pen) or 'expansion' (as if
written with a flexing nib), and they are cursive (the pen remains
on the writing surface) or interrupted (the pen is lifted between
strokes, and makes only downstrokes). Noordzij's view was that
of a producer; it allowed the topic of letterforms and typography
to be a matter of immediate presence – at the work-table or on the
classroom blackboard. As he put it: 'For me there is ... not much
difference between teaching and research: in teaching I address my
future colleagues, and in research into writing I meet colleagues
from the past.' (Noordzij, *De streek*, p. 5.)

As part of the polemical effort to found typography in the practice of writing, Noordzij undertook periodic assaults on a historically determined view of typography: as found especially in the work of
Stanley Morison – the Monotype typeface revivals and his writings
– and, less so, in Updike's *Printing types*. Against Morison's stress on
the 'engraved' character of typographic letters, Noordzij proposed
an opposing stress on – a belief in – the fundamentally written
character of all letters.[5] Against any historical or normative view,

Noordzij offered an anarchist-craftsman's theory of knowledge. Thus, in typical style, in his bulletin *Letterletter*, he wrote: 'Usually serifs are considered in relationship with the terminals of the letters in Roman inscriptions. For me stone cutting is an entirely different subject that might be treated in a lapidary number of *Letterletter*. If you cannot wait that long, take a chisel and invent the story of stone cutting yourself. At the scaffold the tools and the stone demand an approach that cannot be invented at the desk of a scholar.' (*Letterletter*, no.11, p.1.)

Noordzij's students – his 'future colleagues' – did begin, in the later 1980s and in the 1990s, to show the fruits of his teaching: there arose what can be called a school of 'Hague type designers'.[6] But the remarkable flourishing of type design in the Netherlands in these years was more than just the work of this school: it derived rather from the broader typographic culture of the country. Noordzij himself made little contribution to the stock of usable typefaces. Those that he published were brilliant essays that, for the most part, remain unfinished and mostly unavailable to anyone except their maker. The idea that writing is the determining factor in typography thus came back to haunt its proponent: a fully workable typeface requires that it be put through the mill of 'justification' (spatial fitting of the characters), as well as adaptation for different technical

4. 'Broken scripts and the classification of typefaces', *Journal of Typographic Research*, vol.4, no.3, pp.213–40. This prompted two pieces in vol.5, no.1 of this journal: Walter Tracy's 'Type design classification' (pp.59–66), and a bitter letter from the American Alexander Nesbitt (pp.82–4) accusing Noordzij of Germanophobia, incorrect history, and the mistaken belief that writing is the sole foundation of typography. Noordzij replied (pp.85–7) in kind.

5. Morison's stress on engraving, as well as his nuanced view of the history of type, can be seen, for example, in his discussion of the background to Perpetua; see his *A tally of types*, especially at pp.99–100; and see also the quotation from Morison in chapter 11, p.137 above. Noordzij's overstated opposition to Morison can be seen in an essay of 1980, used as the text for the specimens in Lommen & Verheul, *Haagse letters*: 'The assertion that printing types and handwriting are unrelated is brilliantly presented by the Englishman Stanley Morison ...'. Morison asserted no such thing.

6. See Lommen & Verheul, *Haagse letters*, which is constructed around the figure of Noordzij.

formats. Until this process of making a typeface publicly usable has
been accomplished, it remains just a means of private expression
– like handwriting.

Letters as bits

Developments in text-composition and printing technology in this
period have been so great that they require a more detailed, more
technical discussion than is the case with earlier phases. As already
discussed (chapter 11), photocomposition and the widespread
adoption of lithographic printing had seemed to institute a dematerialization of printing. In the 1970s, this tendency had been taken
further: in composition, with the introduction of systems that store
letter images as digital information in the memory of a computer,
rather than as photographic negatives. The development of digital
storage coincided with the introduction of cathode ray technology.
CRT machines and also (later) those that use laser technology had
helped to introduce what can be seen as a new era of composition:
that of digital typesetting, after metal and after photocomposition.
With this dematerialization – the reduction of mechanical motion
and the introduction of computer processing – there came very
significant advances in speed of composition: the persistent goal of
all inventions in this field.

The directly visible effect of digital processing had been a further undermining of the identities of letters. Forms that had been
normalized and then secured by their material embodiment, in the
days of metal composition, were unsettled by photographic techniques. In digitization, by the nature of the process, letters become
fragmented. The norms established in hot-metal composition, of
letterform category (roman, italic, bold) and of letterspace, now had
no material necessity and were frequently modified or ignored. In
this context, ideals of quality in typography have needed defending:
by demonstration and by argument that is historically informed,
but which is without the bibliophilic nostalgia that has been so
strong a motive in the culture of typography. By the 1990s it had
become clear that typographic quality was possible with the newest
techniques. The crudities of much photocomposition had been
left behind, and in many respects (especially in the fitting together
of letters) the quality of good hot-metal composition had been

improved upon. Only the just-perceptible relief of good letterpress printing could not be replaced.[7]

Here, as always, technology should be assessed in more than just technical terms. Certainly in comparison with the best quality in photocomposition and lithographic printing of the 1970s and early 1980s, the metal technologies of the preceding years provided quality more dependably and more cheaply, and so was available to a wider section of producers – and thus users or readers too. (The persistence of letterpress in economically disadvantaged cultures – as well as in the richest portions of the most advantaged – has provided suggestive evidence here.)

Among the applications of the digital computer in typography was its use in running typesetting programs, and as a tool in the design of sets of letterforms. Notable explorations in this field, from the late 1970s, were the TeX and Metafont projects of Donald Knuth and his associates, based at Stanford University in California. TeX and its derivates, Plain TeX and LaTeX, were essentially typesetting programs; Metafont was a computer language that would assist the design of a family of fonts – a typeface. The vision that Metafont offered was that all the elements of a font could be generated from the design of just one letter; and, as well, a family of variants of slope or stroke-width could also be produced. The letterforms of Metafont were generated from the strokes of an imaginary pen; but, as others were soon to suggest, making letterforms as outlines would be the way forward for making typefaces. Early published results of this project were visually crude and found to be illegitimate by the typographically initiated: as a mathematician and computer scientist, Knuth was an outsider and apparently without the 'eye' that follows from years of immersion in the typographic heritage.

This conflict was the ancient one of the rationally correct against the aesthetically satisfying: letters that were exactly describable, as all computer-generated forms must be, did not look quite

7. Polymer-plate printing, in which DTP-set text is then made into a raised printing surface, seems not to be an answer to this conundrum. Rather, in the eerie perfection of its image, it reminds us that the quality of letterpress depended on slight irregularities and imperfections in the height of the type, in the image of its 'face', and thus in its printed image.

right, in comparison with those freely drawn by hand. In the project of the 'romain du roi', the hand of the punchcutter took control and the ideal forms of the engraved plates remained ideal. But now, the means of direct implementation of rationalized forms are available, at any size: the ubiquity of highly simplified, dot-matrix letterforms provides the most obvious instance of this. Knuth's Metafont was an exemplary case of modern typography: a project of technical advance, developed in open, published dialogue with critics, whose programs were published and placed in the public domain. This renunciation of commercial interest helped to characterize the project as an 'academic' one: of value primarily as a tool for thinking about typeface design. Other developments in digital typography, also emerging largely from the same forcing ground on the west coast of the USA – where energetic commercial entrepreneurship joined up with scientific research – proved to have enormous practical consequences.

The moment of PostScript

Two closely linked technical developments may be emphasized in summarizing the changes in typography of the mid- to late-1980s. The first element was the introduction of the 'personal computer', and especially the Apple Macintosh, which, as well as being small and affordable to individual purchasers, was operated by visual analogue (rather than merely through keyboard codes) with results that were quite exactly displayed on a screen.[8] The second element was computer languages that could describe all the elements of a printed page – letterforms, line and half-tone images – and could instruct any output device built to receive such instructions. The same description was then equally capable of being transmitted to high-resolution imagesetters (the successors to traditional text composing machines) and low-resolution laser printers (the successors to typewriters and other such office-equipment machines). Typically, text would be sent to the latter for proofing, and perhaps also to print copies for informal circulation, and then set finally on a high-resolution device. There is an area of intersection between the commercial interest of the manufacturing companies, which make particular devices, and the interests of users of these devices, who want easy and fluid communication between machines and programs. Frequently this became an area of conflict and difficulty: the technical advances seemed to promise an opening of the field, which was then seen to be against the interest of the very companies introducing these advances. The history of the PostScript page description language, developed by Adobe Systems in California, has demonstrated this pattern: from protection through code-encryption of typefaces and non-disclosure, and then to publication of this information, under pressure from commercial rivals.

It was in Silicon Valley – roughly, the corridor between San Jose and San Francisco, with a focus at Stanford University – that the PostScript revolution was seeded and first developed. Early in 1983 a few paragraphs in *The Seybold Report on Publishing Systems* gave the news of the opening move:

> Two veterans of Xerox PARC [Palo Alto Research Center], John Warnock and Charles Geschke, have formed a new company in Mountain View, California, called Adobe Systems ... A central feature of the Adobe approach will be a compact, high-level picture ['page' is the more usual term] description language into which images will be converted. The descriptions in this language are independent of output device resolution. Furthermore, character fonts [i.e. typefaces] are treated like other graphic elements (except that some extra data about them is provided, and some extra operations are available) so that operations like rotation, screening, etc, can be applied to text just as they can to other graphic elements ... the initial product is expected to be available within twelve to eighteen months. (*Seybold Report*, vol. 12, no. 9, 17 January 1983, p. 12. My comments are inserted between square brackets.)

This was the typical Silicon Valley move: people left a university or commercial research centre to start a company which could develop

---

8. The phrase 'personal computer' is here used to mean any computer used by one person at one time. A more limited sense of the term is any such small computer that is not made by Apple Computer Inc. This follows from the nature of the IBM personal computer, introduced in 1981, which ran on an operating system made by Microsoft (MS-DOS). In the 1980s most PCs, apart from those made by Apple, ran on this operating system.

and market their invention. The invention was a page description language that could be the common ground between computer and printer. Text and pictures were treated in the same descriptive terms.

Towards the end of 1983, *Seybold* published a further report on Adobe's software package, which by now had the name of PostScript. 'Adobe is particularly proud of its technique for generating high-quality modest-resolution bit-mapped characters "on the fly" without any need for bit-by-bit editing. It licenses original artwork from companies such as ITC and digitizes the fonts itself.' (*Seybold Report*, vol.13, no.6, 28 November 1983, p.22.) As the report went on to explain, Adobe would not be a hardware manufacturer, but would earn revenue from selling licenses for the use of its software in computers and printers. By early 1985 *Seybold* reported that PostScript was beginning to be the standard page-description language for output printing and typesetting devices of all sorts. (*Seybold Report*, vol.14, no.9, 28 January 1985, p.3.)

The deep implications of PostScript for typefaces – or 'fonts' as they would now become popularly known – were as follows.[9] Typefaces were now no longer tied to any particular typesetting or printing device. In all previous systems of mechanical composition of type, both metal and photographic, typefaces had been a part of the composing system and had thus to be made or adapted by the particular machine manufacturer. But now the same data of description could drive any output device which had the software installed, and at any resolution. Typeface design processes changed fundamentally too. In the days of mechanical composition, designs were drawn on paper and then interpreted and adapted by company draftspeople, for photographic reproduction and fitting into the metrics of a particular composing machine. But when font design software packages became commercially available, there was no longer any barrier between drawing and the final product. So the way was open to the individual designer to set up as his or her own typeface producer. The hold on typeface design of the old composing-machine companies – Linotype and Monotype, above all – had been steadily weakened through the photocomposition era, with the spread of low-quality copies or adaptations of their existing typefaces (a leader here was the Compugraphic Corporation in the USA, established 1960), the rise of the licensing company International Typeface Corporation (established 1970), and with the development of rub-down lettering (notably the Letraset company, established in the UK in 1959) and strike-on-impact composition (notably the IBM Composer, in use from 1961). But now the grip of the old companies was broken.

PostScript was one of the essential components of what became known as 'desktop publishing' (DTP). The term was a marketing slogan, coined in January 1985 by Paul Brainerd, president of the Aldus Corporation, another Silicon Valley start-up company that had then just been formed to develop and market the PageMaker page-layout software package. The essential components of desktop publishing became these: the Apple Macintosh computer (launched in January 1984), the Apple LaserWriter printer (launched in January 1985), and PageMaker (launched in January 1985). Though there were soon rivals and, in some respects, superior products on the market. The principal rival to the Apple Macintosh – its ubiquitous all-conquering shadow – was Microsoft's Windows interface, overlaid on top of the operating system (MS-DOS) that this company had made for the IBM personal computer and its many clones.

The first LaserWriter was provided with just four typefaces (or nine fonts): Times (Medium, Medium Italic, Bold, Bold Italic) Helvetica (Medium, Bold); Courier (Medium, Bold); Symbol (Medium). By the end of 1985, the possibilities of PostScript were just beginning to be exploited. Adobe announced its first fonts for sale in a dull list of existing designs, mostly bought from ITC: Avant Garde Gothic, Benguiat, Bookman, and so on. (*Seybold Report*, vol. 15, no. 5, 4 November 1985, p. 39.) As it happened, one good typeface had just been designed specifically for low-resolution laser-printer output. This was Lucida, designed by Kris Holmes with Charles Bigelow, then a professor of digital typography at Stanford, a close colleague

9. In the days of hand-set metal type, a 'font' in English was a set of characters of any one size and style: say, 8 point Baskerville Italic. In this example the 'typeface' was Baskerville. Such a font was given a separate price and each could be bought separately: so one could buy the 8 point italic without the 8 point roman. With the coming of typesetting that generated multiple styles and sizes from a single set of master characters, this distinction broke down: 'typefaces' became 'fonts'.

of Donald Knuth, and among the typographers who had collaborated on the TeX and Metafont work. (Others included Richard
Southall, Matthew Carter, and Hermann Zapf.) It would be some
years before the new software companies began to harness their
local typeface design intelligence. In January 1986 the LaserWriter
Plus was launched, with several of the Adobe/ITC fonts built in to it.
They now became the familiar repertoire of downmarket, generic
desktop publishing.[10] In 1986 also, Fontographer was launched by
the Altsys Corporation in Richardson, Texas (a rare exception to the
Silicon Valley rule). Until its recent displacement by FontLab, Fontographer was the dominant design program for typeface designers
working on Macintoshes.

Font wars

Adobe Systems made two formats for PostScript fonts: Type 1 and
Type 3 (there was no Type 2).[11] The Type 3 specification was pub-
licly available, but it was inferior to the unpublished Type 1 format.
Notable among the features of Type 1 was the 'hinting' of fonts:
the capacity of the font information to adapt for optimum charac-
ter form on low-resolution devices, most importantly on screens.
Behaving like any self-interested commercial concern, Adobe kept
Type 1 to itself, reaping the rewards. It did however develop a com-
mercial product (Display PostScript – later developed as Adobe Type
Manager) which could visualize PostScript data on screen.

   This was the background against which rivals to PostScript
Type 1 began to be developed. For a time, the font industry became
fevered, with shareholders' meetings and industry conferences
becoming theatres of high drama. It was in this atmosphere that the
term 'font wars' became current. In an unlikely alliance, Apple and
Microsoft joined forces to develop a new format that would be an
alternative to PostScript Type 1. In 1991 this was launched as True-
Type. The font format was Apple's, while Microsoft made the imag-
ing technology (TrueImage, which never functioned properly and
soon fell by the wayside). Adobe's response was to issue Adobe Type
Manager, their software for improving the display of Type 1 fonts on
screens and the output of these fonts on non-PostScript printers.
And in 1990 it had also published the Type 1 format specifications.
Thus, belatedly, the knowledge for making fully workable fonts

was available, and the way was open for hundreds of one-person typefoundries to bloom. In opening up its secret, Adobe was bowing to the inevitable: the Type 1 format had already been 'reverse-engineered' (by the Bitstream typefoundry in Boston).

The TrueType format had advantages over PostScript Type 1 in allowing designers to control character shape at particular sizes. The smaller the size, the wider and bolder the characters could and should become – for visually satisfactory results. This ancient wisdom had been lost in the technologies of photocomposition and of PostScript type. TrueType also required only one file to hold data, where PostScript Type 1 needed two. TrueType had been conceived of as a displacing rival to Adobe's technology, but by the time it was released a pact between the companies had been agreed, whereby the two formats could co-exist, running on any computing platform for which they had been fitted.

The 1990s saw a game of leapfrog, as the main participating companies – Adobe, Apple, Microsoft were those most visible to typographers – developed a succession of modifications to extend their products. As always in the history of typography, there could be no pure 'design'. Rather, design was inextricably intertwined with technics and commerce. Despite its superiority over Type 1, TrueType never quite found its place – perhaps entrapped by its association with Microsoft's Windows, and thus not part of a designer's world. Apple went ahead with attempts to develop more sophisticated font formats, most especially in its QuickDraw GX project. Adobe developed its Multiple Masters format, which offered infinite formal sophistication, and perhaps for this reason was hardly taken up by designers. Then in 1996, in a surprise move, Adobe and Microsoft announced that they would develop a new font format, OpenType, which would combine PostScript and TrueType. The same file would run on PCs and on Macintoshes. The fonts would possess the

10. See the discussion by type industry insiders at: <www.xnet.se/xpo/typetalk/>.
11. In this section I rely on two accounts by industry insiders: 'The history of fonts' by L. Leurs at <www.prepressure.com/fonts/history01.htm>, and 'Type 1, TrueType, OpenType' by Tom Arah at <www.designer-info.com/Writing/font_formats.htm>.

formal sophistication of TrueType. And further, OpenType would incorporate the Unicode character set of 64,000 glyphs in one package, and thus would be capacious enough to represent any of the world's languages.[12] This was certainly a huge advance on the old 256 glyph limit of the previous standard (extended ASCII), which had excluded scripts such as Arabic or Chinese from proper typographic representation, and allowed full representation of Latin-script languages (small capitals, alternative sets of numerals) only by add-on 'expert sets'. The first OpenType fonts were released in 2000. The new format promised an end to the font wars. Though for as long as typography is made with tools that are sold on the market, there will be rivalries, conflicts of interest, incompatibilities.

Legibility wars

The technical disputes of those years began to be accompanied by some fighting on the front of style and visual appearance. As the younger font designers began to get their work into commercial circulation, there was discussion. This erupted especially in the pages of *Emigre*, in debates that spilled over now and then into the other graphic design magazines. It was primarily a North American affair, drawing sustenance from the explosion on the US campuses of what became known as 'Theory' (broadly: a set of ideas taken from the poststructuralist writers in France, in which 'difference' and plurality were prized, in which any notion of centrality was disparaged and disbelieved, in which the world consisted most importantly of 'discourse'). Things were quieter in the United Kingdom, and quieter still on the European mainland, not to speak of everywhere else in the world. The pragmatic Neville Brody got on with the work, while his in-house theorist, Jon Wozencroft, wrote apocalyptic prose that ranged way beyond mere graphic design.[13] In 1986, the magazine *Octavo* was established in London by the design group 8vo: young Weingartians, fresh from Basel, and bitingly critical of British commercial design (in which category they included Neville Brody). True to their education, 8vo's interest was in graphic design rather than typefaces. Through the eight issues of the publication, they proudly used only one typeface – the immaculate and thoroughly Swiss Unica (designed in the 1970s by André Gürtler, Erich Gschwind, and Christian Mengelt at Basel). Only in 1990, in the seventh of *Octavo*'s predetermined eight issues, did they join the growing discussion of legibility, in 'Type and image' by Bridget Wilkins.

The 'legibility' discussion was then taking off in *Emigre*. This was the time of the 'Do you read me?' issue (no.15, 1990). It was there that VanderLans and Licko formulated the words that would become the slogan of the magazine and font foundry: 'Typefaces are not intrinsically legible. Rather, it is the reader's familiarity with faces that accounts for their legibility.'[14] Beside this thought was placed the idea that typefaces and typography should be personally expressive, in contradiction to the idea that text should be an invisible container of thought. Two sources were found for the theory of invisible typography that was then opposed: the Swiss or Swiss-inclined modernists of the 1950s and 1960s, and Beatrice Warde's notion of the 'crystal goblet'. Warde's broadly anti-modernist essay of 1932 was thus given a second life, but as 'straw man': dug up, only to be pilloried with derision and buried with the corpse of Swiss modernism. Behind these attacks there worked a politics of identity: a peculiarly Protestant-American interpretation of the post-structuralist theory of 'difference', which lapsed back into a simple espousal of the liberty of the individual. Typography was a matter of personal expression, and its products could not be separated from their makers: any criticism of the product was thus a comment on the makers and – but in quite abstract terms – on the clan or class to which they belonged. While this view had the appearance of radicalism (those at the margins of society were given their due), it could have no grip on the social, intersubjective processes of making texts and reading them.

The pursuit of the personal politics of legibility reached a climax in the mid-1990s in the theory issues of *Emigre*: from the first small (near A4) format issue (no. 33) to the 'Mercantile' issue

12. In distinction to the old typographic term 'character', 'glyph' has become current, meaning: the visible forms that are used to display encoded text. For example, the characters 'f' and 'i' can be represented by a single glyph, the fi ligature.

13. See the concluding section ('Language') to Brody, *The graphic language of Neville Brody*, pp.156–9.

14. From an editorial display accompanying an interview between Licko and Vanderlans: *Emigre*, no.15, 1990. p.12.

(no. 42), which signalled the magazine's turn to a more concerted
commercial policy. From that point, in 1997, like any trade magazine, *Emigre* was sent free to customers in the USA.[15]

   A poetics of style
In 1992 Robert Bringhurst's *The elements of typographic style* was
published in Vancouver. The author had come to typography
from outside the sphere of design and printing; he was doubly an
outsider in being Canadian in a field that had been defined, predominantly, in the USA and Europe. He was a poet and a critic of
literature and art, with considerable learning and expertise in the
native cultures and languages of North America; by this time he was
also a book designer and evidently had a very extensive command
of the knowledge of typography. Bringhurst's book took the model
of the manual of literary style and applied it to the more visual and
technical domain of typography. *The elements of typographic style*
soon became established as a desk-companion to which book designers (especially) could turn for illumination on all the disparate
questions that their work must entail – choice of typeface, choice of
page format, disposition of text on a page, use of diacritics, technical terminology, and so on.
   In its first context of the struggle to establish standards in the
new domain of desktop publishing, and the squabbles over 'legibility', *The elements of typographic style* found its place: a serene yet
richly detailed overview besides which shoddy contemporary production could be measured and improved (it was a practical work).
The book was evidently written by a poet and had an incantatory
manner, yet the material was well structured and included simple,
well-judged illustrations. This 'scriptural' quality was emphasized
by the numbered maxims that punctuated the discussion; in the
second edition (1996) these were reprised at the end of the book. In
this respect, and in others too, Bringhurst joined hands with other
recent charismatic writers – Christopher Alexander (in his 'Pattern
Language' books) or Edward Tufte (the set of books started with *The
visual display of quantative data*). A comparison with Tufte, whose
books are recommended in *The elements*, suggests that while both
these writers may enjoy a certain cult status and while both have
the omnivorous, driven passion of the late arriver in their field of

discovery, it is Bringhurst who is the more practical – because less messianic and more modest in tone and means.

The flavour of *The elements of typographic style* was immediately signalled by the advocating words of Hermann Zapf on the back cover of both its editions: 'I wish to see this book become the Typographers' Bible.' In some of its manner, *The elements* was certainly biblical. It was also Zapfian: it suffered from over-polishing and a lack of realism – a lack of what might seem ungainly grit in the detail. Bringhurst's thought and his information were spoiled by overwriting. For example, a good point about the difference between logotypes (logos) and type becomes obscured by the simile: logos are like candy or drugs, type like bread. (*The elements of typographic style*, 2nd edn, 1996, p. 49.) In part these remarks about *The elements* make an aesthetic judgement, from one who prefers the strong (also delicate) sculptural quality of a Frutiger to the calligraphic perfume of much of Zapf's work. Yet, as in any aesthetic judgement, there is a wider judgement here too. For all its learning, for all the width of its reference, Bringhurst's book lacked a critical or historical sense. In this vision, concentrated so exclusively on the well-resolved product and neglecting the dimension of process (and thus the unfinished, the disputed, the failed and discarded), there could be no power of explanation.

A practical example

In the sphere of typeface design, aside from the eruption of the new young font designers, there were some notable contributions that exemplify the notion of critical thinking embodied within the design and making process – within form. The prime case is the work of Matthew Carter, who emerged out of a long and varied learning period, primarily with Mergenthaler Linotype in New York (1965–71), to produce substantial typefaces for photocomposition (ITC Galliard, a loose revival of sixteenth-century types cut by Robert Granjon), for CRT typesetting (Bell Centennial, a sanserif for telephone directories), then for digital typesetting proper (Bitstream Charter, an ahistorical roman, whose formal details were

15. In 2003, from no. 64, *Emigre* began to appear as thematically unified small books, co-published with Princeton Architectural Press.

conditioned by the constraint of cutting down the work of computer processing). Carter – son of Harry Carter, pre-eminent British
typographer and historian of typography – had a natural access to
the history of the activity: both in his early days as part of the group
who in the mid-1950s helped to sort and identify the holdings of
the Plantin-Moretus archives in Antwerp, and then later in his entry
into the American type industry. (It seems clear that the British type
world, such as it was by the 1960s, could offer him no worthwhile
position.) In 1981, with Mike Parker (another British expatriate, also
one of the Plantin archives group), he left Mergenthaler Linotype to
join in establishing Bitstream, an early purely digital type company.

   Matthew Carter's achievement was to ride the waves of technical advance, without losing sight of the notion of quality and the
lessons of history, and to show again that the deepest contributions in typography are often made in-house, semi-anonymously,
and for highly 'industrial' uses (newspapers, telephone directories,
display screens). His path shows an engagement with problems and
challenges as they come up – for whatever language-script (he has
been interested to work outside the Latin canon), in whatever style
(historical or not), and for whatever medium (print, screen). In this
respect, Carter can be placed properly in the company of the twentieth-century masters of type design – a Dwiggins or a Frutiger. The
new conditions of type manufacture, of the small digital typefoundry run by the designers themselves, while seeming to be a liberation may rather be a discouragement to design – by introducing a
small cult of the designers and their personalities, and by cutting
out the challenge of the large and necessarily impersonal commission.

   Reform and research
The coming of desktop publishing took away the impetus from the
effort of reform that had been evident in Europe, and especially in
Britain, in the 1960s and 1970s. These campaigns were conducted by
typographers and others in the industry, in the national and international standardization organizations, in professional and educational forums. Most notable in this loose movement of reform was
the effort to introduce the metric system to typography. For a while,
as photocomposition and lithographic printing came to displace

metal, there seemed to be some hope that machine manufacturers and printers could be persuaded to leave behind the irrationality of using both a common cultural unit (inch or millimetre) and the typographic one (the Anglo-American or Didot point). Further, a metric point would resolve the long-term anomaly of the two typographic points, as well as joining typography to the common world of production. At the same time, much of the seeming terminological and procedural muddle of letterpress typography, especially as it had been transferred to the bodiless sphere of lithography and photocomposition, could now be cleared up. The measurement of type could be done by what one actually saw displayed (capital height and x-height), rather than by reference some mysterious 'body' surrounding the image of the letter. The terminological hangovers from letterpress could be reformed too. Thus the unclear term 'leading' (originally, strips of lead inserted between lines of type) would be replaced by an unambiguous measurement from baseline to baseline in lines of text. Much consideration was given also to the work of specifying for production. Success in production then depended on clear instructions from the typographer to those running the machines of composition and reproduction. The presence in this process of computers – the large 'mainframe' computers that in those years were being introduced into the processes of text composition – only intensified the need for clarity of description.

The computers introduced into typography in the 1980s were, however, of a different order from those considered by the Typographers' Computer Working Group in Britain in the 1960s and 1970s. The new machines sat on the desk of the designers, who did not formulate instructions but rather composed the pages themselves. The software that began to be supplied for this work was written for the most part by computing engineers in North America, largely innocent of typography and the possibilities for its reform. The model of typography that they and the sales departments of their companies followed was regressive: they imagined assemblies of metal type gripped in rectangular frames, and wrapped their products in the language and the myths of metal printing. The first assumption of desktop publishing was that the user would work in inches. The typographic point was now rationalized to an even 1/72 part of an inch (as against a 1/72.27 part). Though so quick and so fine was the processing of the new device that perhaps it made no difference what the units of measurement were. Users could enter the units in which they were working, and the machine would accept those and display the result in its preferred units, as near as made no difference. In the new conditions, in which display screens and printers now played determining roles, and were calibrated in yet other units (dots per inch, pixels per inch), instant machine translation of measurement systems saved the day. But the description of type size would remain unresolved: based on a dimensional reference (the em square) which might be clear to those originating the product, but which was entirely opaque to users.

Information design

To some extent the energies of the reformers of the 1960s and 1970s were subsumed into what began to be known, towards the end of the 1970s, as 'information design'.[16] This field of practice was characterized by a much greater theoretical consciousness than was usual in graphic design (or typography). The attempt of information design was to use research and reflection in the work of making products and systems that could be useful in the world. This newly designated field, with its echoes of the thoroughly quantified 'information theory' of Claude Shannon's work in the Bell Laboratories in the 1940s, now provided a home for staple components of an enlightened typography: research into legibility of typefaces and into the effectiveness of particular pages or configurations of text, the ordering and classification of the materials of the typography, an emphasis on processes of production on a large scale and their co-ordination, the harnessing of technics through the development and standardization of instructional procedures. All this was by contrast to the habitually one-off and almost untutored nature of graphic design, and its celebration in the cult of the designer.

In great contrast to the 'theory' that figured in the 'legibility wars', the theories of information design have been modest and often unashamedly empirical. And while the legibility warriors set themselves the hopeless task of importing into practice a theory that was one of reception, imagining that it could inform production, information designers have begun to learn the limits of what research into the reception or use of products might really tell us.

As the history of legibility research shows, it is only in more extreme conditions – of low illumination, or severely degraded output, or partially sighted readers – that clear results can be found. In average conditions it seems that human beings can read and process adequately any text that interests them – and that choice of typeface and manner of typesetting make no significant difference. Then there is much to be said for a pragmatic approach that tempers 'good form', and the wisdom of craft approaches, with the hard lessons of user-testing – when time and money allow for that.

The story of the design practice MetaDesign provides some illustration of these themes. Founded in 1983 in Berlin by the German typographer Erik Spiekermann, MetaDesign – as its name suggested – hoped to introduce a more reflective approach to graphic design than was usual. It engaged in all the usual tasks of graphic design, and though, for obvious practical reasons, could not usually include research into effectiveness into its design processes, it did often show intelligence and critical consciousness in its work – in the modern tradition. The ambition of MetaDesign was to bring this intelligence to the largest design tasks, usually then in Germany given to advertising agencies. Quite soon the practice was working for the Deutsche Bundespost (the German Post Office), redesigning much of its printed output in detail. Spiekermann and his colleagues were virtuosi of forms design. Especially after 1989, with the unification of Germany and Berlin in particular, MetaDesign was able to realize some of the hopes for design as a socially vital activity. Their work on signing and information-provision for the Berliner Verkehrs-Vertrieb (the Berlin transport authority) was the great demonstration of these ideals. But with the fearless plunge into designing for large organizations, so MetaDesign itself changed. By the end of the 1990s the practice had the makings of being a small empire, with offices also in San Francisco and London. Soon (in 2000) Spiekermann was pushed out of the company, and then (in 2001) MetaDesign was sold to an international 'branding firm' of

16. Among the events in the identification of information design were the NATO Conference on Visual Presentation of Information, held at Het Vennenbos in the Netherlands in 1978, and the founding in 1979 of *Information Design Journal*.

the most nebulous kind. This passage, which could be amplified by other case-histories of the time, was from the straightforward to the overblown, from the real to the specious.

Debates over the modern

In the period under focus in this chapter – from 1973 through to the present – the debate over the modern has been relentless, and so loud and contradictory that it is tempting to resign from it and forsake the use of the term altogether. Descriptions of what has happened, rather than a fight over slogans and terms, will get us nearer to the truth. But in drawing this book about the modern to a close, it is necessary to provide at least a sketch of what has been said: that, too, is what has happened.

Modernism, in its post-1945 Western variety, came to a halt in the 1970s. It was followed by what became known, above all in architecture, as postmodernism. Broadly, the term denoted an espousal of all the things that modernism was said to have rejected. Postmodernism was said to describe the embrace of complexity (as against simplicity), of non-rectangularity (as against the grid), of popularity (as against elitism), of diversity (against monoculture), of the old (against the new), and so on. But already, as the last opposition on this list begins to show, the categories became muddled. Postmodernism was sometimes, with justice, seen as simply the next stage of modernism. (Figures such as the composer John Cage or, from a later generation, the architect Rem Koolhaas, can be understood as at once very modernist and very postmodernist.) And different cultures provided notably different contexts for work: the slow-moving Swiss culture was very different from the more febrile culture of the United Kingdom, and both, in turn, were quite other than the cultures of the United States – often very slow to change (Iowa), and often very quick (urban California).

With the dissolution of the Soviet Union in the early 1990s, a fundamental point of reference in ideas and views of the modern was changed. Modernism in the earlier twentieth century, but much less so in its post-1945 remembrance, had been tied to the idea of political revolution, and – however brutal and stale that focus of political change had been, almost from its outset – the landscape of power now changed. Although, in its corruption and oligarchic nature, the Soviet world had become a force against the modern, it also gave some evidence for the view that the really radical and ruthless force for change was capitalism, not socialism. Certainly, since the end of communism, and with less impediment from socialist and social-democratic forces, the pace of change has quickened: the enlargement of the market to global proportions, the spread of the transnational corporations, the spread of English as a world language, the near-universal adoption of rationalized ways of building, the adoption of the internet as a genuinely global carrier for the traffic of communication. In this context, the idea of modernity carries very mixed meanings. 'Modernity' (as distinct from 'modernism') comes to seem a code-word for capitalism, rather than for enlightenment. The style of this latest phase in the West is an imitation of an earlier and rather more authentic moment of modernizing: the pop culture of the mid-1960s, when sanserifs and geometry were discovered or perhaps rediscovered for the first time.

Global prospects

A hopeful claim might be that with the increasing intermeshing of cultures – the migration of peoples to the developed West, as much as the spread of capital and technics to the now developing parts of the world – some unexpected and genuinely humane results will follow. In typography, the best evidence for this is in the emergence of small centres of design and production in places that have been without any culture of the activity, unless it was a very old and subsequently broken one. For example, some of the most serious and inventive work in typeface design is being done in places and for language-scripts that have been on the periphery of the American and North European forcing grounds: the Czech Republic, Russia, Greece, Portugal, Spain, and – though one might say that there the tradition was hardly broken – Italy. In Latin America schools and centres of design show signs of new life. Arabic typography and type design is now the subject of considerable investigation. Now that the technics of adequate typographic representation for Arabic or similarly complex language-scripts is available (at a certain price), results must begin to follow.

The phrase 'democratization of typography' has become common, referring to the wide availability of the tools of production for type and typographic design. One may take this with some scepticism: after all, for the majority, the generation and production of these tools is still largely in the hands of a few corporations – though the open source software movement may provide an alternative. If 'democracy' implies a spreading of power to the people, this is the wrong description for what is going on here: it is more a simple spreading of typography among the masses. The astonishing development in this period has not been the contribution of any designer or writer, but rather the spread of the means of making sophisticated typography to anyone with a computer. The domain of typography has been opened up, as never before, and there is a much wider interest in the activity now than there was even twenty years ago. The internet provides the platform for this enlarged and changed culture of typography: of practical example, of sales and exchange of tools, of discussion and sharing of knowledge. The printed page becomes both less prevalent (overtaken by electronic transfer and display) and more important (a stable record of knowledge that will outlast the transience of digital formats). The great negative of the modern – irrevocable and disastrous damage to the natural world – gathers terrifying pace. Enlightenment thus proceeds, amid much babble and confusion. The watchwords remain: doubt, critique, reason, hope.

14   Examples

Items are shown here in one of three reductions: to 33, 40 or 50 per cent. Same-size details are added, to show things of special interest. In books, page counts refer to the total number of pages in an item, whether the pages carry numbers or not.

1. A system of measuring type
Diagram engraved by G. Quineau, Paris, c. 1700
340 x 223 mm, intaglio
This document, never formally published, survives among
the materials left from the work of the Académie des
Sciences in investigating and systematizing printing. Its
importance is that it shows the application of rational
principles to the measurement of type. Until that time there
had been no explicit system of measurement of printing
materials, and sizes of type had been described merely by
the informal set of names deployed. This system, devised by
Sébastien Truchet, is as follows. At the bottom we see a scale
showing one 'ligne' – then part of the officially recognized
system of measurement in France – divided into 204 parts.
In the five rows above are: the major vertical dimensions of
a font (x-height, capital-height, the whole body), and then the
capital-height and whole body dimensions of larger sizes.
Sizes are graduated in steps. Thus, in the fifth row, from the
left, the sizes are: 37 lignes and 68/204ths, 32 lignes, 26 and
136/204ths, and so on. The whole is a prevision of the point
systems that were later adopted as the means of ordering
typography.

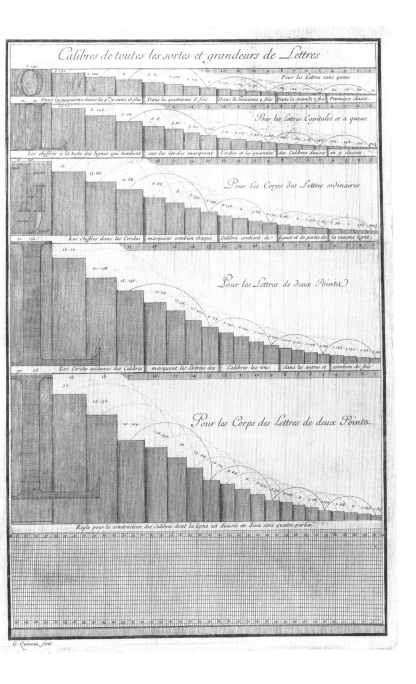

Calibres de toutes les sortes et grandeurs de Lettres

Pour les Lettres sans queue

Dans la cinquieme classe la p.ᵉ y entre 16 fois | Dans la quatrieme 8 fois | Dans la troisieme 4 fois | Dans la seconde 2 fois | Première classe

Pour les Lettres Capitales et a queue

Les chiffres a la teste des lignes qui tombent | sur les Cercles marquent | l'ordre et la quantité | des Calibres divisés en 5 classes

Pour les Corps des Lettres ordinaires

Les Chiffres dans les Cercles | marquent combien chaque | Calibre contient de | lignes et de partie de | la mesme ligne

Pour les Lettres de deux Points

Les Cercles au dessus des Calibres | marquent les Entrées des | Calibres les vns | dans les autres et | combien de fois

Pour les Corps des Lettres de deux Points

Regle pour la construction des Calibres dont la ligne est divisée en deux cens quatre parties

G. Quineau fecit

185

2. Fertel's manual

Martin Dominique Fertel, *La Science pratique de l'imprimerie*, Saint-Omer: Fertel, 1723

252 x 195 mm [this trimmed copy], 322 pp, letterpress

From the first substantial French manual for printers, the spread (below) shows the characteristic method of Fertel's book. A typical (imagined) title-page is shown on the right-hand page, with an explanation and annotations on the left. Here as elsewhere, Fertel is concerned with the way typography and the form of the book can structure information: the title-page becomes a means of signalling content in some detail (the two-column list of themes). At the foot of the example, Fertel points to the 'M' on a new signature of his own text.

LA SCIENCE
PRATIQUE
DE L'IMPRIMERIE.

CONTENANT
DES INSTRUCTIONS TRÉS-FACILES
POUR SE PERFECTIONNER DANS CET ART.

ON Y TROUVERA UNE DESCRIPTION DE toutes les pieces dont une Presse est construite, avec le moyen de remedier à tous les défauts qui peuvent y survenir.

Avec une Methode nouvelle & fort aisée pour imposer toutes sortes d'impositions, depuis l'In-folio jusqu'à l'in cent-vingt-huit.

De plus, on y a joint des Tables pour sçavoir ce que les Caracteres inferieurs reçoivent & ce que leur font superieurs, & un Tarif pour trouver, d'un coup d'œil, combien de Formes contiendra une copie d'imprimer, très-utile pour les Auteurs & Marchands Libraires qui font imprimer leurs Ouvrages à leurs dépens.

Le tout representé avec des Figures en bois & en taille douce.

A SAINT OMER,
Par MARTIN DOMINIQUE FERTEL, Imprimeur & Marchand Libraire, rue des Epeciers, à l'Image de Saint Bertin.

M. DCC. XXIII.

AVEC APPROBATION ET PRIVILEGE DU ROI.

Explication de la troisième Démonstration, avec un modèle pour les Additions au bas des pages, distinguées par des lettrines entre deux parenthèses.

QUAND il y a plusieurs périodes dans une première page & que la première a quelque rapport aux mots essentiels (a) du titre, on peut faire cette première période de lettres capitales de différente grosseur, en faisant une ligne courte avec les premiers mots de ladite (b) période, lorsqu'elle arrive immédiatement après une ligne longue, comme il se rencontre dans cette Démonstration.

Les autres (c) périodes suivantes, doivent être du bas de casse, les unes de caractère romain, & les autres d'italique que alternativement, & de différents corps.

Lorsque le nom &, les *qualités* d'un *Auteur* se rencontrent immédiatement après quelques lignes de caractère romain du bas de casse, on doit faire les *qualités* du bas de casse italique & le *nom* de l'*Auteur* de caractère italique de même caractère, en observant de séparer les lettres capitales d'une grosse ou d'une fine espace, suivant que le terrain de la place le permettra.

Quand il y a à la fin d'un titre les mots de *nouvelle Edition*, &c. qui ne peuvent entrer en une ligne de capitales, comme il se voit dans la cinquième Démonstration de ces premieres pages, on doit les faire du bas de casse italique lorsqu'ils suivent quelques lignes de romain de bas de casse : Si au contraire, ils sont précedés d'une période qui sera de bas de casse italique, on doit faire ces mots (d) de *nouvelle Edition &c* du bas de casse d'un caractère romain, comme il se voit dans la présente Démonstration.

(a) Voyez les lignes des nombres 4. & 5.

(b) Voyez le mot de Communion, qu'il se met le plus distinctement au nomb. 3.

(c) Voyez les trois périodes qui sont le nomb. 6. 7. & 8.

(d) Pour le mot de nouvelle Edition &c. voyez le nomb. 8.

INSTRUCTION

INSTRUCTION
POUR FAIRE SA PREMIERE
COMMUNION;
TRÉS-UTILE
POUR LA JEUNESSE
CHRÉTIENNE.

AVEC UNE ADDITION DE TROIS LEÇONS
pour ceux qui font plus avancés

*Par le Revernd Pere CHIFFLET, de la Compagnie
de JESUS.*

Nouvelle Edition, augmentée de plusieurs Actes de Vertus, &
de Prieres pour assister à la Sainte Messe.

ECCE PANIS ANGELORUM

A BRUXELLES,
Chez EUGENE HENRY FRICX, Imprimeur du Roy,
vis-à-vis de l'Eglise de la Madeleine.
M. DCC. VII.
Avec plusieurs Approbations, & Privilege du Roy.
☞ Cette page est la Squunte.

3. Music printing and the 'Dutch taste'
Leopold Mozart, *Grondig onderwys in het be-
handelen der viool*, Haarlem: Enschedé, 1766
280 x 220 mm, 280 pp, letterpress
Techniques and systems of reproducing
musical notation by letterpress printing
type, rather than from engraved plates, were
developed in the middle of the eighteenth
century. This book shows an early use of
typeset music, and also one of its technical
advantages: music and text could be set and
printed in one process only. The music type
was cut for Enschedé by J.M. Fleischman.
The text typeface shows characteristic
'Dutch' features of that time: lateral conden-
sation and a slightly ungainly purposeful-
ness.

84   ONDERWYS IN HET

§. 22.

Het is heel wat anders, wanneer de Comprijs de Strykaart door een Verbindingssteken antwoord. By voorbeeld:

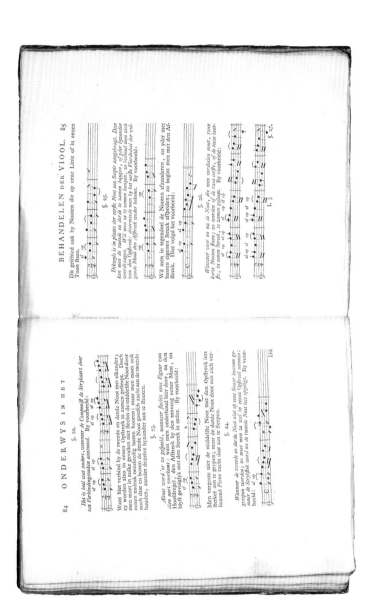

Want hier verbind hy de tweede en derde Noot met elkander; zy worden alzo in eenen Opstreek te zamen getleeft. Doch men moet in zulke gevallen niet flechts de middelfte Noot door eenen indruk tweeverdig haaren hooren: maar men moet ook noch daar en boven de derde Noot gantsch zacht aan de tweede houden, zonder dezelve byzonder aan te stooten.

Altoos word 'er zo gespeeld, wanneer flechts eene Figuur van dien aart voorkomt: want men onderhoud hier door, na den Hoofdregel, den Aftreek by den aanvang eener Maat, en blyft gevolglyk met den Streek in order. By voorbeeld:

Men vergeete niet de middelfte Noot met den Opstreek iets sterker te grypen; maar die derde Noot door een zich verliezent Piano zacht daar aan te sleepen.

§. 24.

Wanneer de tweede en derde Noot niet op eene Snaar kunnen gegreepen worden; zo moet men ze wel in eenen Opstreek neemen: maar de Stryfflag word na de tweede Noot iets opgeligt. By voorbeeld:

Dit

BEHANDELEN DER VIOOL.   85

Dit geschied ook by Nooten die op eene Linie of in eenen Toon staan.

§. 25.

Dikwyls is in plaats der eerste Noot een Sospir aangebragt. Dan kan men de tweede en derde te zamen haggen, of flet byzonder voordraagen. Wil men ze te zamen hangen, zo behind men zich van den Opstreek: daarmede men by ter eerfte Pärdehel der volgende Maat den Aftreek weder bekomt. By voorbeeld:

Wil men in tegendeel de Nooten afzonderen, en yder met haaren eigenen Streek affpeelen; zo begint men met den Aftreek. Hier volgt het voorbeeld:

§. 26.

Wanneer voor en na de Noot, die men verdeelen moet, twee korte Nooten staan; zo worden of die eerste twee, of de twee laatste, in eenen Streek, te zamen gesleept. By voorbeeld:

§. 27.

L 3

4. An approach to book design

J.J. Rousseau, *Dictionnaire de musique*, vol. 2 (*Oeuvres de J.J. Rousseau, avec des notes historiques*), Paris: Lefèvre, 1819

212 x 130 mm, letterpress, with intaglio plates

This volume from a collected edition of Rousseau's writings shows a certain tradition in typography and book-making well established – and the use of Didot 'modern' types. The configuration of the content shows the ease with which the neoclassical manner could handle most kinds of book-work. Yet there are subtleties of treatment here that lift this edition above the norm: the use of small capitals and italics for the coding of special terms and for headings; the fractions and maths signs; and especially the engraved pull-out plates at the end of the book, which can thus accompany the text as one turns the pages. The copy shown has survived in what must be its first paper-covered cased binding; the pages are uncut.

OEUVRES
DE
J. J. ROUSSEAU,
AVEC DES NOTES HISTORIQUES.

DICTIONNAIRE DE MUSIQUE, TOME II.

A PARIS,
CHEZ LEFÈVRE, LIBRAIRE,
RUE DE L'ÉPERON, N° 6.

M. DCCC. XIX.

A PARIS,
DE L'IMPRIMERIE DE CRAPELET.
1819

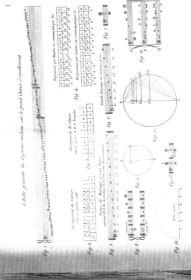

Échelle générale du système moderne sur le grand Clavier à resoudissement

chez l'intervalle en abaissant le son supérieur, ou élevant l'inférieur seulement d'un ½, aussitôt le son produit descendra d'un ton. Faites la même opération sur le *semi-ton* majeur, et le son produit descendra d'une quinte.

Quoique la production du troisième son ne se borne pas à ces intervalles, nos notes n'en pouvant exprimer de plus composé, il est pour le présent inutile d'aller au-delà de ceux-ci.

On voit dans la suite régulière des consonnances qui composent cette table qu'elles se rapportent toutes à une basse commune, et produisent toutes exactement le même troisième son.

Voilà donc, par ce nouveau phénomène, une démonstration physique de l'unité du principe de l'harmonie.

Dans les sciences physico-mathématiques, telles que la musique, les démonstrations doivent bien être géométriques, mais déduites physiquement de la chose démontrée : c'est alors seulement que l'union du calcul à la physique fournit, dans les vérités établies sur l'expérience et démontrées géométriquement, les vrais principes de l'art ; autrement la géométrie seule donnera des théorèmes certains, mais sans usage dans la pratique ; la physique donnera des faits particuliers, mais isolés, sans liaison entre eux et sans aucune loi générale.

Le principe physique de l'harmonie est un, comme nous venons de le voir, et se résout dans la propor-

tion harmonique : or ces deux propriétés conviennent au cercle ; car nous verrons bientôt qu'on y retrouve les deux autres extrêmes de le monde et du son ; et quant à la proportion harmonique, elle s'y trouve aussi, puisque dans quelque point C (*Planche* 1, *figure* 9) que l'on coupe inégalement le diamètre A B, le carré de l'ordonnée C D sera moyen proportionnel harmonique entre les deux rectangles des parties A C et C B du diamètre par le rayon, propriété qui suffit pour établir la nature harmonique du cercle : car bien que les ordonnées soient moyennes géométriques entre les parties du diamètre, les carrés de ces ordonnées étant moyens harmoniques entre les rectangles, leurs rapports représentent d'autant plus exactement ceux des cordes sonores, que les rapports de ces cordes ou des poids tendeurs sont aussi comme les carrés, tandis que les sons sont comme les racines.

Maintenant, du diamètre A B (*Planche* 1, *fig.* 10), divisé selon la série des fractions ½ ⅓ ¼ ⅕ ; lesquelles sont en progression harmonique, soient tirées les ordonnées C, C G ; G G ; c, c e ; e e ; g, g g.

Le diamètre représente une corde sonore, qui, divisée en pareilles raisons, donne les sons indiqués dans l'exemple O de la même *Planche*, *figure* 11.

Pour éviter les fractions, donnons 60 parties au diamètre, les sections contiendront ces nombres entiers BC $=\frac{1}{2}=$ 30 ; BG $=\frac{1}{3}=$ 20 ; Bc $=\frac{1}{4}=$ 15 ; Be $=\frac{1}{5}=$ 12 ; Bg $=\frac{1}{6}=$ 10.

5. Mass-producing the classics

Charles Montesquieu, *Considérations sur les causes de la grandeur des Romans et de leur décadence*, Paris: Borrani, [no date]

140 x 85 mm, 236 pp, letterpress

In the 1790s the Didots (Firmin and Pierre l'aîné, with Louis-Etienne Herhan) developed their version of the stereotype process and began to apply it in book production. In stereotyping, metal plates were made from pages of type. The procedure was well suited to printing established or classic texts in large numbers (type was preserved, the text was stabilized). The type is a Didot roman, with the rough, slightly irregular appearance that must be the result of stereotyping and then multiple printing from the plates. Its (first?) owner dated this book '26 Sept '88'; and the ornaments of the border on the cover suggest that kind of date for publication. Yet the typography of the pages – fixed by stereotype – seems to date from early in the century.

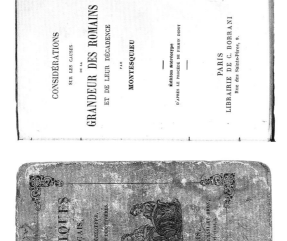

du vingtieme: la puissance de Rome étoit donc à celle d'Athenes, dans ces divers temps, à-peu-près comme un quart est à un vingtieme, c'est-à-dire qu'elle étoit cinq fois plus grande.

Les rois Agis et Cléomenes voyant qu'à Sparte du temps de Lycurgue (1), il n'y en avoit plus que neuf mille citoyens (2), et qu'il n'y en avoit plus que sept cents, dont à peine cent possédoient des terres (2), et que tout le reste n'étoit qu'une populace sans courage, ils entreprirent de rétablir les lois à cet égard (3); et Lacédémone reprit sa premiere puissance, et redevint formidable à tous les Grecs.

Ce fut le partage égal des terres qui rendit Rome capable de sortir d'abord de son abaissement; et cela se sentit bien quand elle fut corrompue.

Elle étoit une petite république lorsque, les Latins ayant refusé le secours de troupes qu'ils étoient obligés de donner, on leva sur-le-champ dix légions dans la ville (4). « A peine à « présent, dit Tite-Live, Rome, que le monde « entier ne peut contenir, en pourroit-elle faire

(1) C'étoient des citoyens de la ville appelés proprement Spartiates. Lycurgue fit pour eux neuf mille parts; il en avoua trente mille aux autres habitans. Voyez Plutarque, vie de Lycurgue, tom. 1, p. 177, édit. de Cassac.—(2) Voyez Plutarque, vie d'Agis et de Cléomenes, t. 7, p. 365.—(3) Voyez Plutarque, ibid., p. 370, 371, 372.—(4) Tite-Live, premiere decade, l. 7, ch. 25, &c. fut quelque temps après la prise de Rome, sous le consulat de L. Furius Camillus, et de Ap. Claudius Crassus.

« autant si un ennemi paroissoit tout-à-coup « devant ses murailles; marque certaine que « nous ne nous sommes point agrandis, et que « nous n'avons fait qu'augmenter le luxe et les « richesses qui nous travaillent. »

« Dites-moi, disoit Tiberius Gracchus aux « nobles (1), qui vaut mieux, un citoyen ou un « esclave perpétuel; un soldat ou un homme « inutile à la guerre? Voulez-vous, pour avoir « quelques arpents de terre plus que les autres « citoyens, renoncer à l'espérance de la con-« quête du reste du monde, ou vous mettre en « danger de vous voir enlever par les ennemis « ces terres que vous nous refusez? »

(1) Appien, de la Guerre civile, l. 1, ch. 11.

CHAPITRE IV.

1. Des Gaulois. 2. De Pyrrhus. 3. Parallele de Carthage et de Rome. 4. Guerre d'Annibal.

LES Romains eurent bien des guerres avec les Gaulois. L'amour de la gloire, le mépris de la mort, l'obstination pour vaincre, étoient les mêmes dans les deux peuples; mais les armes étoient différentes. Le bouclier des Gaulois étoit petit, et leur épée mauvaise: aussi furent-ils traités à-peu-près comme, dans les derniers siecles, les Mexicains l'ont été par les

CHAPITRE IV.

1. Des Gaulois. 2. De Pyrrhus. 3. Parallele de Carthage et de Rome. 4. Guerre d'Annibal.

LES Romains eurent bien des guerres avec les Gaulois. L'amour de la gloire, le mépris de la mort, l'obstination pour vaincre, étoient les mêmes dans les deux peuples; mais les armes étoient différentes. Le bouclier des Gaulois étoit petit, et leur épée mauvaise: aussi furent-ils traités à-peu-près comme, dans les derniers siecles, les Mexicains l'ont été par les

6. A treatise on legibility

James Millington, *Are we to read backwards? or, what is the best print for the eyes?*, London: Field & Tuer, [1883]

140 x 112 mm, 100 pp, letterpress

Millington's pamphlet was an early and informal survey of legibility – research into the topic was then just getting under way. The style of the series, as elsewhere in Field & Tuer's publications, was one historical revival, showing an interest in pre-industrial letterforms and styles of printing. In this context, the handful of pictures to illustrate possibilities of presenting text in other ways (white out of black, or in a boustrophedon arrangement) seem rather startlingly graphic and forward-looking. The plate showing a disturbed reading image (below left) is the frontispiece of the book.

THE VELLUM-PARCHMENT SHILLING SERIES
OF MISCELLANEOUS LITERATURE.

ARE WE TO READ

BACKWARDS?

OR,

What is the Best Print for the Eyes?

BY

JAMES MILLINGTON.

WITH AN INTRODUCTION BY

R. BRUDENELL CARTER, F.R.C.S.

(ILLUSTRATED.)

ONE SHILLING.

LONDON:

Field & Tuer, Yᵉ Leadenhalle Presse, E.C.

Simpkin, Marshall & Co.; Hamilton, Adams & Co.

[COPYRIGHT]

Plate—5.

But when a boy leaves school for university or college, he learns if botany be a branch of his studies, that the word for tea is a contraption of the Chinese *T'sia* or *Tcha, Cha.* This is right enough; and he is also taught that there are three distinct species of the tea plant, all belonging to the natural family Ternstromiaceæ, namely *Thea viridis*, or green tea; *Thea Bobea,* and black tea; *Thea Assamensis,* which gives us the tea-plant of India. Assam, At most examinations he would run the risk of being plucked, it

Plate—2.

English as she is spoke.

We expect then, who the little book (for the care what we wrote him, and for her typographical correction) that may be worth the acceptation of the studious persons, and especially of the Youth, at which we dedicate him particularly.

The column in Portuguese which runs through out the original work is genuine, and only a number of the English leaves are given to enable the reader to form a just idea of the multitudinous attempts to follow the footsteps of "English as she is spoke" by the aid of a French dictionary and a phrase-book.

It is to be hoped the essence of "Guide" by which this short sketch is intended to serve as translation—and, so far as may be, elucidation—is now a fair specimen of Portuguese or Brazilian educational literature; if such as the case the schoolmaster is indeed

A MILE A MINUTE!

or,

How it looks in a Railway Carriage.

[See page 79

195

7. De Vinne's manuals
Theodore Low De Vinne, *The practice of typography*,
New York: The Century, 1900–4

190 x 130 mm, 406 + 478 + 484 + 478 pp, letterpress
De Vinne's four *Practice of typography* books put forward
an approach to printing that is mundane, and yet interested – in rich, subtle detail – in both technique and textual
meaning. Together they provided (and still provide) anyone
working in the production of printed matter with an extraordinary compendium of knowledge. The spread shown
here, from *Correct composition*, is quite typical of the ways
in which De Vinne uses the pages of his own books to enact
the points he makes. The *Practice of typography* books feel
almost perfectly made, in the disposition of their material,
in the way in which they lie compactly in the hand.

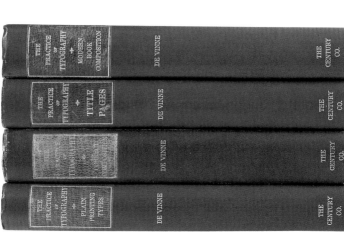

The following words or phrases usually appear in italic, with their proper accents:

ab ovo	*en passant*	*locum tenens*
ancien régime	*fait accompli*	*mise en scène*
bête noire	*grand monde*	*noblesse oblige*
comme il faut	*hors de combat*	*raison d'être*
de quoi vivre	*inter alia*	*sans cérémonie*
de trop	*jeu d'esprit*	*tour de force*

The phrases prima facie and ex officio, when used to qualify the nouns that follow, are frequently put in roman; but when used as adverbs they may be set in italic. The compositor may need special instruction for these cases.

Prima-facie evidence.
The evidence is, *prima facie*, convincing.
An ex-officio member of the committee.
The Speaker is, *ex officio*, the chairman.

Note also that these words may be connected with a hyphen when they are used as qualifiers.

In works on bibliography the titles of all books specified in the text are usually put in italic, as:

Storia Critica de Nic. Jenson.
Lettres d'un Bibliographe.
Hints on Decorative Printing.

This method, approved by all bibliographers, is to be preferred to the commoner practice of setting titles in roman and inclosing them with quotation-

marks. A different method is observed for foot-notes, not only by bibliographers, but by modern historians: the name of the author, the title of the book, and the date and description are always set in roman lower-case, without the use of small capitals, italic, or quotation-marks.

1 Santini, *Storia Critica de Nic. Jenson*, Lucca, 1796-98 (3 parts), 8vo, p. 19.
2 Madden, *Lettres d'un Bibliographe*, Paris, 1886, 8vo., sixième série, p. 116.
3 Savage, *Hints on Decorative Printing*, London, 1882, 4to, chap. ii.

In the texts of magazines and journals, and in all ordinary book-work, the titles of cited books are frequently and needlessly put in roman lower-case between quotation-marks, as in

"Introduction to the Classics," vol. ii, p. 555.
"Gentleman's Magazine," 1785, p. 91.

The full names of magazines and newspapers were formerly always set in italic, but they often appear now in roman lower-case quoted.[1] A recent practice is to select italic for the name (but not always the place) of the paper, as London *Times* or *New*

[1] Some editors still adhere to the old usage, putting the name of the book or magazine in italic, and reserving quotation-marks for the heading of any article referred to in the publication. This is a nice distinction, but the specification of the article could be made equally clear by using roman lower-case for the name or title, and beginning each important word with a capital letter, as has been the custom for the specification of book titles.

8. Reformed German typography

Karl Theodor Körner, *Werke*, Leipzig: Insel Verlag, 1906

166 x 95 mm, 480 pp, letterpress

This collected edition of Körner's works is part of the Großherzog Wilhelm Ernst edition of German classic texts, published in twenty-one volumes by the Insel Verlag (1905–11). It is a pocket edition, using the reformed German typography of the moment – breaking free of blackletter and also Jugendstil. As explained in the colophon (shown in detail), the title lettering was drawn by Eric Gill, in his first commission from Harry Kessler. But the main feature of this series, in purely material terms, is the exceptional refinement and durability of the book-object: achieved by the very thin (Bible) paper, and the soft leather binding. It is indeed a real pocket book.

KOERNERS WERKE

GROSSHERZOG WILHELM
ERNST AUSGABE

Diese Ausgabe wurde heraus-gegeben im Auftrage von Alfred Walter Heymel, Harry Graf Kessler und Emery Walker-lai-tten den Druck, der besorgt wurde von Poeschel und Trepte in Leipzig. Eric Gill zeichnete die Titel. Herausgeber dieses Bandes ist: Werner Deetjen

ZRINY

EIN TRAUERSPIEL IN FÜNF AUFZÜGEN

PERSONEN

SOLIMAN DER GROSSE, türkischer Kaiser. MEHMED SOKOLOWITSCH, Großwesir. IBRAHIM, der Begler-beg von Natolien. ALI PORTUK, oberster Befehlshaber des Geschützes. MUSTAFA, Pascha von Bosnien. LEVI, Solimans Leibarzt. Ein Bote. Ein Aga. NIKLAS, GRAF VON ZRINY, Ban von Kroatien, Dalmatien, Slawonien, Tavernikus in Ungarn, Obrister von Sigeth. EVA, geborne GRÄFIN ROSENBERG, seine Gemahlin. HELENE, ihre Tochter. KASPER ALAPI, WOLF PAPRUTOWITSCH, PETER VILACKY, LORENZ JURANITSCH, ungarische Hauptleute. FRANZ SCHERENK, Zrinys Kammerdiener. Ein Bauer. Ein ungarischer Hauptmann. Ungarische Hauptleute und Soldaten. Türken.

(Die Zeit der Handlung ist das Jahr 1566, der Schauplatz in der ersten Hälfte des ersten Akts in Belgrad, dann teils in..., teils vor der ungarischen Festung Sigeth.)

ERSTER AUFZUG
1. AUFTRITT

Zimmer im Palais des Großherrn zu Belgrad.

Soliman (*sitzt tiefsinnig, den Kopf auf die Hände gestützt, im Vordergrund*), Levi (*kommt durch den Haupteingang*).

LEVI Mein kaiserlicher Herr hat mein verlangt?——
Ihr habt mich rufen lassen, großer Sultan?——
Der Sklave harrt auf seines Herrschers Wink.
(*Beiseite*) Noch immer keine Antwort——
                  (*Laut*) Herr und Kaiser!
Verzeihst dem treuen Knecht!—Seid Ihr krank?
Herr, Ihr seid krank!
SOLIMAN.   Wär ichs, du hilfst mir nicht!
LEVI. Doch, großer Herr, doch!—Traut dem alten Diener!
Wenns einer kann, ich kanns. Ich gab Euch Proben
Von meiner Treue wie von meiner Kunst.
Seit vierzig Jahren schleicht mein scharfes Auge
Dem Wandeln Eures Lebens forschend nach.

Was ich von hohen Meistern früh erlernte,
Was die Natur mir später selbst bekannt,
Auf Euch begrenzt ich alles Wissens Ende.
Ich kenne Eures Lebens tiefsten Bau,
Vertraut mit seinen Kräften, seinen Wünschen.
Des Arztes Kunst sei allgemeines Gut,
Wohl weiß ich das und mocht es treu erfüllen,
Denn Euer Wohl war mir der Menschheit Leben:
Ein Held und Kaiser gilt ein ganzes Volk!
SOLIMAN. Ich kenne dich und kenne deine Treue,
Und deine Kunst hat sich mir oft bewährt;
Drum hab ich dein verlangt.—Sprich unverhohlen!
Wie weit steckst du noch meines Lebens Ziel?
Zeig dich, wie oft dich innerdar gefunden,
Als treuen Knecht mit offnem, gradem Sinn!
Wie lange soll ich leben?—Ich will Wahrheit!
LEVI. Herr! Diese Frage kann nur der dort lösen,
An diesen Rätseln schiefest meine Kunst.
SOLIMAN. O Stümperei des armen Menschenwitzes!
Des Lebens innern Bau wollt Ihr verstehn,
Der Räder heimlichstes Getrieb berechnen
Und wißt doch nicht, wie lang das Uhrwerk geht,
Wißt nicht, wenn diese Räder stocken sollen!
LEVI. Mein großer Herr, schmäht nicht die edle Kunst
Die enge Grenze ward von Gott gezogen,
Und in die stille Werkstatt der Natur
Hat keines Menschen Auge noch geschn.
Erklären mögen wir des Lebens Weise,
Sein Keimen, seine Blüten, seinen Tod,
Doch in das Chaos ferner Möglichkeiten
Verbirt sich traurig der bedrängte Geist,
Wenn ers versucht, dem Rätsel abzulauschen,
Was sechs Jahrtausende noch keinem Ohr vertraut.
Ich kann Euch sagen: dieser Nerven Stärke,
Des Feuer, das im Höllenzug glüht,
Und Eurer Seele rüstige Begeistrung,
Die deuten mit auf manches volle Jahr.
Das deuten der gütge Gott noch zugemessen;
Das Euch der gütge Gott noch zugemessen;
Doch nicht bestimmen mag ichs mit Gewißheit.

9. George's typography

Stefan George, *Der Stern des Bundes*, Berlin:
Georg Bondi, 5th impression, 1922
205 x 150 mm, 116 pp, letterpress

This is one of the books from the uniform edition of
George's work. The typeface is an adapted and augmented
sanserif, which shows moves towards a single alphabet,
although capital letters are employed at the start of lines
and occasionally for emphasis. One likely inspiration for
this approach to letterform design and text-setting is early
German orthography. In its visual simplifications, George's
'new typography' was part of a larger attitude to life and its
reform: but a life confined to aesthetics, and looking away
from contemporary reality. The less than simple lettering on
the cover (presumably by Melchior Lechter) shows the style-
world out of which George was moving.

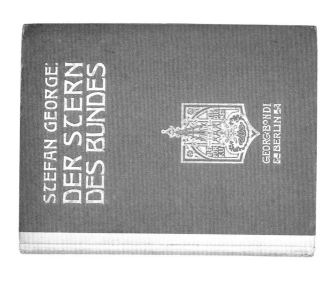

Du hausgeist der um alte mauern wittert
Noch schaudmgrung süchtig unter bogen kauert
Aus trümmern daseins überbleibsel saugend:
Strich deine hand auf schal- und unrenscherbe
So stand fast körperhaft vor uns dein denkbild:
Von goldnen säulen schlang sich blumenkette
Erzbecken rauchte neben purpurlagern
Verstrickt in allen formen der umarmung
War milch- und rosenleib und kupferbrauner
Dort schlichen zage füsse durch die pforte . . .
Doch wenig blieb im tag vom schattenchore
Es schwand der spuk: die üppig wirren prächte
Des weißes Rom mit dem die könige buhlen.

Fragbar ward Alles da das Eine floh:
Der geist entwand sich blindlings aus der siele
Entlaufne seele ward zum törigen spiele –
Sagbar ward Alles: drusch auf leeres stroh.
Nun löst das herz von wut und wahn verschlackt
Von gärung dunkelheit gespinst und trubel:
Die tat ist aufgerauscht in irdischem jubel
Das Bild erhebt im licht sich frei und nackt.

Fragbar ward Alles da das E
Der geist entwand sich blindli
Entlaufne seele ward zum töri
Sagbar ward Alles: drusch au
Nun löst das herz von wut u
Von gärung dunkelheit gespin
Die tat ist aufgerauscht in ir
Das Bild erhebt im licht sich

10. Larisch's 'ornamental lettering'

Rudolf Larisch, *Unterricht in ornamentaler Schrift*

Vienna: K. K. Hof- und Staatsdruckerei, [1905], 11th edn, 1934

236 x 150 mm, 122 pp, letterpress

In this book Larisch gives a detailed description of his approach to the production of lettering. His teaching lay behind much German-language lettering practice, into the 1930s. The approach is a pluralist, liberal one. His fundamental writing implement (the 'Quellstift') dictates no strong form; emphasis is placed on the spacing between letters and on the overall pattern. Larisch worked with reproduction in mind and is careful here to indicate the size at which examples are shown – true size ('Wirkliche Größe') or by how much reduced.

38

Erhöhung der ornamentalen Reizfähigkeit von heute konventionell erſcheinenden Buchſtabenformen durch Gruppierung. Abdruck der eingefärbten Papierſchnittpatrone

Wirkliche Größe

die DIFFERENZIERUNG DURCH DEN ZWECK, dem ornamentale Schrift zu dienen hat, Hand in Hand zu gehen.

Man soll unterscheiden lernen, in welchen Fällen dekorative Rücksichten frei geübt und sonstige gestaltende Absichten ungehemmt verwirklicht werden können, bei welchen Verwendungsarten dagegen ausschließlich der Mitteilungszweck bestimmend erscheint. Auch muß man sich stets vor

39
Papierschnittschablone
Gegenbild von Nr. 38. (Das Ergebnis des Patronierens.)
Weißüberstrahlung. Wirkliche Größe

91

37
Zeitungskopf
Gotik (9. Kursübung) wegen der Fleckenwirkung verwendet
1/3 der wirklichen Größe

Differenzierung durch den Zweck

Mit diesem Feingefühl für die Unterordnung jeder Einzelheit zugunsten der Gesamterscheinung hat die stete Rücksicht auf

38
Erklärung der ornamentalen Reizfälligkeit von heute konventionell erscheinenden Buchstabenformen durch Gruppierung. Abdruck der eingeritzten Papierschnittspatrone
Wirkliche Größe

90

11. Johnston's pedagogy

Edward Johnston, *Manuscript & inscription letters*, London:
Pitman, [1909], 4th impression, 1920
310 x 253 mm, 16 sheets, letterpress
Johnston intended these sheets as a 'working supplement'
to his *Writing & illuminating, & lettering* (1906). They consist
of a number of alphabets in different 'hands' or styles – the
second plate here (no. 6) shows the most widely influential

of his model hands – supplemented by sheets showing other useful material. Plentiful annotation is provided. In this, as throughout his work, Johnston stayed true to the principle of active creation, not passive copying. The sheets convey the spirit of the blackboard lecturer in dialogue with students. In the strong ethical charge of his work, and its trust in the pen as the generator of forms, Johnston took an opposite line to that followed by Larisch.

12. Gill's politics

Eric Gill, *Unemployment*, London: Faber & Faber, 1933

167 x 105 mm, 32 pp, letterpress

Gill's typography and his social and religious views are combined in this pamphlet, from a time of severe crisis in Britain. It was one of the large number of essays that he wrote through most of his adult life. *Unemployment* was printed by Hague & Gill, which by then used a Monotype caster and a powered printing press. The small mechanized workshop was evidently within the realm of the good for Gill, who here attacks industrialism, capitalism, and the women's movement. Typefaces used are Gill Sans (on the cover), Perpetua (for the main text), Joanna (for the appendixes on 'Matriarchy' and 'Higher things').

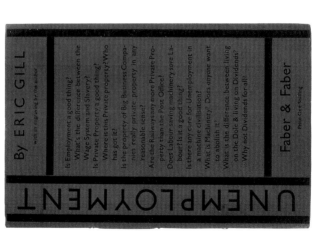

UNEMPLOYMENT

By ERIC GILL

with an engraving by the author

Is Employment a good thing?
What's the difference between the Wage System and Slavery?
Is Private Property a good thing?
Where is this Private property? Who has got it?
Is the property of Big Business Companies really private property in any reasonable sense?
Are the Railways any more Private Property than the Post Office?
Does Labour saving machinery save Labour? Is it a good thing?
Is there any cure for Unemployment in a machine civilisation?
What is Machinery? Does anyone want to abolish it?
What is the difference between living on the Dole & living on Dividends?
Why not Dividends for all?

Faber & Faber

Price One Shilling

UNEMPLOYMENT

¶IT IS absolutely necessary to have principles, that is things that come first, the foundations of the house. What we want to know is: what principles of common sense are relevant to the matter of human work.

a

1

It is a movement of women who quite rightly recognize that they can go out to work and bear children too. No man can serve two masters; and no woman can mind her house and her children and a machine in the factory as well. (See Appendix 1.)

¶When James Watt invented his steam engine these developments were of course unknown & unexpected. Nobody could have foreseen what we now see. They thought of machinery as they thought of their old tools—things to help men in their work. It never occurred to them that machinery would or could do away with work. And it was more than fifty years after the time of James Watt before they began to realize that the chief power of machines was not to help but to displace human labour, to do away with human labour.

This was not realized because, to start with, machinery was not used all over the world but only in a few countries—and these countries were able to sell their vastly increased factory products to all the other countries.

But gradually every country has introduced machinery. The strange & ludicrous thing is that most of them have set up their machine industries by borrowing money to pay for it from us. We made such enormous profits from the sale of our manufactures that we were able to lend our savings to help our customers to set up their own factories. London became the great money lenders of the world. And England was able to exact tribute

18

---

from everyone else. We wanted the other countries to buy our manufactures & yet we lent them money to set up factories of their own. The war of 1914-18 saw the climax of the process and made the foreign countries finally independent of England. English foreign trade has gone never to return. Foreign countries do not want our goods because they can manufacture their own.

Meanwhile the real meaning of factory machinery has become clear. Factory machinery does not help men to do their work better, to make better things; factory machinery helps the factory owner or to do without the men altogether. Machinery does not improve the work; it displaces the men. Labour saving machinery does in fact save labour. There are now in England between three & ten million people whose labour is unnecessary. In the whole world there are perhaps fifty millions of people whose labour is not needed.

¶NOW in any period of history there are bound to be many unemployed persons—persons whose labour is not required to keep the world going.

1. Young children and students at school & college.
2. Old people and mentally and physically incapable people.
3. People on holidays or resting.
4. Ornamental people—the idle rich; that is people who live upon their own or other peoples' savings.

The improvement of machinery under the Capitalist system has increased the number of people whose la-

19

13. American letters

W.A.Dwiggins, *Layout in advertising*, New York: Harper, [1928], revised edition, 1948

208 × 140 mm, 202 pp, letterpress

Dwiggins's intensely practical manual for graphic design – or commercial art – has the quality of a vastly experienced practitioner speaking to an apprentice at the drawing board. The many explanatory drawings, often placed in the margins, encourage this impression. As the jacket of the book suggests, Dwiggins's formal writing for reproduction was of a piece with his graphic design work. *Layout in advertising* was first published in 1928, the same year as Tschichold's *Die neue Typographie*. The huge contrast of style and manner between the two books represents the gulf then between the modern spirit in the USA and in Central Europe.

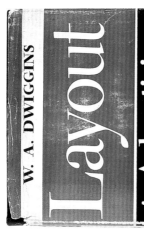

Technique

Scale of texture

55. As the size of the type increases above 12 point, the "break-back" problem diminishes in importance.

When rules, or ornaments, or pictures in line are used in conjunction with type, the good appearance of the piece will depend upon a proper regulation of the scale of texture between type and ornament. Faults of texture scale destroy the suavity of the design; falsely scaled parts refuse to settle into the general scheme; they stand out as accidental blots.

The type face sets the texture scale. The strokes of some kinds of type characters meet each other crisply and sharply; the strokes of other kinds flow together like liquids. The thick-and-thin strokes of some fonts do not vary strikingly in weight; in other faces the strokes are sharply contrasted in thickness. These characteristic details need to be echoed in the lines of the ornament or picture. The rule does not imply that there should be no solid blacks in such designs; it means that the line parts of a drawing—the gray parts—need to harmonize with the linear characteristics of the type with which it is used. There is no texture relation between type and half-icons, so in the case of half-icons no problem of texture scale arises.

Indention

Indention is an aid to legibility. The space made by indention at the beginning of a paragraph is a device for attracting attention. The first few words of a paragraph are (or should be) important. People, reading casually, try the first few words, and then—if the text is not particularly succulent—drop to the next paragraph and try that. The entrance into a paragraph, therefore, needs to be vigorous.

Leaded paragraphs

A 1-em indent is achieved by inserting more leads between paragraphs than occur between lines of the text. This device is practicable if the story of the text breaks up into sections that are not much related out

to another. But if the sense of the copy is continuous from paragraph to paragraph—if the story runs right along—the leaded breaks are too emphatic—they make the reading bumpy. Leaded paragraphs do not help the looks of the page.

First line flush

Left to his own devices, the average compositor will indent the first line of a body of text. The first word of the first line is *the* critical word of that particular body of text. Let it start flush, at least. Granted that indention attracts attention, but not to the first line, because the force of blank space is dissipated here by the much larger blank area above the lines. Reinforce the first line, by an initial dropping into the text or striking up above it, by caps and small caps, by jutting the line out beyond the body-matter—at least by starting it flush with the text.

If there are two lines of displayed matter that tend to arrange themselves as a longer and a shorter line, do not space out the shorter line to make it come even with its mate. Lay hold of the chance for variety that the uneven lengths provide and let the lines have their natural spacing. *Naturalness* is a key word. The gaps that vary the edge of a body of displayed matter set long and short make a valuable pattern—for catching the eye. But it is not commendable practice to juggle lines into the shape of a vase; it is not natural for type to fall into the form of a vase.

Long and short lines

Letter-spacing is to be applied to capitals, only—not to lower-case, or to black letter (Old English). Letter-spacing is an ornamental device. It does not increase legibility. It makes a decorative pattern, if you want pattern.

Letter- spacing

There is a general tendency, in setting body matter either by hand or on a machine, to get more space between words than is convenient to the eye. It is easier to do it that way; but the practice not only

Word spacing

14. The left-wing book

André Reuze, *Giganten der Landstrasse*, Berlin: Büchergilde Gutenberg, 1928

240 x 170 mm, 200 pp, letterpress

Reuze's report on the Tour de France was a cross-category work, typical of that time: a 'novel', but also documentary in spirit and illustrated by photographs. This translation (from the French), published by the German printing trade union's Büchergilde Gutenberg, was appropriately designed by Georg Trump in a non-literary spirit. The Büchergilde's larger-than-novel-sized format provided a good basis for this. Photographs are interspersed in the text, which is set asymmetrically around the centre of the book; oversized page numbers add a further touch here. An experiment is performed by ranging the last line of paragraphs from the right.

klärung dieses langen Rennens. Wie überall, muß auch beim Rennsport die Flagge die Ware decken; und die Helden der Landstraße sind letzten Endes nichts weiter als rasende Plakatsäulen! Da aber jede Reklame, die Geld kostet, wieder Geld einbringen muß, lautet der Befehl: Krepiere ...
aber fahre! ..."

Maingry schüttelte stumm den Kopf.

Ravenelle fuhr fort:

„Sie haben doch näher schon einmal im Kasino irgendeines Kurorts die kleinen Pferdchen' laufen sehen? Der Uneingeweihte kann sich nur ganz selten erklären, welcher Mechanismus dieses Pferdespiel eigentlich belebt. Forscht er aber nach, dann entdeckt er hinter dem Spielleiter eine Finanzgruppe, die diese Unterhaltung organisiert, um die Spieler mit ihrem Geld anzulocken ... Hier, mein Lieber, rollt dasselbe Spiel auf der Landstraße, und auch hier sind die Karten mehr oder minder gut gemischt!"

Inzwischen nahm der Aufruf der Fahrer seinen Fortgang.

„Wer ist denn eigentlich das dunkelblaue Trikot mit weißem Stern, das scheinbar keinen Kopf hat?" fragte Maingry.

„Das ist der Seengalturger Sambo-Takori. ‚Kakaodiie' genannt, ein früherer Schiffskoch, und ein Fahrer, der in der tollsten Hitze am besten kurbelt! Ich möchte wissen, was dem kleinen Chevillard fehlt! Sehen Sie doch, wie nervös er ist!"

Chevillard lief mit seiner Rückennummer hastig die Reihen des Publikums ab.

„Den fehlt gar nichts!" sagte Tampier. „Er hat sich bloß in den Schädel gesetzt, daß ihm irgendeine hübsche Maus seine Rückennummer aus Trikot nähen soll, weil er sich einbildet, daß ihm das Glück bringt!"
Ravenelle suchte mit Maingry nach einer kleinen Dame, die Chevillards Wunsch entsprechen könnte, und entdeckten schließlich ein reizendes Mädchen, das auch sofort bereit war, dem Rennfahrer seinen Wunsch zu erfüllen.

Als der Rückennummer angenäht war, zog Chevillard die Mütze vom Kopf und gab der Kleinen einen herzhaften Kuß.

Die übrigen Fahrer brüllten:

„Mensch, paß bloß auf, sonst stehste wie'n Einer! ..."

„Das ist gegen die Brenbestimmungen!"

„Fünfzig Eier Strafe kost' dich das!"

Doch der dicke Ausrufer unterbrach diese Unterhaltung, wich an den Bürgersteig zurück und rief:

„Achtung! ... Fertigmachen!" Alles schwieg.

Die Fahrer setzten den rechten Fuß aufs Pedal und standen mit der linken Fußspitze auf dem Boden.

22

Die Autos stellten sich in die Reihe.

Dann wurden die Wagmütüren aufgeschlagen. Licht blitzte auf, die Motoren begannen zu rattern, die Kraftwagen setzten sich langsam in Bewegung. Der Dicke sah auf seinen Chronometer und sagte dann, ganz einfach:
„Los!"
Die Räder rollten!
Im Lichterwirbel sah man vorgereckte Köpfe, ein Meer von Schultern und das Gewoge tretender Beine.

„Viel Glück, Tampier!" rief eine helle Frauenstimme.

Rasender Beifall tobte.

Ravenelle war in den Wagen gesprungen.

„Also, Boost, los!"

Ein Rennfahrer aber war neben ihnen geblieben und tastete mit der rechten Hand über die Holzkisten der Karosserie: Tampier.

„Ich muß Holz anfassen!" erklärte er. „Irgendeine dumme Gans hat mir ‚viel Glück' zugerufen. Unter Garantie ist das ein Brangschein auf fünf-

23

15. Tschichold's pedagogy
Jan Tschichold, *Eine Stunde Druckgestaltung*, Stuttgart:
Wedekind, 1930
297 x 210 mm, 100 pp, letterpress
In one of the series of 'Eine Stunde' ('in one hour') books
that Wedekind published, Tschichold gives a short course
in design for print. For the most part quite practical, with a
strong emphasis on standardization of formats, the book is
introduced by one of his most stirring statements, 'Was ist
und was will die Neue Typografie?' The practical bulk of the
work proceeds by demonstration, with frequent use of 'good'
contrasted with 'bad' examples. Shown here is a spread on
letterheads: 'the common unstandardized and undesigned
letterhead'; 'unstandardized and "moderne" in style'; 'standardized but undesigned'; and (right page) Tschichold's own
work: 'standardized and designed'.

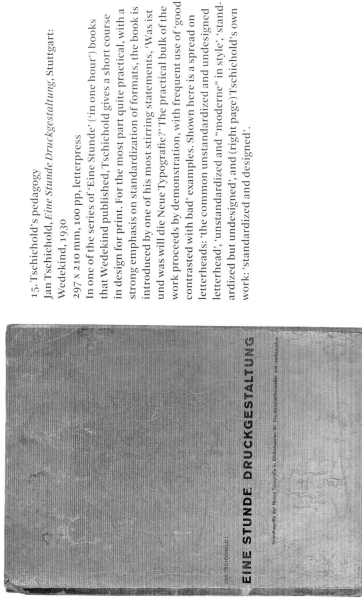

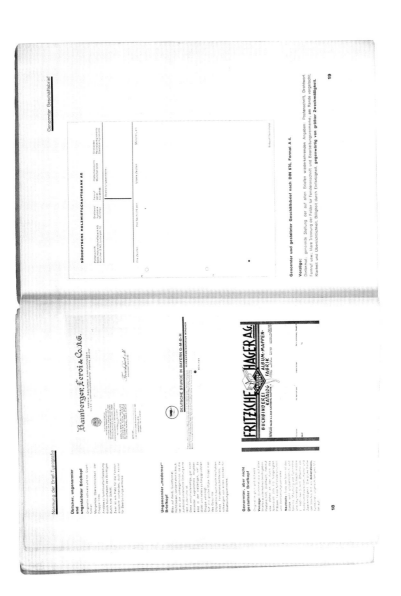

Üblicher, ungenormter und ungestalteter Briefkopf

Ungenormter „modederner" Briefkopf

Genormter, aber nicht gestalteter Briefkopf

Vorzüge:

Nachteile:

SÜDDEUTSCHE HOLZWIRTSCHAFTSBANK AG

Genormter und gestalteter Geschäftsbrief nach DIN 676, Format A 4.

Vorzüge: genormte Stellung der auf allen Brüuten wiederkehrenden Angaben, Postanschrift, Drahtwort, Fernruf usw.; klare Trennung der Felder für Fensteranschrift und Bearbeitungsvermerke, am Rande vergleichbt; Klarheit und Übersichtlichkeit. Billigkeit durch Einfachigkeit. **gegenwärtig von größter Zweckmäßigkeit.**

16. Early information design
K. Lönberg-Holm & Ladislav Sutnar, *Catalog design*,
New York: Sweet's Catalog Service, 1944
208 x 148 mm, 72 pp, letterpress

The booklet expounds an approach to the design of catalogues, and, by extension, to the design of information in book (or codex) form. The opportunities that the book format offers, page by page, for repetition and for fresh announcement, are discussed and illustrated. Sutnar, an exponent of the new typography in Czechoslovakia, had been stranded in the USA in 1939. This booklet exemplifies the approach it describes, and shows the Central-European modernist sensibility at work in the USA. It is spiral-bound, and approximates to the DIN A5 format. So too, the typefaces (Futura and Bodoni) are those favoured by European modernists. Sweet's was an information systems company, issuing catalogues of industrial and architectural products. Sutnar held a long-term consultancy with them. A larger work by these authors, *Catalog design progress*, was published by the same company in 1950.

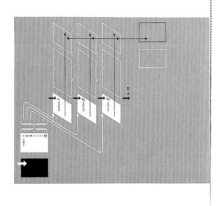

Diagram of catalog containing twelve sections—each section consisting of one visual unit, with covers, and so designed that it may be used separately—the whole contained within general covers. White arrows trace information flow from index to sections; black arrows, the flow from cover to cover within individual sections and, finally, to catalog's back cover.

product—*building hardware*

problem—*To devise a simple information pattern, this extensive line of products requires classification according to use needs. The problem is that of arranging a complex field of information so as to give architects and building contractors a quick impression of each product's advantages and to enable them to check each type against their specific needs.*

pattern—*Analysis suggests first the classification of information according to product types, features, applications; next, its organization in self-contained sections, each covering the specific features and range of applications of one product type.*

215

17. Sandberg's typography
Alexander Calder, Amsterdam: Stedelijk Museum, 1959
258 x 187 mm, 24 pp, letterpress

The booklet is one of the series of Stedelijk Museum catalogues designed by Sandberg from 1945 through to the early 1960s. The typical components of his design work are evident here: the use of 'wholemeal' papers and (in strong contrast) coated white paper for the pictures; text set unjustified in long lines, with considerable space between lines of text; bold sanserif used for text setting; lowercase setting where possible. The atmosphere achieved is one of informality and openness: it breathes modernism, but a modernism that is opposite to the grey authoritarian ideology of ill-repute. This is primarily a German-language publication, for the showings of the exhibition in Germany and Switzerland.

alexander calder

216

calder und die „mobiles"

manchmal weiss man nicht recht, wo beginnen mit einem vorwort

vor allem über calder

also an ihm ist rund

sein kalk, seine finger, seine nase, sein wesen, seine herzliche gesinnung,

aus seinem runden mund dringen kurze sätze

die schnell immer rollende, wie humor

und die grossen finger formen diffizile konstruktionen,

glupp wie weidenzweige mit feinen blättern im frühjahr

das material, womit er arbeitet: eisendraht, eisenblech, aber auch gleichgewicht

seine farben kuntsic schwarz, zuweilen rot, weichlich blau, gelb oder weiss

die quelle seiner inspiration: alles, was sich sanft bewegt, eine flagge, eine girlande, ein fisch, die sterne

im beginn suchte er mechanische mittel, um seine plastiken in bewegung zu bringen,

nun macht er es einfacher, der leitzug und der wind treiben seine werke

er weiss seine gunst launen auf dem werk zu überragen

ein mal mit „mobilise" von calder ist wie frühlicher welk freisster formen, das ruhig und rhythmisch

mit der wurde der weiken lingo ähnlichkeit,gefallen geometrische figuren in der luft beschreibt

figuren ohne ende und ohne beginn

wer calder sagt, sagt: bewegung

er ist der erste, der dies element in die bildende kunst einführte

er ist nach der erste aner, kunter, der einen beitrag zur entwicklung dieser künste liefert

plötzlich sehen wir, wie aus andere bänder ganz andere formen entstehen

zeichnen und erstes konstrucktionen, noch inzilten fassen fest auf dem grund errichtet,

obwohl ein arms in die höhe gestrecke: „stabilse"

räuschbröcken; skupkären, frühige kächsen oder nur signals und zeichen

sie bilden hrem den hauptteil dieser ausstellung.

« doch darüber spricht georges sallas und so brauchen wir hier darauf nicht näher einzugehen,

so passen dem aanschaue noch besser zum modell ihres schöpfers

doch die mytentwenter calders allsmplick sind erner, leicht und schwer zugleich,

meisten wir, glaube ich, irgendwo in der mitte suchen,

mitten zwischen den „mobilse" und „stabilse"

sandberg

18. The Penguin paperback
Patience Gray & Primrose Boyd, *Plats du jour*,
Harmondsworth: Penguin Books, 1957
180 x 111 mm, 304 pp, letterpress

As an instructional work, this is a more thoroughly designed instance of the mass-published paperback than the usual continuous-text Penguin book could be. If not actually designed by Hans Schmoller, it was made at that time when he was in charge of typography at Penguin. The illustrations (by David Gentleman) are unusually well integrated into the whole, and move from the wonderfully decorative (as on the cover), to being also 'technical illustration' (as on the spread shown). Throughout, the typography is both sophisticated and relaxed in its articulation of an information-rich but friendly text. The whole is a fine testament to the virtues of the new traditional approach.

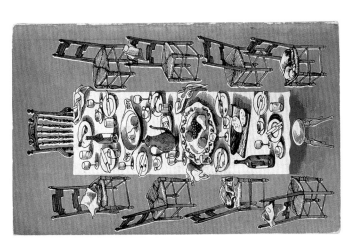

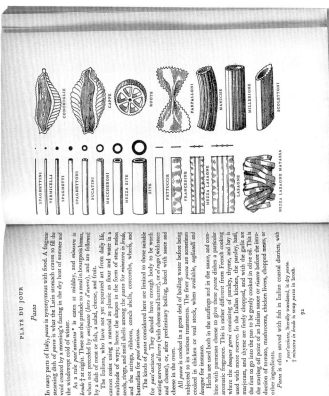

SPAGHETTINI · VERMICELLI · SPAGHETTI · SPAGHETTONI · BUCATINI · MACCHERONI · MEZZA ZITE · ZITE · FETTUCCIE · FRANCESINE · MEZZA LASAGNE · LASAGNE · MEZZA LASAGNE MATASSA

CONCHIGLIE · CAPPE · RUOTE · FARFALLONI · MANICHE · MILLERIGHE · SCOLETTONI

PLATS DU JOUR

Pasta

In many parts of Italy, *pasta* is synonymous with food. A fragrant steaming dish of *pasta* is what the Latin stomach craves to fill the void created by a morning's fasting in the dry heat of summer and the windswept cold of winter.

As a rule *pasta asciutta* * is eaten at midday, and *minestra in brodo* † at night. These are the prelude to a meal in bourgeois homes, when not preceded by *antipasto* (*hors d'œuvre*), and are followed by a dish of meat or fish, a salad, cheese, and fruit.

The Italians, who have not yet separated art from daily life, cannot resist using a material as plastic as flour and water in a multitude of ways; hence the shapes in the form of stars, melon seeds, rings, and snail shells among the *pasta* for *minestra in brodo*, and the strings, ribbons, conch shells, corncombs, wheels, and butterflies for *pasta asciutta*.

The kinds of *pasta* considered here are limited to those suitable for *pasta asciutta*. They should have enough body to be worth eating served *al burro* (with cheese and butter), or *al sugo* (with sauce and cheese), or, after preliminary boiling, baked with sauce and cheese in the oven.

All *pasta* is cooked in a great deal of boiling water before being subjected to its various treatments. The finer *pasta* are sometimes cooked in chicken or veal stock, when available, *tagliatelli* and *lasagne* for instance.

Herbs are used both in the stuffings and in the sauce, and combine with parmesan cheese to give these *pasta* dishes a particular aromatic fragrance. This is rather different from French cooking where the *bouquet garni* consisting of parsley, thyme, and bay is used with more reserve. In the Italian kitchen, the parsley, basil, marjoram, and thyme are finely chopped, and with the garlic are the first to go into the pan to be gently cooked in olive oil. This is the starting off point of an Italian sauce or *risotto* before the introduction of tomato, mushrooms, chicken livers, chopped meats, or other ingredients.

Pasta is often served with fish in Italian coastal districts, with

* *pasta asciutta*, literally translated, is dry *pasta*.
† *minestra in brodo* is soup *pasta* in broth.

92

19. Gerstner's typography

Karl Gerstner, *Designing programmes*, London: Tiranti, 1964 (enlarged edition, 1968)

250 x 177 mm, 112 pp, lithography

Gerstner's book contains 'four essays and an introduction' on the idea of programme, and moves seamlessly from a discussion of typefaces, through typographic design, to art, and to visual method more generally. Typography is thus just part of a large aesthetic vision. The midway page size of the book, and its two-column format, carry well quite a wide variety of texts and pictures, and the whole work escapes from the stiff formalism that can be seen in several of the expositions of Swiss typography of that time. This is the English-language edition of the book.

Karl Gerstner:
Designing
Programmes

Programme as morphology
Programme as logic
Programme as grid
Programme as photography
Programme as literature
Programme as music

Programme as typeface
Programme as typography
Programme as picture
Programme as method

Alec Tiranti Ltd., London W.1.

Programme as Grid

In the grid a programme? Let me put it more specifically. A fine grid is considered as a proportional regulator, a system, it is a programme par excellence. Superdraw is a proportional method, but not a programme. Unlike, say, the (geometrical) module of Le Corbusier, which is, of course, be used as a grid but is primarily a proportional. Albert Einstein said of the module: "It is a scale of proportions that makes the bad difficult and the good easy". That is a programmatic statement of what I like to be the aim of "Designing Programmes".

The typographic grid is a proportional regulator for compositions, tables, pictures, etc. It is a formal programme to accommodate x unknown items. The difficulty to find the balance, the maximum of conformity to a rule with the maximum of freedom. Or: the maximum of constants with the greatest possible variety.

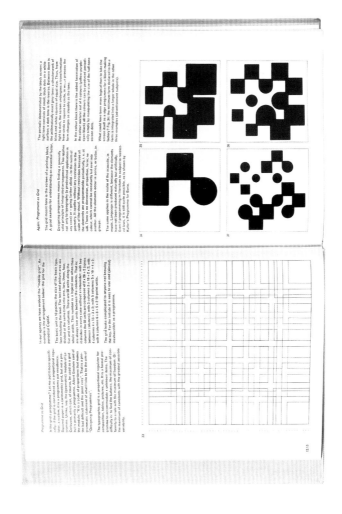

In our agency we have evolved the "mobile grid". An example is the arrangement below: the grid for the periodical *Capital*.

The basic unit is 10 points; the size of the basic typeface including the lead. The text and picture area are divided at the same time into nine fields, four, two five and six columns. There are 58 units along the whole width. This number is logical one when there are always two units between the columns. That is, it divides in every case without a remainder: with two columns the units are composed of 2 x 28 + 2 (units between columns); with 3 columns 3 x 18 + 8 x 2; with 4 columns 4 x 13 + 3 x 2; with 5 columns 5 x 10 + 4 x 2; with 6 columns 6 x 8 + 5 x 2 (8-point units).

The grid looks complicated to anyone not knowing the key. For the initiate it is easy to use and (almost) inexhaustible as a programme.

Again: Programme as Grid

The grid recurs here as the screen of a printing block. A good example for understanding an essential factor.

Designing programmes means finding a generally valid principle of integrated arrangement. This applies not only to typography (a predestined application in any case) but to any visual signal — to the realm of geometry. It applies without any restriction to the realm of the visual. Without restriction because all the elements are programmable, i. e. all are programmable periodically, i. e. at will. There is no dimension, proportion, form, no colour, which cannot be converted into one and another. All the elements occur in series, or better, in groups.

The same applies in the realm of the acoustic, in music. Composing is different, because the elements have not been produced naturally but artificially. Even if programming in form here is subject to restricted laws, it is still quite possible, as is shown by Kutter's Programme for Boris.

The periodic, demonstrated by the block screen: a light tone consists of small, black dots on a white surface; a dark tone in the reverse. Between them is the arithmetically exact grey tone: a chesswork of black and white squares of equal size. Thus, from light to dark, the screen undergoes a transformation. From white in square to circle, in which process the form changes all visibility to the first.

In the colour block there is the added fascination of the colour mixture out of 4 colours (yellow-purple-cyan-black) all the colours can be produced periodically simply by manipulating the size of the half-tone screen dots.

What could have been more logical than to take the screen itself as a sign-programme for a block making factory? Fig. 34: the minimum form declared to be a block, and its accumulation into a larger whole in the other three examples (advertisement subjects).

34

35

26

27

20. Image as information

Habitat catalogue 1975, Wallingford: Habitat Designs, 1974
297 x 210 mm, 112 pp, lithography

This retail catalogue succeeds, through highly organized photography, in combining 'selling' images of its goods with quite detailed information about them. A good part of the design work thus lies in directions to the photographer. Behind the highly coloured scenography lies a certain honesty of purpose. But the catalogue shows a shift from the time (as in example 18) when line drawings were made to describe such goods. A few years on from this, the photography would be yet more scenic and less informational. The text here would have been photoset and the pages probably made up by hand as film, by printshop workers.

223

Natalia Ginzburg
La strada che va in città

Einaudi

21. The Italian paperback

Natalia Ginzburg, *La strada che va in città*, Turin: Einaudi, 1997

195 x 115 mm, 88 pp, lithography

One of the 'Nuovi Coralli' books published by Einaudi: the first edition in this format appeared in 1975, and this printing (1997) differs in the series style for the cover design. The typeface of the series is Simoncini Garamond, used here in a relatively large size for this short text. The typography is of great simplicity, dignity and directness: without rhetoric. The sections are sewn, and the whole ensemble (including its white coated-board cover) makes a robust and usable item of mass production.

Natalia Ginzburg
La strada che va in città

Einaudi

Al paese di mia zia ci andai su un carro. Mi accompagnò mia madre. Prendemmo una strada fra i campi perché non mi vedesse nessuno. Io portavo un soprabito di Azalea, perché i vestiti miei non mi stavano più bene e mi stringevano in vita. Si arrivò di sera. La zia era una donna molto grassa, con degli occhi neri sporgenti, con un grembiale di cotone azzurro e le forbici appese al collo, perché faceva la sarta. Cominciò a bisticciare con mia madre per il prezzo che dovevo pagare nel tempo che sarei rimasta con lei. Mia cugina Santa mi portò da mangiare, accese il fuoco nel camino e sedutasi vicino a me mi raccontò che anche lei sperava di sposarsi presto, «ma per me non c'è fretta», disse ridendo forte e lungamente. Il suo fidanzato era il figlio del podestà del paese ed erano fidanzati da otto anni. Lui adesso era militare e mandava delle cartoline.

La casa della zia era grande, con delle alte camere vuote e gelate. C'erano dappertutto dei sacchi di granturco e di castagne, e ai soffitti erano appese delle cipolle. La zia aveva avuto nove figli, ma chi era morto e chi era andato via. In casa c'era solo Santa, che era la minore e aveva ventiquattro anni. La zia non la poteva soffrire e le strillava dietro tutto il giorno. Se non si era ancora sposata era perché la zia, con un

pretesto o con l'altro, le impediva di farsi il corredo. Le piaceva tenersela in casa e tormentarla senza darle mai pace. Santa aveva paura di sua madre, ma ogni volta che parlava di sposarsi e lasciarla sola piangeva. Si meravigliò che io non piangessi, quando ripartí mia madre. Lei piangeva ogni volta che sua madre andava via per qualche affare in città, anche sapendo che prima di sera sarebbe tornata. In città Santa non c'era stata che due o tre volte. Ma diceva che si trovava meglio al paese. Pure il paese loro era peggio del nostro. C'era puzzo di letamaio, bambini sporchi sulle scale e nient'altro. Nelle case non c'era luce e l'acqua si doveva prendere al pozzo. Scrissi a mia madre che dalla zia non ci volevo più stare e mi venisse a riprendere. Non le piaceva scrivere e per questo non mi diede risposta per lettera, ma fece dire da un uomo che vendeva il carbone di aver pazienza e restare dov'ero, perché non c'era rimedio.

Cosí restai. Non mi sarei sposata che in febbraio ed era soltanto novembre. Da quando avevo detto a mia madre che mi doveva nascere un figlio, la mia vita era diventata cosí strana. Da allora m'ero dovuta sempre nascondere, come qualcosa di vergognoso che non può essere veduto da nessuno. Pensavo alla mia vita d'una volta, alla città dove andavo ogni giorno, alla strada che portava in città e che avevo attraversato in tutte le stagioni, per tanti anni. Ricordavo bene quella strada, i mucchi di pietre, le siepi, il fiume che si trovava ad un tratto e il ponte affollato che portava sulla piazza della città. In città si compravano le mandorle salate, i gelati, si guardavano le vetrine, c'era il Nini che usciva dalla fabbrica, c'era Antonietta che sgridava il com-

2.2. Dutch public design

PTT Telecom, telephone cards, 1994
54 x 85 mm, lithography

The four lowest-value cards from a set of standard cards issued by the Dutch telecommunications organization – in the short period between coin-operated phone boxes and the age of the cell phone. The design, by Karel Martens, works with overprinted coloured numbers: arrayed not randomly, but determined – via a letter-number code – by the words of the Dutch national anthem. As the view recedes, the value of the card increases. On the other sides, the value and directional arrow become the main graphic elements, with the memory chip proudly displayed. The material is recyclable plastic.

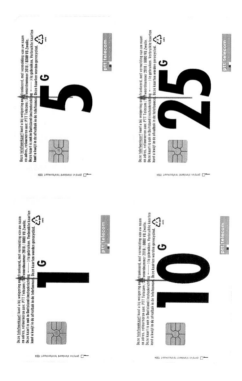

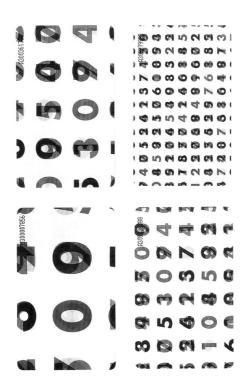

227

23. Digital book-making

Verb: processing, Barcelona: Actar, 2001

240 x 170 mm, 288 pp, lithography

The very packed pages of this work show our present means of text and image assembly at full stretch. It is a 'digital book' especially in the sense it gives of being made by editors and designers, authors and subjects, working together on the same files of data. A habitual device is the caption imposed over photographs, which become no longer separate and perhaps estranged, but are instead part of the overall narrative. Full colour is used throughout, on paper that is mostly matt, but includes an interlude of coated stock for a predominately pictorial section – cinematic in effect. This was the first of the *Verb* 'boogazines' (serially appearing books) from Actar, designed under the direction of Ramon Prat.

AN EXPRESSION OF STATES
AND RELATIONS WHICH IS
INFLECTED, WHICH EVOLVES A PROCESS SHAPED BY DIFFERENT
TYPES OF INFORMATION BEFORE,
DURING AND AFTER A BUILDING IS
MATERIALIZED.

VERB architecture boogazine

PUBLISHED THREE TIMES A YEAR WITH
THEMATIC CONTENTS, A COLLECTABLE BOOK
RATHER THAN A MAGAZINE
(ALSO PUBLISHED IN FRENCH AND SPANISH)

The roof garden consists of 20 m² of lawn and concrete slabs

The exterior handrails are of reinforced plastic.

The main facades consist of sheets of insulating glass in anodised aluminium or galvanised steel frames, and slightly tinted sheets of translucent reinforced plastic.

The side walls are above ground level of in-situ reinforced concrete, cement-rendered light-coloured.

79.50 m

24.10 m

2.80 m

24. A historical-critical edition

H. v. Kleist, *Die Familie Schroffenstein* (Band 1/1, *Sämtliche Werke, Brandenburger Ausgabe*, edited by Roland Reuß & Peter Staengle), Frankfurt a.M: Stroemfeld, 2003

275 x 175 mm, 564 pp, lithography

This spread from a volume of this major edition of Kleist's writings shows the method of this way of editing. A primary document of the text – in this case, Kleist's handwritten pages – is reproduced on one page, and facing it is a typographic version that attempts to transcribe every significant word or sign or mark. Elsewhere in the volume a straightforward transcription of the first printed text is given. Readers and scholars are thus provided with the important materials for a study of this work. The Kleist edition is one of a number following these principles being published by Stroemfeld, which includes editions of Kafka (also edited by Reuß and Staengle) and Hölderlin. A special feature that makes possible this approach is that the editor (Roland Reuß) is also the typesetter. The act of setting the text, in QuarkXPress, is part of the act of interpreting and transcribing Kleist's (to modern, non-German eyes) often impenetrable script. Yet the interpretation is done with great fidelity and restraint – qualities that permeate every part of the design of these dignified books.

Rodrigo.

    Ja, grad' heraus, Antonio.

Es gab uns Gott das seltne Glück, daß wir

Der Feinde Schaar leichtfaßlich, unzweideutig,

Wie eine runde Zahl erkennen. Gossa.

In diesem Worte liegt's, wie **Gift in einer Büchse Und weils jetzt drängt** eben **die** ~~In einer Büchse – Und weils jetzt nicht Zeit ist~~

Zu makeln, ein zweideutig Körnchen Saft

Mit Müh herauszuklauben, nun so machen

Wir's kurz, und sagen, Du gehörst zu Gossa.

    Antonio.

Bei meinem Eid, da habt ihr Recht. Niemals

War eine Wahl mir zwischen Euch und sie.

Doch muß ich mich entscheiden, auf der Stelle

Thu ich's, wenn so die Sachen stehen. Ja, sieh,

Ich spreng' auf alle Schlösser im Gebirg,

Empöre jedes Herz, bewaffne

Wo ich es finde, das Gefühl des Rechts,

Den Frech-Verläumdeten zu rächen. ⌐**Nmr. 2.**

Dem Recht der Rache weigern würde? Nun,
Du Thor, wie könnt' ich denn dies Schwerdt, dies gestern
Empfangene, dies der Rache
Geweihte so mit Wollust tragen? Doch
Nichts mehr davon, das kannst Du nicht verstehen.
Zum Schlusse – Wir, wir hätten, denk' ich, nun
Einander nichts zu sagen mehr[?] – 'Leb' wohl'
          Nein

Ich seh in' sie, doch des [z]Gerichts's Stimme
Rühmet ihre Schönheit – 'Wohl So in der Preis
Es werth.

Antonio

Wer meinst Du das?

Rodrigo

Ich meine', 'Jnfjusä –

Antonio

Lafz gut sein, kann es selbst mir übereizen.
Du meinest, weil ein schöner Fürst sich zeigt,
Der doch zum Unglück blüß von Allen's tüllet,
So schlug ich meine Ritter(her troß
Und barng, ihr Leich' an meiner Ehre Angel
So habe er off?

Rodrigo

Zu, qraß' herum, Antonio.

Es gab am Gott das schöne Glück, daß wir
Der Freude Schaar lu's leidlich, untereidentig,
War nur runde Zahl erkennen, Genoa.
Ich denn Worte lergt's, wie **Gift in einer Buche**
Und weils gratt dränge etwas   du
Inzwerer Buchsen – Und weils prau nicht Zeit ist
Zu zählen, ein zweidentig Keinrelben Salt
Mit Mich heranwälsllalten, nun so machen
Wir kurz, und sagen, Du, geliebst zu Genoa.

Antonio

Bei meinem Eid, du habt Ihr Recht. Normals
War eine Wahl mir zwischen Euch und sie
Doch mull ich nach rauschreiben, auf der Stelle
Hier ich's, wenn so die Sachen stehen. Ja, vieh,
Ich spreng' aul alle Schlösser im Gebirg.
Enpore jede Herz, herauffne
Wes ich's finde, das Gefühl des Rechts,

Des Frech-Verdammütren zu riehen.   / Snnz. z.

Rodrigo

So löten
Wer denn einander weiter nichts zu sagen?

---

f Rodrigo.

Das
Gefühl des Rechts! O Du Marktschreier der   ...
Natur, nicht Einen wird Dein Auftrit tragen.
Und schreiend an der Ecke werden sie
Allein Dich sterben lassen - Des Gefühl
Des Rechts! Als ob's zu einem Mensch'en Innern
Lus anders auch als dieses gabe - Denker Du,
Halt's la die Brust, wenn ums Schuld noch denckts

Dem Recht der Rache weigern würde? Nun,
Du Thor, wir könn' ich's denn dies Schwredt, dirs gestern
Empfangene, dies dir Rache
Geweihte so mit Wollust tragen? Doch
Nichts mehr davon, das kannst Du nicht verstehen
Zum Schlusse - Wer, wer hatten, denk' ich, uns
Umander nichts zu sagen nicht?] Lebt' wohl
Sean

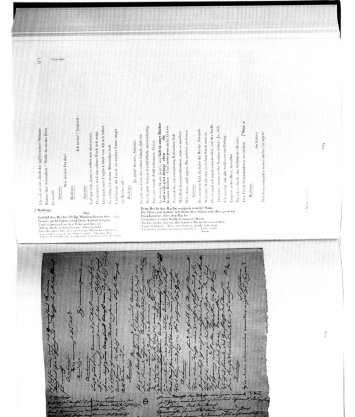

QUI 12 FEV

EDIÇÃO LISBOA

12 de Fevereiro de 2004
Ano XIV • Nº 5073
€0,80 (IVA incluído)

Director JOSÉ MANUEL FERNANDES
Directores adjuntos: NUNO PACHECO
e MANUEL CARVALHO
e-mail: publico@publico.pt

PÚBLICO

www.publico.pt

SÉRIE Y HOJE **NOVO DVD**
"A Maldição do
Escorpião de Jade"
de Woody Allen
POR APENAS
MAIS € 8,9
P42

AGORA ÀS QUINTAS
Na compra do PÚBLICO, o Guia do
Lazer fica por apenas € 0,50
Ver cupão de desconto de € 0,30 na última página

Amanhã
novo
álbum

TINTIM
O TEMPLO DO SOL
P48
POR APENAS
MAIS € 4

IRAQUE

Mais de 100 mortos em menos de 24 horas

Em menos de 24 horas morreram mais de 100 iraquianos em dois atentados suicidas com carros armadilhados. Em comum, as vítimas tinham uma característica: queriam juntar-se às forças da ordem iraquianas. **P12**

Raides israelitas matam 15 palestinianos na Faixa de Gaza **P13**

BICENTENÁRIO DA MORTE DE

KANT

Hoje, quando se completam dois séculos sobre a morte de Kant, o filósofo dos direitos humanos é recordado na Alemanha com várias iniciativas. Em Portugal as comemorações ficam para mais tarde. **P22/3**

GOVERNO

PSD quer obrigar SNS a cumprir lei do aborto

O PSD acrescentou um ponto ao projecto de resolução sobre medidas que previnam o aborto, propondo ao Governo que obrigue o Serviço Nacional de Saúde a cumprir a actual lei de interrupção voluntária da gravidez. **P11**

SOCIALISTAS

Ferro Rodrigues faz apelo à coesão no PS

Ferro Rodrigues fez ontem um apelo à coesão e combatividade no PS, depois de tanto Jorge Coelho como João Soares terem manifestado disposição para liderarem o partido. **P8**

Governo quer proibir tabaco nos locais de trabalho e venda de álcool nas auto-estradas

PLANO NACIONAL DE SAÚDE PREVÊ TAMBÉM LIMITAÇÃO DA VENDA DE ÁLCOOL NOS RECINTOS DESPORTIVOS E NAS UNIVERSIDADES E A SUBIDA DOS PREÇOS DO TABACO **P25**

Tribunal de Contas aponta ilegalidades na privatização das Cervejas da Madeira

O Tribunal de Contas levantou dúvidas quanto à legalidade do procedimento adoptado pelo governo regional na privatização da Empresa de Cervejas da Madeira. Mas a responsabilidade pelo incumprimento da lei, argumenta o executivo de Alberto João Jardim, está extinta por amnistia. As questões jurídicas suscitadas na auditoria do Tribunal de Contas residem, essencialmente, na não observância da Lei Quadro das Privatizações que o governo madeirense entendeu não seguir, alegando competências próprias. **P19**

Economia nos EUA crescerá cinco por cento este ano

PABLO MARTINEZ MONSIVAIS/AP

O presidente da Reserva Federal dos EUA, Alan Greenspan (na foto), sempre prudente nas análises que faz em público, traçou ontem um quadro optimista da economia dos Estados Unidos **P19**

LISBOA CORREDORES "BUS" VÃO SER ISOLADOS POR MUROS DE BETÃO

Separadores de betão vão impedir ocupação por carros particulares das vias dedicadas aos transportes públicos lisboetas, que terão em breve mais 21 quilómetros exclusivos para circular. A ideia, inspirada em Paris, foi ontem anunciada por Santana Lopes numa visita à cidade. **LOCAL**

SEGURANÇA MARÍTIMA CADILHE CRITICA OPÇÃO POR LISBOA PARA SEDE EUROPEIA

Miguel Cadilhe, presidente da Agência Portuguesa de Investimento, lançou ontem um repto à Universidade do Porto – que reclame junto do Governo a instalação na cidade do Porto da futura Agência Europeia de Segurança Marítima. **LOCAL**

25. The modern newspaper
Público, Lisbon & Porto, 2004
400 x 280 mm, 48 pp, lithography
Established in 1990, *Público* is an example of the new breed
of small-format newspapers. The founders' high-minded,
liberal aim was to open up a new public forum for discussion of current affairs, presented through fresh typographic
structures. Regional supplements are added, and a 'side-
plate' of books and now DVDs is issued every week. With all
this *Público* has become the newspaper of the Portuguese
intelligentsia. The front page acts as a contents page to the
whole, then the first few pages carry reflective articles, with
hard news following. The tendency, here as in many other
newspapers of the recent period, is towards the magazine.
Colour is reserved for the front and back pages; inside the
typography is serious and dignified, with a Bodoni used for
the headlines. The basic design – since altered somewhat –
was by Henrique Cayatte.

Postscript on reproduction

The artefacts reproduced as 'examples' in this book attempt to provide some visual illustration of its themes. No strict rules governed the choice of examples. Some of them are actually discussed in the text. Some were chosen just because they show things that are not otherwise mentioned: this is particularly so with the last examples, of recent work, which raise the question of what modern typography may be in the years in which this book has been written. In this second edition of the book I have also tried to choose examples different from those in the first, and borne in mind other books that I have produced since 1992, which present material that overlaps with this one.

From the reservoir of printed matter deposited over three hundred years, what should one show? The possibilities may seem to be almost infinite. But in the event – when it comes to actually locating examples and reproducing their images in a book – the process of selection becomes considerably clarified. It was decided to confine the images to a separate 'chapter' and to use a different paper for this purpose. Forty-eight pages were allocated for this. It was decided to show artefacts not often reproduced before, in freshly-made photographs, with a caption that would give some physical description and refer to points of interest. It then became a matter of finding suitable things, which one could lay one's hands on – gently – and place before a camera and lights. Libraries and archives may not be the best sources here. Heavy fees, bureaucratic obstacles, uncertain technical quality: all of these things lead the reproducer away from these institutions and towards the private archive, which may be small and arbitrary, but is at least friendly and unrestricted.

This pressure towards the things that happen to be easily available has helped to confirm one of the arguments of the text. Printing and typography are in service of the ordinary and the everyday. The pamphlet, the invoice form, the trade catalogue, the flimsily-made novel: these are the staples of printing, and it seems right to give them full attention. If they are not more prominent here, this is partly due to the difficulty of finding old examples of ordinary printing: they perish and are discarded, or else may be found only in unfriendly libraries. It will be clear, then, that this collection of examples is not a 'canon' of modern typography: such a notion seems beside the point of typography. Rather, these examples are just a 'continuation by other means' of the essay.

How exactly to photograph and then print these examples is another area of dilemma and finally unresolvable contradiction. One strong wish has been to show that these artefacts are indeed artefacts. Books, for example, have weight, texture, smell, as well as kinetic possibilities when their pages are turned. When opened, a book may not lie flat, and even if it does, 'flat' will include a valley through the middle. Paper may be torn and stained. At some point in its history, a book's pages may have been ruthlessly trimmed, nastily rebound, or embellished by library stamps. Letterheadings should have been written and typed on; postage stamps licked, stuck and franked. All of these things are the reality of the artefacts of typography. How or whether one shows any of this in reproduction should be a matter of serious consideration.

In the first edition of this work we used black-and-white printing for the pictures, arguing that this gives 'some distance from the artefact', and perhaps a 'critical distance' that gives room for reflection. In this new edition we have tried colour – again in the spirit of experiment, and after seeing what good realist colour photography can achieve. As in the first edition, we have presented the objects cut out from any background. Readers might compare the two results.

Sources of the examples

The examples shown here all belong to private collections with the exception of the first four, as indicated below. We are grateful to these libraries for permission to reproduce these things in their collections.

The British Library: Music Library [Hirsch 1.420]: 3
The London Library: 2, 4
St Bride Printing Library: 1

15   Sources: commentary

1   Modern typography

The following are among the works that have been found useful throughout the writing of this book. They are grouped in the four categories (which are far from mutually exclusive) suggested in this chapter.

The *Journal of the Printing Historical Society* (from 1965) has provided a forum for printing history; the *Bulletin* of this Society – now incorporated into the *Journal* – has also been an informative voice. These are published from London. Since 1979, the American Printing History Association has published *Printing History*, covering a wider field that extends more into history of typography. Among contributions to printing history, Twyman, *Printing 1770–1970*, stands out, as a synopsis and in its suggestions for new approaches, supported by a long bibliography; its exemplary illustrations are a substantial contribution in their own right. Twyman, *Breaking the mould*, makes the case for the importance of lithography in any historical discussion of printing.

The principal journal of bibliographical history is *The Library* (from 1889), published by the Bibliographical Society in London. The Dutch journal *Quaerendo* (from 1971) has its base in this kind of history, but has published articles of prime importance to typography. Gaskell, *A new introduction to bibliography*, is more than its title suggests: it is also a history of printing, and provides many leads for research. Hellinga, *Copy and print in the Netherlands*, is exceptional in its examination of copy and layouts as indications of design and production processes; it is also notable for its own typographic design. D. F. McKenzie provided instances of bibliographical history that escape the confines of the category: for example, his essay 'Typography and meaning: the case of William Congreve' in Barber & Fabian, *Buch und Buchhandel in Europa,* and also given in his selected essays, *Making meaning*. See also his wide-ranging lectures *Bibliography and the sociology of texts*.

Two books stand out among the contributions from general historians: Febvre & Martin, *The coming of the book*, and Eisenstein,

The printing press as an agent of change. The former is brisker and
more simply informative; the latter is more theoretically concerned,
and is provided with a splendidly thorough bibliography and index.
Eisenstein's main thesis of the 'fixity' brought by printing has by
now been thoroughly aired. Johns, *The nature of the book*, provides a
critique using the case of science publishing in seventeenth-century
England. Steinberg, *Five hundred years of printing*, was widely read
in the absence of any better text. Darnton's writings have shown
the kind of fruits that can be discovered by the 'history of the book'.
Books and society in history, edited by Carpenter, contains essays by
leading historians and includes a survey by Darnton of the whole
field. The four-volume *Histoire de l'édition française* covers every
aspect and phase of its subject – if summarily – with abundant visual
illustration. The Society for the History of Authorship, Reading &
Publishing (SHARP) has a website <www.sharpweb.org> that provides a good gateway to this now large field of activity.

Updike's *Printing types* remains a prime example of the history
of typography, and of the fruitful interaction of practice and history,
despite the qualifications and updatings that it requires. Morison's writings also remain useful, if their polemical purposes are
understood and allowed for. Harry Carter's work is also enlivened
by practical experience, as well as by scholarship expressed with
remarkable economy. In comparison with these writers, A. F. Johnson's contributions are peaceful, but still worthwhile. Day, *Book
typography 1815–1965*, is a substantial collection of essays, divided
by country. Two more recent British writer-practitioners can be
mentioned here: Walter Tracy, whose *Letters of credit* remains
a very helpful guide to type design, and whose late miscellany,
The typographic scene, can be contrasted with the present book.
Sebastian Carter, *Twentieth century type designers*, provides a useful
introduction to the technics of making type, up to the photocomposition period. Another practitioner-writer's book – Hollis, *Graphic
design* – is indeed the 'concise history' it claims to be. Baudin, *L'Effet
Gutenberg*, is a maze-like work arguing for continuities especially
between writing and typography, with splendid black-and-white
photographs of key books. Among the journals that have published
contributions of quality: *The Fleuron* (1923–30); *Signature* (1935–40,
1946–54); *Typography* (1936–9); *Alphabet and Image* (1946–8);

Typographica (1949–67); *Motif* (1958–66); *Alphabet* (1964). These
were all published from Britain, and – though one could mention
some American and certain Continental journals – the list indicates
the extent of the British commitment to a historically informed
culture of typography. This impetus has now left the ordinary (if
high-class) trade and retreated to the world of craft printing, from
which sphere the journal *Matrix* (from 1981) now emanates; in the
USA, *Fine Print* (1975–90) published material of interest to those
outside the clan of fine printers, some of which was collected in
the anthology edited by Bigelow. *Typography Papers* (from 1996),
from the Department of Typography at the University of Reading,
has published distinguished contributions to the field. The 'Questions de la typographie' web pages maintained by Jacques André at
<www.irisa.fr/faqtypo/Welcome.html> provide many useful leads.

Not all information can be found in print or on the internet.
Museums and exhibitions of printing and typography – such as
those in Mainz, Offenbach, Antwerp, Lyons – can provide important
resources. A series of critical articles on these museums, by Frans
Janssen, was published in the journal *Quaerendo* (from 1980).

2   Enlightenment origins

The edition of Moxon, *Mechanick exercises*, by Davis and Carter,
provides copious material for an understanding of printing before
industrialization. Moxon himself appears as a subject in Johns,
The nature of the book. Fertel's manual has been discussed by Giles
Barber: 'Martin-Dominique Fertel and his "Science pratique de
l'imprimerie", 1723', *The Library*, 6th series, vol. 8, no. 1, 1986; see
also Barber, *French letterpress printing*, for a list that suggests the
growth of published discussion of typography in France. André
Jammes's work on the 'romain du roi' was published in English
in the *Journal of the Printing Historical Society*, no. 1, 1965; a full
account is his *La Naissance d'un caractère*. Jammes's pioneering
work is now supplemented and extended by Mosley's writing: in his
essays on the work of the Académie des Sciences (see the remarks
on measurement in this period, below) and as the leading author
in the wonderfully illustrated bicentenary catalogue from Lyons (*Le
Romain du roi*). Useful documentation is provided by an anthology
of texts and plates from the *Encyclopédie*: Barber, *Book making in*

Diderot's 'Encyclopédie'. Darnton, *The business of enlightenment*, is a minutely detailed history of the publishing of the later, popular edition of the *Encyclopédie*. Dreyfus, *Aspects of French eighteenth-century typography*, is a survey of the field, as well as a special study of type specimens. *Revolution in print*, edited by Darnton and Roche, contains primary research on French publishing and printing in the later eighteenth century. Eisenstein's *Grub Street abroad* is a spirited survey of the 'French cosmopolitan press'.

Social-historical aspects of measurement are discussed in Kula's *Measures and men*, which includes an account of the introduction of the metric system in France. This can be supplemented by Alder's *The measure of all things*: a lively and very detailed account of the working-out of the metric system. On the development of standards for paper and for type, there is a brief but fundamental consideration in Froshaug, *Typographic norms*. Graham Pollard set out the factors informing the development of book formats in 'Notes on the size of the sheet', *The Library*, 4th series, vol. 22, nos. 2–3, 1941. E. J. Labarre, *Dictionary and encyclopaedia of paper and paper-making*, has good articles on 'size' and 'standardization'. The early history of the point system of measurement was outlined by Updike in his *Printing types*, vol. 1, and by Walter Tracy, 'The point', *Penrose Annual*, vol. 55, 1961 (whose material was resumed in the same author's *Letters of credit*). But these acounts must now be qualified by Mosley's essays in this field: 'Illustrations of typefounding engraved for the *Description des arts et métiers* of the Académie Royale des Sciences, Paris, 1694 to c.1700', *Matrix*, no. 11, 1991; and 'French academicians and modern typography', *Typography Papers*, no. 2, 1997; and in the commentaries in his edition of Fournier's *Manuel typographique*. Andrew Boag provided an invaluable overview of the whole history in 'Typographic measurement: a chronology', *Typography Papers*, no. 1, 1996.

A concise account of the development of modern-face roman types is available in Johnson, *Type designs*. Fournier's life and work are described in a monograph by Hutt. Mosley's edition of the *Manuel typographique* provides full and up-to-date documentation of Fournier's work. Accounts of the work of the Didot family are not easily available. Two articles by Veyrin-Forrer, in her *La Lettre et la texte*, discuss the typefaces of François Ambroise and Pierre

François. James's *Les Didots* is a useful catalogue. The best short
survey in English may be: Walter Tracy, 'Didot: an honoured name
in French typography', *Linotype Matrix*, no. 24, 1956 (reprinted in the
Bulletin of the Printing Historical Society, no. 14, 1985). For a rare attempt to discuss text arrangement in this period, see Nicolas Barker,
'Typography and the meaning of words: the revolution in the layout
of books in the eighteenth century', in Barber & Fabian, *Buch und
Buchhandel in Europa*.

3   The nineteenth-century complex

Good synoptic accounts of the industrialization of printing are provided by Gaskell, *A new introduction to bibliography*, and Twyman,
Printing 1770–1970. For a corrective to ideas of a sudden triumph of
mechanization, see: Raphael Samuel, 'The workshop of the world:
steam power and hand technology in mid-Victorian Britain', *History
Workshop*, no. 3, 1977.

For new typefaces in this period, Gray, *Nineteenth century ornamented typefaces* is a standard but also lively account; see also the
same writer's 'Slab-serif type design in England 1815–1845', *Journal of the Printing Historical Society*, no. 15, 1980–1. Sanserif in this
period is discussed by Gray, and most importantly by James Mosley,
The nymph and the grot. See also Tracy, *Letters of credit*. Old-face
types are treated by Johnson, *Type designs*, and in a ground-break-
ing article by G. W. Ovink, 'Nineteenth-century reactions against the
didone type model', *Quaerendo*, vol. 1, nos. 1 & 4, 1971.

For surveys of pre-twentieth-century histories of typography,
see Morison's 'On the classification of typographic variations' in
his *Letter forms*. See also the lists of literature given in Faulmann,
Illustrirte Geschichte. Other useful guides to literature are: P. Gaskell,
G. Barber, & G. Warrilow, 'An annotated list of printers' manuals to
1850', *Journal of the Printing Historical Society*, no. 4, 1968, & no. 7,
1972; and Barber, *French letterpress printing*.

The mechanization of composition is well documented in:
Legros & Grant, *Typographical printing-surfaces*; Moran, *The composition of reading matter*; Huss, *The development of printers' mechanical typesetting methods*. For a detailed account of the major reform
of measurement in this period, see: Hopkins, *Origin of the American
point system*. On the history of legibility research, see: Pyke, *Report*

on the legibility of print; Spencer, *The visible word*. Lawrence Wallis provides good background information in his article 'Legros and Grant: the typographical connection', *Journal of the Printing Historical Society*, no. 28, 1999.

4   Reaction and rebellion

On the typography of Morris, Sparling, *The Kelmscott Press and William Morris*, written under his shadow, is an important document. Among the plentiful recent literature, Peterson's *The Kelmscott Press* is the most complete account. The Pierpont Morgan Library collection, *William Morris and the art of the book*, stands out, though it lacks critical judgement. A more modest exhibition catalogue, the William Morris Society's *The typographical adventure of William Morris*, is still useful. Peterson, *A bibliography of the Kelmscott Press*, is helpful beyond its nominal scope. Morris's writings on typography are gathered in *The ideal book*.

The private press movement is sufficiently described by Franklin, *The private presses*, and Cave, *The private press*. Walker, who merits a longer study, is treated in Franklin's brief *Emery Walker*. The Doves Press is fully described by Tidcombe. Ashbee's typography is the subject of a chapter in Crawford, *C.R.Ashbee*. Lethaby's life and work are documented in Rubens, *William Richard Lethaby*. Johnston (the man rather than his work) is well conveyed in the engaging biography by his daughter Priscilla: *Edward Johnston*. His Underground type is now documented in the monograph by Howes.

On aestheticism in trade printing, see: V. Ridler, 'Artistic printing', *Alphabet and Image*, no. 6, 1948; Gray, *Nineteenth century ornamented typefaces*. And for the wider context, see: Aslin, *The aesthetic movement*.

5   Traditional values in a new world

Thompson, *American book design and William Morris*, is an exhaustive but uncritical chronicle of its subject, covering all the people who took some inspiration from Kelmscott. Its bibliographies are extensive. Blumenthal, *The printed book in America*, covers the whole history of book-printing in the country, from the 'fine-printing' point of view. Much the same approach informs the survey by

James M. Wells in Day, *Book typography*. Recent historical work may be found in the journal *Printing History*. Most of the literature on individual designers is contemporary: appreciations by colleagues or autobiographical texts. Apart from De Vinne (essentially a nineteenth-century figure), those whose work most needs critical reappraisal are Updike and Dwiggins. Updike's printing is documented in his *Notes on the Merrymount Press* and in American Institute of Graphic Arts, *Updike*; his occasional essays have now been collected in *The well-made book*. Some of Dwiggins's essays were collected in his MSS by WAD; his thoughts on methods of designing typefaces, in WAD to RR, are of considerable interest. Dwiggins was the subject of a contemporary tribute: Bennett, *Postscripts on Dwiggins*; among recent essays, see especially: Gerard Unger, 'Experimental no. 223, a newspaper typeface designed by W. A. Dwiggins', *Quaerendo*, vol. 11, no. 4, 1981. There are evaluations of the typefaces of Goudy and Dwiggins in Tracy, *Letters of credit*, and there is a biography of Goudy by Bruckner.

6   New traditionalism

There is no extended history of British new traditionalism, but Barker, *Stanley Morison*, helped by an excellent index, amounts to this, as well as fulfilling the immediate biographical task. Otherwise, the literature, in periodicals, memoirs and biographies, is plentiful but dispersed. A major gap is a history of the Monotype Corporation, though a centenary issue of the *Monotype Recorder* (new series, no. 10, 1997) provides a good framework for this; Mike Parker's brief introduction to his edition of Morison's *A tally of types* suggests the kind of critical approach that would be needed. The Curwen Press is documented by Herbert Simon, *Song and words*, and also in Oliver Simon, *Printer and playground*. The Nonesuch Press is conclusively described in Dreyfus, *A history of the Nonesuch Press*. Celebratory histories of both the Double Crown Club and the Society of Typographic Designers (*Fit to be styled a typographer*) were written by Moran.

Moran, *Stanley Morison*, is a narrow work and not comparable to Barker's full biography, but it has useful illustrations. These books were the occasion for a searching discussion by G. W. Ovink: 'Two books on Stanley Morison', *Quaerendo*, vol. 3, no. 3, 1973. Meynell, *My lives*, and Simon, *Printer and playground*, are the autobiographies of central figures. Though not an orderly account, Gill's *Autobiography* has his spirit: something that has eluded his biographers, who have all been weak on his lettering and typographic activity. The best extended account here is: Wolfgang Kehr, 'Eric Gill als Schriftkünstler', *Börsenblatt für den deutschen Buchhandel* (Frankfurt), no. 77a, 1961. A special study, but of wide illumination is: James Mosley, 'Eric Gill's Perpetua type', *Fine Print*, vol. 8, no. 3, 1982 (and reprinted in the anthology *Fine Print on type* edited by Bigelow). Beatrice Warde was the subject of a substantial memorial issue of *Monotype Recorder*, vol. 44, no. 1, 1970; there is also much about her in Barker, *Stanley Morison*.

7   Cultures of printing: Germany

For Germany, Schauer, *Deutsche Buchkunst*, is much the most substantial history of the subject. Besides its text, it has exemplary illustrations in a separate volume, and an extensive bibliography. The book's limitations are those of its subject: a concern with the 'art of the book' at the expense of everyday printing. The essay by Schauer in Day, *Book typography*, condenses the arguments of his book, and extends their time-span. Rodenberg, *Deutsche Pressen*, is now itself a historical example, but its thorough annotations are still useful, though the scope is narrow (private and small press books). Rodenberg's later *Größe und Grenzen der Typographie* is a wide-ranging and rapid international survey of traditionalist book design. Schmidt-Künsemüller, *William Morris und die neuere Buchkunst*, is a rare discussion of the ideas (less the products) of the printing reform, with special emphasis on Germany: without pictorial illustration, but thoroughly documented.

Most of the leading designers have been the subject of contemporary 'Festschriften' or monographs. These, as well as the periodical literature, are listed by Schauer in *Deutsche Buchkunst*. Among works published since Schauer's book, Mardersteig, *The Officina Bodoni*, stands out. Schneidler's work is now described in the book edited by Schumacher-Gebler. Koch is fully treated in the monograph by Cinamon. Sichowsky, *Typographie und Bibliophilie*, is an anthology of statements by printers and designers; among them, Eckmann, Poeschel, Weiß, Ehmcke.

The Deutscher Werkbund is now well documented. Among the English-language books, Schwartz provides a history of ideas; the best single history in English remains Campbell, *The German Werkbund*.

8   Cultures of printing: the Low Countries

Useful essays in Day, *Book typography*, by Gerard Blanchard and Maximilien Vox himself tend to confirm my remarks in this chapter; see also the compendious *Dossier Vox*, edited by Magermans and Baudin.

For Belgium, see Fernand Baudin's essay in Day, *Book typography*, and also his article: 'La Formation et l'évolution typographiques de Henry van de Velde', *Quaerendo*, vol. 1, no. 4, 1971; vol. 2, no. 1, 1972. For an international survey of 'art nouveau' lettering, with special attention to Belgium and Germany, see: Roswitha Riegger-Baurmann, 'Schrift im Jugendstil', *Börsenblatt für den Deutschen Buchhandel* (Frankfurt), no. 31a, 1958.

For the Netherlands, see the article by G. W. Ovink in Day, *Book typography*, which has references to further literature. Among more recent contributions, the monograph on Van Krimpen, *Adieu aesthetica*, by Van Faassen and others, shows what can by done by a fresh, revisionist view. The journal *Quaerendo* publishes material on modern-period Dutch topics, as well as on its main topic of pre-industrial typography.

9   The new typography

Tschichold's *Die neue Typographie*, is still the best account of the subject, as well as being a prime specimen of it. Both this text and his first survey, 'Elementare Typographie', have been reprinted in facsimile editions, with useful introductory material. The introductions to the English-language and Spanish-language editions of *Die neue Typographie* (by the present writer and by Josep M. Pujol, respectively) should be consulted. Two books published in the 1960s helped to define the topic: Spencer, *Pioneers of modern typography*, in its first and best edition, can be used as an introductory survey, but its art-movement approach and anthology character are severe limitations; Neumann, *Functional graphic design*, attempts a synthesis, but is marred by quirks and incompleteness. Much more detailed and better illustrated work has since appeared: Fleischmann, *Bauhaus: Drucksachen, Typografie, Reklame,* shows much of the printed matter from the Bauhaus, reproduced to a high standard and well annotated; it also reprints texts by Bauhaus teachers and other contemporaries. Brüning, *Das A und O des Bauhauses,* is a later report, based on the material in the Bauhaus Archiv; among the essays there is a revisionist piece by the present writer, given now in English in his collection *Unjustified texts.* The set of four publications titled *'Typographie kann unter Umständen Kunst sein'* is the best source for material on the Ring Neuer Werbegestalter and on Schwitters as typographer. Drucker, *The visible word*, may be useful as a survey of typography and art in the early twentieth century, but carries the burdens of the dissertation format and a very theoretical understanding of 'materiality'.

There are substantial surveys of the lives and works of Lissitzky (by Lissitzky-Küppers, by Debbaut, and by Tupitsyn), Moholy-Nagy (by Passuth), Schwitters (by Schmalenbach and by Elderfield). Some of their writings on typography may also be found in these books; and see also the anthology by Kostelanetz on Moholy-Nagy, and the edition of Schwitters's *Manifeste und kritische Prosa*. Lissitzky's typographic work is best seen in the catalogue edited by Nisbet.

Tschichold provided a monograph on himself: the *Leben und Werk*. This reprints a pseudonymous autobiographical text, some articles, and bibliographies; it also reproduces an extensive selection of his work. McLean, *Jan Tschichold*, relies uncritically for much of its information on Tschichold's own account and is introductory in character. G. W. Ovink wrote a judicious summary in his article 'Jan Tschichold 1902–74: Versuch zu einer Bilanz seines Schaffens', *Quaerendo*, vol. 7, no. 3, 1978. The present writer's introduction the English-language edition of *Die neue Typographie* discusses the earlier phase of his work at some length; so too does Pujol's introduction to the Spanish-language edition. An extensive selection of Tschichold's writings has been reprinted as *Schriften 1925–1974*.

The tributes to Renner, Tschichold, and Trump, produced by the Typographische Gesellschaft München, are slight though nicely illustrated, and include the only book on the latter designer. Renner's work is treated in Burke's comprehensive account. Cohen, *Herbert Bayer*, is a laudatory monograph; the Bauhaus-Archiv's catalogue of Bayer's German work is more useful. Dutch new typography is conveniently summarized in Maan & Van der Ree, *Typo-foto*.

On standardization, see an official history: B. Holm (ed.), *Funfzig Jahre Deutscher Normenausschuß* (Berlin: Beuth-Vertrieb, 1967); and also a contemporary international survey by the National Industrial Conference Board, *Industrial standardization* (New York: NICB, 1929). A penetrating and accessible exposition of the philosophy of standards can be found in Bruce Martin's *Standards and building* (London: Royal Institute of British Architects, 1971).

The best critical discussion of political book-clubs is the essay by Bühnemann and Friedrich in: Neue Gesellschaft für Bildende Kunst, *Wem gehört die Welt*. This catalogue provides good social-political studies of the art and design of the period. Willett, *The new sobriety*, is a wide-ranging survey.

10   Emigration of the modern

On cultural production under National Socialism, there is useful material in Hinz, *Art in the Third Reich*. A well-documented survey of National-Socialist ideology is available in: Jeffrey Herf, *Reactionary modernism* (Cambridge: Cambridge University Press, 1984). For a brief but interesting special survey, see Hans Peter Willberg's 'Schrift und Typografie im Dritten Reich' in: Typographische Gesellschaft München, *Hundert Jahre Typographie*. For this and earlier topics, Aynsley, *Graphic design in Germany*, provides much fresh illustration.

For contemporary documents of the post-1945 debate over blackletter and roman, see: Klingspor, *Über Schönheit von Schrift und Druck*, and a special issue on 'Sprache und Schrift' of *Pandora* (no. 4, 1946), with contributions by Ehmcke, Renner, and others. A more recent advocate of blackletter was Walter Plata; see his *Fraktur, Gotisch, Schwabacher*. Plata's work, in an earlier form, provoked Gerrit Noordzij's stimulating and wide-ranging critique 'Broken scripts and the classification of typefaces', *Journal of Typographic Research*, vol. 4, no. 3, 1970. Heiderhoff, *Antiqua oder Fraktur?*, is a brief survey, but with a bibliography. Kapr joined the discussion with his *Fraktur*. Bain & Shaw, *Blackletter*, is a useful summary in English. Hartmann's thesis, *Fraktur oder Antiqua*, is exhaustive.

The best English-language source on the clandestine book-printing during the occupation of the Netherlands is Simoni, *Publish and be free*. For Werkman and Sandberg, complete surveys (with English texts) are: Martinet, *Hot printing*; Petersen & Brattinga, *Sandberg*. For a good short survey of the whole phenomenon, with special emphasis on Germany, see: Sibylle Fraser, 'Underground printing in Europe, 1933–1945', *Printing History*, no. 15, 1986. The work of two German book designers in Dutch emigration (Henri Friedlaender and Paul Urban) is fully described by Löbe.

The work of Tschichold at Penguin Books is well described (from personal experience) by McLean, *Jan Tschichold*, and Tschichold himself documented some of the products in his *Designing books*. Schmoller's work is described incidentally in the voluminous literature on Penguins, and in a memorial issue of the *Monotype Recorder*, new series, no. 6, 1987. The Victoria & Albert Museum's catalogue of a retrospective exhibition (1980) is the best published document on Berthold Wolpe. Schleger's work is documented in Pat Schleger's engaging *Zero*; Henrion awaits proper documentation. There is a survey, with case-studies of individuals, by the present writer: 'Emigré graphic designers in Britain: around the Second World War and afterwards', *Journal of Design History*, vol. 3, no. 1, 1990. The field of book design in emigration is now treated by Fischer, *Buchgestaltung im Exil*.

American work in this period (as well as earlier and later) receives coverage in Friedman & Freshman's *Graphic design in America*, and in Remington & Hodik, *Nine pioneers in American graphic design*. The whole range of Sutnar's work is represented in Janáková's monograph, and see the elaborate website <www.sutnar.com>.

11   Aftermath and renewal

For material on new traditionalist typography after 1945, see the notes to the preceding chapters. Here, as for developments in modernist typography of this period, no extended survey has yet been attempted, and investigators must use their initiative in picking ways through the contemporary literature in journals, annuals, and books.

The history of photocomposing techniques is covered in: Phillips, *Computer peripherals and typesetting*; Seybold, *The world of digital typesetting*; Wallis, *Electronic typesetting*; Marshall, *Du plomb à la lumière.* These works provide structures for understanding a bewildering period of invention.

Anthony Froshaug, by the present writer, provides extensive documentation of this designer's work and life. Herbert Spencer's magazine is recorded in Poynor, *Typographica*.

The literature of the Hfg Ulm is now plentiful. The best surveys of the school's work may be: Herbert Lindinger (ed), *Hochschule für Gestaltung Ulm: die Morale der Gegenstände*, Berlin: Ernst & Sohn, 1987 (English-language edition, 1989); Ulmer Museum / Hfg Archiv (ed.), *Ulmer Modelle – Modelle nach Ulm*, Ostfildern-Ruit: Hatje Cantz, 2003. Published twenty years after the closure of the Hfg Ulm, Otl Aicher's *Typographie* provides a summary of his approach, as developed in contemporary conditions.

12 Swiss typography

The phenomenon of Swiss typography has still to be fully analysed: it was marked by a high degree of self-consciousness, and the contemporary literature is abundant. Principal sources would be the books and journals mentioned in this chapter, especially *Typographische Monatsblätter*, which was the leading journal of modernist typography – internationally – over several decades. Substantial monographs are however beginning to appear, notably *Max Bill* (edited by Bürkle), *Richard Paul Lohse* (edited by the Lohse Stiftung), and *Karl Gerstner* (by Gestner himself).

13 Modernism and modernity

It is, of course, too soon to be able to write adequate histories of typography in this period. The following notes concern the discrete topics treated in this chapter.

Wolfgang Weingart's work is presented in his own book, *Wege zur Typographie*; Brody's work is presented in his *The graphic language of Neville Brody* and its follow-up. For Gerrit Noordzij's work, see the bibliographies and other materials at <www.letterror. com/noordzij/>. At the time of writing, the only available English-language book of Noordzij's writings is *Letterletter*: an anthology drawn from his bulletin of that name. Matthew Carter's work is documented and discussed in Re, *Typographically speaking.*

Developments in text composition are summarized by Seybold,

The world of digital typesetting, and by Wallis, *Electronic typesetting*.
Bosshard, *Technische Grundlagen zur Satzherstellung*, is a splendid
compendium of practical and historical knowledge. The most au-
thoritative journal in this field has been *The Seybold Report on Publishing Systems*, published every two weeks since 1971, which provided (and continues to provide) a rich source on the development
of the technics of typography. Between 1986 and 1996, a monthly
Seybold Report on Desktop Publishing was published alongside the
Report on Publishing Systems (it was then replaced by *The Seybold
Report on Internet Publishing*). For an introduction to digital type,
see especially a series of articles by Charles Bigelow in *The Seybold
Report on Publishing Systems*, vol. 10, no. 24, 1981; vol. 11, no. 11, 1982;
vol. 11, no. 12, 1982. In a rush of literature on the topic, Black, *Typefaces for desktop publishing*, stood out as a critically conscious guide.

Certain recent systems of composition are critically discussed,
and general principles suggested, in the course of Williamson,
Methods of book design. Wallis, *Type design: developments 1970–
1985*, is a useful rapid survey of products (rather than systems).
Knuth's work on Metafont and TeX is elaborated in his *Computers
and typesetting*. For its development and the debate over it, see articles in *Visible Language*: vol. 16, no. 1, 1982; vol. 16, no. 4, 1982; vol. 17,
no. 4, 1983; vol. 19, no. 1, 1985. Some practitioners have written help-
fully; see, for example, Matthew Carter's 'Typography and current
technologies', *Design Quarterly*, no. 148, 1990.

The most recent developments in font technology are best followed, as they happen, in reports and reviews on the internet. Berry,
Language, culture, type is a useful collection of essays, especially on
questions of technology and particular 'non-Latin' language-scripts.

On the contemporary debates over typography and graphic design in this period, the best primer may be the first two volumes of
the series *Looking closer: critical writings on graphic design*, edited by
Steven Heller and others (New York: Allworth Press, 1994 and 1997).

Among articles on the reform of typographic measurement, see
especially these by a principal protagonist, Ernest Hoch: 'International unification of typographic measurement', *Penrose Annual*,
vol. 60, 1967; 'The demise of the point system in sight', *Icographic*,
no. 3, 1972. A further substantial contribution is: Séamas Ó Brógáin,
'Typographic measurement: a critique and a proposal', *Professional*

Printer, vol. 27, no. 5, 1983. The long history of this reform is presented in a two-part article by G. W. Ovink, 'From Fournier to metric, and
from lead to film', *Quaerendo*, vol. 9, nos. 2 & 4, 1979. The clearest
statement of rational principles for measurement of letterform size
is: Ernest Hoch & Maurice Goldring, 'Type size: a system of dimensional references', *Typographica*, new series, no. 13, 1966; this is now
reprinted in Burnhill, *Type spaces*, which comments on the question
of measurement by way of an investigation of Aldus Manutius's
printing. Andrew Boag's 'Typographic measurement: a chronology'
(*Typography Papers*, no. 1, 1996) provides a summary.

    At the time of writing (2004), a research project is getting un-
derway at the University of Reading to document the activities of
reform in typography in the UK, under the title 'The optimism of
modernity: recovering modern reasoning in typography'.

    Jeremy Campbell, *Grammatical man* (London: Allen Lane, 1983)
is a popular account of the history and ideas of information theory;
Colin Cherry, *On human communication* (Cambridge, Massachusetts: MIT Press, 1957), is a standard exposition. Information design
can be traced through the *Journal of Typographic Research* (from
1967), which changed its name and broadened its scope as *Visible
Language* (from 1971), and *Information Design Journal* (from 1979).

    Two unpublished theses provide discussion of issues debated in
these years. Each is of much greater analytical power than the material published in the magazines and book-anthologies. They are:
Robert Waller, 'The typographic contribution to language: towards
a model of typographic genres and their underlying structures' (PhD
thesis, Department of Typography, University of Reading, 1987: files
can be downloaded at <www.gem.stir.ac.uk/newframe.html>); Ole
Lund, 'Knowledge construction in typography: the case of legibility
research and the legibility of sans serif typefaces' (PhD thesis, Department of Typography, University of Reading, 1999).

    In tracing the fate of 'the modern' and 'the postmodern', a
fruitful line of debate and analysis can be found in Fredric Jame-
son, *Postmodernism, or, the cultural logic of late capitalism* (London:
Verso, 1991), Perry Anderson, *The origins of postmodernity* (London:
Verso, 1998), and the discussions in *New Left Review* that have surrounded these and associated publications.

16   Sources: bibliography

This bibliography lists those books cited – without further bibliographical description – in the text, including the preceding chapter.
The edition given is that which has been actually used, unless another edition is specified in the notes to the text. Wherever possible, the 'best' edition has been used: later editions of books do not
always improve on their predecessors (e.g. in their illustrations or
in quality of production) and sometimes the last edition has been
passed over in favour of an earlier one. Updike's *Printing types* is an
instance of this. Subtitles are given where they illuminate cryptic
titles.

Aicher, O. *Typographie*, Berlin: Ernst & Sohn, 1988
Alder, K. *The measure of all things: the seven-year odyssey that transformed the
    world*, London: Little, Brown, 2002
American Institute of Graphic Arts (ed.) *Updike: American Printer*, New York:
    AIGA, 1947
Aslin, E. *The aesthetic movement: prelude to art nouveau*, London: Elek, 1969
Aynsley, J. *Graphic design in Germany, 1890–1945*, London: Thames &
    Hudson, 2000
Bain, P. & P. Shaw (ed.) *Blackletter: type and national identity*, New York: The
    Cooper Union / Princeton Architectural Press, 1998
Barber, G. (ed.) *Book making in Diderot's 'Encyclopédie'*, Farnborough: Gregg,
    1973
—   *French letterpress printing: a list of French printing manuals and other
    texts in French bearing on the technique of letterpress printing 1567–1900*,
    Oxford: Oxford Bibliographical Society, 1969
—   & B. Fabian (ed.) *Buch und Buchhandel in Europa im achtzehnten
    Jahrhundert*, Hamburg: Hauswedell, 1981
Barker, N. *Form and meaning in the history of the book: selected essays*,
    London: British Library, 2003
—   *Stanley Morison*, London: Macmillan, 1971
Baudin, F. *L'Effet Gutenberg*, Paris: Éditions du Cercle de la Librairie, 1995
Bauhaus-Archiv (ed.) *Herbert Bayer: das künstlerische Werk 1918–1938*,
    Berlin: Bauhaus-Archiv, 1982
Bennett, P. A. (ed.) *Postscripts on Dwiggins*, 2 vols, New York: Typophiles, 1960
Berry, J. D. (ed.) *Language, culture, type: international type design in the age of
    Unicode*, New York: ATypI / Graphis, 2002
Bigelow, C, & P. H. Duensing & L. Gentry (ed.) *Fine Print on type*, San
    Francisco: Fine Print, 1989

Black, A. *Typefaces for desktop publishing: a user guide*, London: Architecture Design and Technology Press, 1990

Blumenthal, J. *The printed book in America*, London: Scolar Press, 1977

Bosshard, H. R. *Technische Grundlagen zur Satzherstellung*, Berne: Bildungs-verband der Schweizerischer Typografen, 1980

Bringhurst, R. *The elements of typographic style*, 2nd edn, Vancouver: Hartley & Marks, 1996

Brody, N. *The graphic language of Neville Brody*, London: Thames & Hudson, 1988

—   *The graphic language of Neville Brody 2*, London: Thames & Hudson, 1994

Bruckner, D. J. R. *Frederic Goudy*, New York: Abrams, 1990

Brüning, U. (ed.) *Das A und O des Bauhauses*, Berlin: Bauhaus Archiv, 1995

Buddensieg, T. (ed.) *Industriekultur: Peter Behrens und die AEG 1907–1914*, 2nd edn, Berlin: Gebr. Mann Verlag, 1981 (in English as: *Industriekultur*, Cambridge, Massachusetts: MIT Press, 1984)

Burke, C. *Paul Renner*, London: Hyphen Press, 1998

Bürkle, J. C. (ed.) *Max Bill: Typografie, Reklame, Buchgestaltung*, Sulgen / Zurich: Niggli, 1999

Burnhill, P. *Type spaces: in-house norms in the typography of Aldus Manutius*, London: Hyphen Press, 2003

Burt, C. *A psychological study of typography*, Cambridge: Cambridge University Press, 1959

Campbell, J. *The German Werkbund: the politics of reform in the applied arts*, Princeton: Princeton University Press, 1978

Carpenter, K. E. (ed.) *Books and society in history*, New York: Bowker, 1983

Carter, H. *A view of early typography*, Oxford: Clarendon Press, 1969 (reprinted, London: Hyphen Press, 2002)

—   (ed.) *Fournier on typefounding: the text of the 'Manuel typographique'*, 2nd edn, New York: Franklin, 1973 (now reprinted within Mosley's edition of the *Manuel typographique*)

Carter, S. *Twentieth century type designers*, 2nd edn, London: Lund Humphries, 1995

Cave, R. *The private press*, 2nd edn, New York: Bowker, 1983

Cinamon, G. *Rudolph Koch: letterer, type designer, teacher*, London: British Library, 2000

Cobden-Sanderson, T. J. *The ideal book or the book beautiful*, London: Doves Press, 1901

Cohen, A. A. *Herbert Bayer: the complete work*, Cambridge, Massachusetts: MIT Press, 1984

Crawford, A. *C. R. Ashbee*, New Haven: Yale University Press, 1985

Crutchley, B. *To be a printer*, London: Bodley Head, 1981

Darnton, R. *The business of enlightenment: a publishing history of the 'Encyclopédie' 1775–1800*, Cambridge, Massachusetts: Harvard University Press, 1979

— *The kiss of Lamourette: reflections in cultural history*, London: Faber & Faber, 1990

— & D. Roche (ed.) *Revolution in print: the press in France 1775–1800*, Berkeley: University of California Press, 1989

Day, K. (ed.) *Book typography 1815–1965: in Europe and the United States of America*, London: Benn, 1966

Debbaut, J. (ed.) *El Lissitzky*, London: Thames & Hudson, 1990

De Vinne, T. L. *The practice of typography*, New York: Century; comprises: *A treatise on the processes of type-making* (1900); *Correct composition* (1901); *A treatise on title-pages* (1902); *Modern methods of book composition* (1904)

Dreyfus, J. *Aspects of French eighteenth-century typography: a study of type specimens in the Broxbourne Collection at Cambridge University Library*, London: Roxburghe Club, 1982

— *A history of the Nonesuch Press*, London: Nonesuch Press, 1982

— *The work of Jan van Krimpen*, London: Sylvan Press, 1952

Drucker, J. *The visible word: experimental typography and modern art, 1909–1923*, Chicago: University of Chicago Press, 1994

Dwiggins, W. A. *Layout in advertising*, revised edn, New York: Harper, 1948

— *MSS by WAD*, New York: Typophiles, 1947

— *WAD to RR: a letter about designing type*, Cambridge, Massachusetts: Harvard College, 1940

Ehmcke, F. H. *Ziele des Schriftunterrichts: ein Beitrag zur modernen Schrift-bewegung*, 2nd edn, Jena: Diederichs, 1929

Ehrlich, F. *The new typography and modern layouts*, London: Chapman & Hall, 1934

Eisenstein, E. *Grub Street abroad: aspects of the French cosmopolitan press from the age of Louis XIV to the French Revolution*, Oxford: Clarendon Press, 1992

— *The printing press as an agent of change: communications and cultural transformation in early-modern Europe*, 2 vols, Cambridge: Cambridge University Press, 1979

Elderfield, J. *Kurt Schwitters*, London: Thames & Hudson, 1985

Faassen, S. v, K. Sierman & S. Hubregtse, *Adieu aesthetica & mooie pagina's! J. van Krimpen en het 'schoone boek'. Letterontwerper & boekverzorger 1892–1958*, The Hague: Meermanno Museum, 1995

Faulmann, K. *Illustrirte Geschichte der Buchdruckerkunst*, Vienna: Hartleben, 1882

Febvre, L. & H.-J. Martin, *The coming of the book: the impact of printing 1450–1800*, London: New Left Books, 1976 (from the French: *L'Apparition du livre*, Paris: Albin Michel, 1958)

Fertel, M. D. *La Science pratique de l'imprimerie*, Saint-Omer, 1723 (facsimile, Farnborough: Gregg, 1971)

Fischer, E. *Buchgestaltung im Exil, 1933–1950*, Wiesbaden: Harrassowitz, 2003

Fleischmann, G. (ed.) *Bauhaus: Drucksachen, Typografie, Reklame*, Düsseldorf: Edition Marzona, 1984

Fournier, P. S. *Manuel typographique*, Paris, 1764 & 1766 (facsimile, ed. J. Mosley, 3 vols, Darmstadt: Technische Hochschule Darmstadt, 1995)

— *Modèles des caractères de l'imprimerie*, Paris, 1742 (facsimile, ed. J. Mosley, London: Eugrammia Press, 1965)

Franklin, C. *The private presses*, London: Studio Vista, 1969

— *Emery Walker*, Cambridge: University Printer, 1973

Friedman, M. & P. Freshman (ed.) *Graphic design in America*, New York: Abrams, 1989

Froshaug, A. *Typographic norms*, Birmingham: Kynoch Press, 1964 (text reprinted within Kinross, *Anthony Froshaug: Typography & texts*)

Gaskell, P. *A new introduction to bibliography*, revised edn, Oxford: Clarendon Press, 1974 (reprint, New Castle, Delaware: Oak Knoll, 2000)

Gerstner, M. *Karl Gerstner: review of 5 x 10 years of graphic design etc.*, ed. M. Kröplein, Ostfildern-Ruit: Hatje Cantz, 2001

— *Kompendium für Alphabeten*, Teufen: Niggli, 1972 (in English as: *Compendium for literates*, Cambridge, Massachusetts: MIT Press, 1974)

— *Programme entwerfen*, Teufen: Niggli, 1964 (in English as: *Designing programmes*, London: Tiranti, 1968)

— & M. Kutter, *Die neue Graphik*, Teufen: Niggli, 1959

Gill, E. *An autobiography*, London: Cape, 1940

— *An essay on typography*, 2nd edn, London: Dent, 1936

Goudy, F. W. *Typologia: studies in type design & type making*, Berkeley: University of California Press, 1940

Gray, N. *Nineteenth century ornamented typefaces*, 2nd edn, London: Faber & Faber, 1976

Hartmann, S. *Fraktur oder Antiqua: der Schriftstreit von 1881 bis 1941*, Frankfurt a.M: Lang, 1998

Heiderhoff, H. *Antiqua oder Fraktur? zur Problemgeschichte eines Streits*, Frankfurt a. M: Polygraph, 1971

Hellinga, W. G. *Copy and print in the Netherlands*, Amsterdam: North-Holland, 1962

Hinz, B. *Art in the Third Reich*, Oxford: Blackwell, 1980

Histoire de l'édition française, 4 vols, Paris: Promodis, 1982–6

Hollis, R. *Graphic design: a concise history*, 2nd edn, London: Thames & Hudson, 2001

Hopkins, R. L. *Origin of the American point system for printers' type measurement*, Terra Alta: Hill & Dale Press, 1976

Howes, J. *Johnston's Underground type*, Harrow Weald: Capital Transport, 2000

Huss, R. E. *The development of printers' mechanical typesetting methods: 1822–1925*, Charlottesville: University Press of Virginia, 1973

Hutt, A. *Fournier: the compleat typographer*, London: Muller, 1972

Jackson, H. *The printing of books*, London: Cassell, 1938

Jacobi, C. T. *Printing: a practical treatise*, London: Bell, 1893

Jammes, A. *Les Didot: trois siècles de typographie et de bibliophilie, 1698–1998*, Paris: Agence culturelle de Paris, 1998

— *La Naissance d'un caractère: le Grandjean*, Paris: Promodis, 1985

Janáková, I. (ed.) *Ladislav Sutnar: Praha – New York – design in action*, Prague: Argo, 2003

Javal, E. *Physiologie de la lecture et de l'écriture*, Paris: Alcan, 1906

Johns, A. *The nature of the book: print and knowledge in the making*, Chicago: University of Chicago Press, 1998

Johnson, A. F. *Type designs*, 3rd edn, London: Deutsch, 1966

Johnston, E. *Formal penmanship and other papers*, London: Lund Humphries, 1971

— *Writing & illuminating, & lettering*, London: Hogg, 1906 (in German as: *Schreibschrift, Zierschrift & angewandte Schrift*, Leipzig: Klinkhardt & Biermann, 1910)

Johnston, P. *Edward Johnston*, 2nd edn, London: Barrie & Jenkins, 1976

Kapr, A. *Fraktur: Form und Geschichte der gebrochenen Schriften*, Mainz: Hermann Schmidt, 1993

Kautzsch, R. (ed.) *Die neue Buchkunst*, Weimar: Gesellschaft der Bibliophilen, 1902

Kinross, R. (ed.) *Anthony Froshaug: Typography & texts / Documents of a life*, 2 vols, London: Hyphen Press, 2000

— *Unjustified texts: perspectives on typography*, London: Hyphen Press, 2002

Klingspor, K. *Über Schönheit von Schrift und Druck*, Frankfurt a. M: Schauer, 1949

Knuth, D. E. *Computers and typesetting*, 5 vols, Reading, Massachusetts: Addison-Wesley, 1986

Kostelanetz, R. (ed.) *Moholy-Nagy*, London: Allen Lane, 1971

Krimpen, J. v. *A letter to Philip Hofer on certain problems connected with the mechanical cutting of punches*, Cambridge, Massachusetts: Harvard College Library, 1972

— *On designing and devising type*, New York: Typophiles, 1957

Kula, W. *Measures and men*, Princeton: Princeton University Press, 1986

Labarre, E. J. *Dictionary and encylopaedia of paper and paper-making*, 2nd edn, London: Oxford University Press, 1952

Larisch, R. v. *Beispiele künstlerischer Schrift*, 4 vols, Vienna: Schroll, 1900–19

— *Über Leserlichkeit von ornamentalen Schriften*, Vienna: Schroll, 1904

— *Über Zierschriften im Dienste der Kunst*, Munich: Albert, 1899

— *Unterricht in ornamentaler Schrift*, Vienna: Österreichische Staatsdruckerei, 1905

Lee, M. (ed.) *Books for our time*, New York: Oxford University Press, 1951

Legros, L. A. & J. C. Grant, *Typographical printing-surfaces*, London: Longmans Green, 1916

Lissitzky-Küppers, S. *El Lissitzky*, Dresden: VEB Verlag der Kunst, 1967 (in English as: *El Lissitzky*, Thames & Hudson, 1968)

Löbe, K. *Exil-Gestalten: Deutsche Buchgestalter in den Niederlanden 1932–1950*, Arnhem: Gouda Quint, 1995

Lohse Stiftung, *Richard Paul Lohse: konstruktive Gebrauchsgrafik*, Ostfildern-Ruit: Hatje Cantz, 1999

Lommen, M. & P. Verheul, *Haagse letters*, Amsterdam: De Buitenkant, 1996

Maan, D. & J. v. d. Ree, *Typo-foto: elementaire typografie in Nederland*, Utrecht: Veen, 1990

McKenzie, D. F. *Bibliography and the sociology of texts*, 2nd edn, Cambridge: Cambridge University Press, 1999

— *Making meaning: 'Printers of the mind' and other essays*, Amherst: University of Massachusetts Press, 2002

McLean, R. *Jan Tschichold*, London: Lund Humphries, 1975

McMurtrie, D. C. *Modern typography and layout*, Chicago: Eyncourt Press, 1930

Magermans, R. & F. Baudin (ed.) *Dossier Vox*, Ardenne: Rémy Magermans, 1975

Mardersteig, G. *The Officina Bodoni*, ed. H. Schmoller, Verona: Edizioni Valdonega, 1980

Marshall, A. *Du plomb à la lumière: la Lumitype-Photon et la naissance des industries graphiques modernes*, Paris: Éditions de la Maison des Sciences de l'Homme, 2003

Martinet, J. *Hot printing*, Amsterdam: H. N. Werkman Foundation, 1963

Meynell, F. *My lives*, London: Bodley Head, 1971

— & H. Simon (ed.) *Fleuron anthology*, London: Benn, 1973

Millington, J. *Are we to read backwards? or What is the best print for the eyes*, London: Field & Tuer, [1883]

Moran, J. *The composition of reading matter*, London: Wace, 1965

— *The Double Crown Club*, Westerham: Westerham Press, 1974

— *Fit to be styled a typographer: a history of the Society of Typographic Designers 1928–1978*, Westerham: Westerham Press, 1978

— *Stanley Morison: his typographic achievement*, London: Lund Humphries, 1971

Morison, S. *First principles of typography*, 2nd edn, Cambridge: Cambridge University Press, 1967

— *Letter forms*, London: Nattali & Maurice, 1968

— *Politics and script*, Oxford: Clarendon Press, 1972

— *Selected essays on the history of letter-forms in manuscript and print*, 2 vols, Cambridge: Cambridge University Press, 1980–1

— *A tally of types*, 2nd edn, Cambridge: Cambridge University Press, 1973 (reprinted with an introduction by M. Parker, Jaffrey: Godine, 1999)

— *The typographic arts*, London: Sylvan Press, 1949

Morison, S. & D. B. Updike, *Selected correspondence*, London: Scolar Press, 1980

Morris, W. *The ideal book: essays and lectures on the arts of the book*, ed. W. S. Peterson, Berkeley: University of California Press, 1982

Mosley, J. *The nymph and the grot*, London: Friends of the St Bride Printing
    Library, 1999
— with S. de Turckheim-Pey & others, *Le Romain du roi: la typographie au
    service de l'état*, 1702–2002, Lyons: Musée de l'Imprimerie, 2002
Moxon, J. *Mechanick exercises on the whole art of printing* [1683], 2nd edn,
    ed. H. Davis & H. Carter, London: Oxford University Press, 1962
Müller-Brockmann, J. *Gestaltungsprobleme des Grafikers*, Teufen: Niggli,
    1961
Neue Gesellschaft für Bildende Kunst, *Wem gehört die Welt: Kunst und
    Gesellschaft in der Weimarer Republik*, Berlin: NGBK, 1977
Neumann, E. *Functional graphic design in the 20s*, New York: Reinhold, 1967
Nisbet, P. (ed.) *El Lissitzky 1890–1941*, Cambridge, Massachusetts: Harvard
    University Art Museums, 1987
Noordzij, G. *Letterletter*, Vancouver: Hartley & Marks, 2000
— *De streek: theorie van het schrift*, Zaltbommel: Van de Garde, 1987
Owens, L. T. *J. H. Mason 1875–1951*, London: Muller, 1976
Passuth, K. *Moholy-Nagy*, London: Thames & Hudson, 1985
Petersen, A. & P. Brattinga, *Sandberg: a documentary*, Amsterdam: Kosmos,
    1975
Peterson, W. S. *A bibliography of the Kelmscott Press*, Oxford: Clarendon
    Press, 1984
— *The Kelmscott Press: a history of William Morris's typographical
    adventure*, Oxford: Clarendon Press, 1991
Phillips, A. H. *Computer peripherals and typesetting*, London: HMSO, 1968
Pierpont Morgan Library, *William Morris and the art of the book*, London:
    Oxford University Press, 1976
Plata, W. (ed.) *Fraktur, Gotisch, Schwabacher*, Hillsheim: Plata Presse, 1982
— (ed.) *Schätze der Typographie: gebrochene Schriften: Informationen und
    Meinungen von 17 Autoren*, Frankfurt a.M: Polygraph, 1968
Poeschel, C. E. *Zeitgemäße Buchdruckkunst*, Leipzig: Poeschel & Trepte, 1904
Porstmann, W. *Sprache und Schrift*, Berlin: Verlag des Vereins Deutscher
    Ingenieure, 1920
Poynor, R. *Typographica*, London: Laurence King, 2001
Pyke, R. L. [for the Medical Research Council], *Report on the legibility of print*,
    London: HMSO, 1926
Re, M. *Typographically speaking: the art of Matthew Carter*, New York:
    Princeton Architectural Press, 2003
Remington, R. R. & B. J. Hodik, *Nine pioneers in American graphic design*,
    Cambridge, Massachusetts: MIT Press, 1989
Renner, P. *Die Kunst der Typographie*, Berlin: Druckhaus Tempelhof, 1948
— *Mechanisierte Grafik*, Berlin: Reckendorf, 1930
— *Typografie als Kunst*, Munich: Georg Müller, 1922
Rodenberg, J. *Deutsche Pressen: eine Bibliographie*, Zurich: Amalthea-Verlag,
    1925 (with 'Nachtrag', 1930)
— *Größe und Grenzen der Typographie*, Stuttgart: Poeschel, 1959

Rogers, B. *Report on the typography of the Cambridge University Press* [1917], Cambridge: University Printer, 1950

Rubens, G. *William Richard Lethaby*, London: Architectural Press, 1986

Ruder, E. *Typographie*, Teufen: Niggli, 1967

Schauer, G. K. *Deutsche Buchkunst: 1890 bis 1960*, 2 vols, Hamburg: Maximilian-Gesellschaft, 1963

Schleger, P. (ed.) *Zero: Hans Schleger – a life of design*, London: Lund Humphries, 2001

Schmalenbach, W. *Kurt Schwitters*, London: Thames & Hudson, 1970

Schmidt-Künsemüller, F. A. *William Morris und die neuere Buchkunst*, Wiesbaden: Harrassowitz, 1955

Schumacher-Gebler, E. *F. H. Ernst Schneidler: Schriftentwerfer, Lehrer, Kalligraph*, Munich: Schumacher-Gebler, 2002

Schwartz, F. J. *The Werkbund: design theory and mass culture before the First World War*, New Haven: Yale University Press, 1997

Schwitters, K. *Manifeste und kritische Prosa*, Cologne: Dumont, 1981 (vol. 5 of *Das literarische Werk*)

Seybold, J. W. *The world of digital typesetting*, Media, Pennsylvania: Seybold Publications, 1984

Sichowsky, R. v. (ed.) *Typographie und Bibliophilie*, Hamburg: Maximilian-Gesellschaft, 1971

Simon, H. *Song and words: a history of the Curwen Press*, London: Allen & Unwin, 1973

Simon, O. *Introduction to typography*, 2nd edn, London: Faber & Faber, 1963

—   *Printer and playground: an autobiography*, London: Faber & Faber, 1956

Simoni, A. E. C. *Publish and be free: a catalogue of clandestine books printed in the Netherlands 1940–1945 in the British Library*, The Hague: Nijhoff, 1975

Sparling, H. H. *The Kelmscott Press and William Morris master-craftsman*, London: Macmillan, 1924

Spencer, H. *Design in business printing*, London: Sylvan Press, 1952

—   *Pioneers of modern typography*, London: Lund Humphries, 1969

—   *The visible word*, 2nd edn, London: Lund Humphries, 1969

Steinberg, S. H. *Five hundred years of printing*, 3rd edn, Harmondsworth: Penguin Books, 1974 (revised by John Trevitt, London: British Library, 1996)

Thompson, S. O. *American book design and William Morris*, New York: Bowker, 1977

Tidcombe, M. *The Doves Press*, London: British Library, 2003

Tracy, W. *Letters of credit: a view of type design*, London: Gordon Fraser, 1986

—   *The typographic scene*, London: Gordon Fraser, 1988

Tschichold, J. *Designing books*, New York: Wittenborn, 1951

—   *Eine Stunde Druckgestaltung*, Stuttgart: Wedekind, 1930

—   (ed.), 'Elementare Typographie' [*Typographische Mitteilungen*, October 1925], Mainz: Hermann Schmidt, 1986

— *Leben und Werk des Typographen Jan Tschichold*, Dresden: VEB Verlag der Kunst, 1977
— *Die neue Typographie* [Berlin: Bildungsverband der Deutschen Buch-drucker, 1928] facsimile, Berlin: Brinkmann & Bose, 1987 (in English as: *The new typography*, Berkeley: University of California Press, 1995; in Spanish as: *La nueva tipografía*, Valencia: Campgràfic, 2003)
— *Schriften 1925–1974*, 2 vols, Berlin: Brinkmann & Bose, 1991–2
— *Typografische Entwurfstechnik*, Stuttgart: Wedekind, 1932
— *Typographische Gestaltung*, Basel: Schwabe, 1935 (in English as: *Asymmetric typography*, Faber & Faber, 1967)
— *Zur Typographie der Gegenwart*, Bern: Monotype Corporation, 1960
Tupitsyn, M. *El Lissitzky*, New Haven: Yale University Press, 1999
Twyman, M. *Breaking the mould: the first five hundred years of lithography*, London: British Library, 2001
— *Printing 1770–1970: an illustrated history of its development and uses in England*, London: Eyre & Spottiswoode, 1970 (reprint, London: British Library, 1998)
'*Typographie kann unter Umständen Kunst sein*': (1) *Kurt Schwitters: Typo-graphie und Werbegestaltung*; (2) *Vordemberge-Gildewart: Typographie und Werbegestaltung*; (3) *Ring 'neue werbegestalter': die Amsterdamer Ausstellung 1931*; (4) *Ring 'neue werbegestalter' 1928–1933: ein Überblick*; (1–3) Wiesbaden: Landesmuseum, 1990; (4) Hannover: Sprengel Museum, 1990
Typographische Gesellschaft München, *J.T: Johannes Tzschichhold, Iwan Tschichold, Jan Tschichold*, Munich: TGM, 1976
— *Hundert Jahre Typographie: Hundert Jahre Typographische Gesellschaft München*, Munich: TGM, 1990
— *Paul Renner*, Munich: TGM, 1978
— *Vita activa: Georg Trump*, Munich: TGM, 1967
Updike, D. B. *Notes on the Merrymount Press and its work*, Cambridge, Massachusetts: Harvard University Press, 1934
— *Printing types: their history, forms, and use*, 2nd edn, 2 vols, London: Oxford University Press, 1937
— *The well-made book: essays & lectures*, ed. W. S. Peterson, New York: Mark Batty, 2002
Veyrin-Forrer, J. *La Lettre et la texte: trente années de recherches sur l'histoire du livre*, Paris: L'École Normale Supérieure de Jeunes Filles, 1987
Victoria & Albert Museum, *Berthold Wolpe: a retrospective survey*, London: V & A, 1980
Wallis, L. W. *Electronic typesetting: a quarter century of technological upheaval*, Gateshead: Paradigm Press, 1984
— *Type design: developments 1970–1985*, Arlington: National Composition Association, 1985
Warde, B. *The crystal goblet*, London: Sylvan Press, 1955
Weingart, W. *Wege zur Typographie: ein Rückblick in zehn Teilen*, Baden: Lars Müller, 2000

Willett, J. *The new sobriety 1917–1933: art and politics in the Weimar period*,
    London: Thames & Hudson, 1978
William Morris Society, *The typographical adventure of William Morris*,
    ed. R. C. H. Briggs, London: William Morris Society, 1957
Williamson, H. *Methods of book design*, 3rd edn, New Haven: Yale University
    Press, 1983
Windsor, A. *Peter Behrens: architect and designer*, London: Architectural
    Press, 1981

Note on orthography

The transcription of printed text presents problems that, in the present
context of a discussion of typography, are of more than obscure bibliographic interest. In transcribing a printed text, such as the title of a book or
the name of its author, how closely should one keep to the conventions used
in the composition of that text? For example, in one code of bibliography,
blackletter text is transcribed in blackletter, roman in roman. By the same
logic, should one think of transcribing bold as bold, italic as italic? This
degree of fidelity is not possible or needed here. The main area of decision
has been that of capitalization. In book titles, only the first letter of the title
and the first letters of proper names have been capitalized. Though not yet
so common in English, this follows French usage, and has the weight of
rationality behind it. Journal titles, which are in some sense proper or institutional names, are given initial capitals for every important word. In transcribing German text, the presently employed conventions of that language
are followed: all nouns are capitalized. Difficulties arise in the treatment of
'Kleinschreibung' ('kleinschreibung'?): the conscious adoption of lowercase
typography, which is one of the important subjects of this book. Here the
policy has been to transcribe lowercase as capitals, according to the conventions already outlined, in the interests of consistency and rationality. Those
who object to giving an initial capital to an all-lowercase title, as it appears
on a book or magazine (or if it is a commercial logo or trademark), need to
consider whether they would capitalize every letter when referring to the
The Times of London (the masthead of that newspaper is set all in capitals).
By their logic, they should. German new typography called also for a phonetically more accurate orthography. The most frequent and persistent issue
has been treatment of the 'f' sound: as 'f' or 'ph'. Modernist preference has
been for 'Typografie' in place of 'Typographie', 'Grafik' and not 'Graphik'.
As far as possible, these differences in spelling have been maintained here,
at the risk of seeming careless or inconsistent.

Index

The index covers people, companies, institutions, and some key subjects; but 'modern' and related ideas have not been indexed. 'Typefaces' are gathered under that heading. The concept, as now understood, dates from the full commodification of these things (around 1900); references to types before this time may be found through the names of people. Chapter 15 has not been indexed. Material in notes is shown by the suffix 'n'.